Labour's landslide

Labour's landslide

The British general election 1997

edited by
Andrew Geddes and Jonathan Tonge

MANCHESTER UNIVERSITY PRESS
Manchester and New York
distributed exclusively in the USA by St. Martin's Press

Published by Manchester University Press
Oxford Road, Manchester M13 9NR
and Room 400, 175 Fifth Avenue, NY 10010, USA

Distributed exclusively in the USA by
St. Martin's Press, Inc., 175 Fifth Avenue, New York, NY 10010, USA

Distributed exclusively in Canada by
UBC Press, University of British Columbia, 6344 Memorial Road, Vancouver, BC, Canada V6T 1Z2

British Library Cataloguing-in-Publication data
A catalogue record for this book is available from the British Library

Library of Congress Cataloging-in-Publication data applied for

ISBN 0 7190 5158 4 *hardback*
0 7190 5159 2 *paperback*

First published 1997

01 00 99 98 97 10 9 8 7 6 5 4 3 2 1

Typeset and designed by Carnegie Publishing, Lancaster
Printed in Great Britain by Redwood Books, Trowbridge

Contents

List of tables

List of contributors

Philip Cowley is a Lecturer in Politics at the University of Hull. He has published extensively on aspects of the Conservative Party leadership and party elites.

David Denver is a Reader in the Department of Politics and International Relations at the University of Lancaster. Amongst his numerous works on electoral behaviour is *Elections and Voting Behaviour in Britain* (Prentice Hall, 1994).

Steven Fielding is a Lecturer in the Department of Politics and Contemporary History, European Studies Research Institute, at the University of Salford. His most recent book is *The Labour Party: 'Socialism' and Society since 1951* (Manchester University Press, 1997).

Justin Fisher is a Lecturer in Political Science in the Department of Politics and Modern History at London Guildhall University. His publications include *British Political Parties* (Prentice Hall, 1996).

Andrew Geddes is Lecturer in the School of Politics and Communication Studies at the University of Liverpool. During academic year 1997–98 he is a European Forum Fellow at the European University Institute in Florence, conducting research on EU immigration policy. His publications include *Britain in the European Community* (Baseline, 1993).

Ian Holliday is Senior Lecturer in Government at the University of Manchester. His recent publications include *The British Cabinet System* (with Martin Burch, Prentice Hall, 1996) and *The NHS Transformed* (Baseline, 1995). He is a co-editor of *Developments in British Politics 5* (Macmillan, 1997) and of the journal *Party Politics*.

James Mitchell is Senior Lecturer in the Department of Government at the University of Strathclyde. Amongst his extensive list of publications is *Conservatives and the Union* (Edinburgh University Press, 1990).

Lucy Peake is completing a Ph.D. in the Department of Politics at the University of Southampton. Her research focuses on the consequences of increasing numbers of women MPs in Britain. She has also worked as a researcher on the British Representation Study.

Shamit Saggar is a Senior Lecturer in Government at Queen Mary and Westfield College, University of London. He is the co-director of the 1997 Ethnic Minority Election Study within the 1997 British Election Study. His new edited book, *Race and Electoral Politics*, is published by UCL Press.

Jonathan Tonge is a Lecturer in Politics at the Department of Politics and Contemporary History, European Studies Research Institute, at the University of Salford. He is author of *Northern Ireland: Conflict and Change* (Prentice Hall, 1997) and co-editor (with Chris Gilligan) of *Peace or War? Understanding the Peace Process in Northern Ireland* (Avebury, 1997).

Mark Wickham-Jones lectures in Politics at the University of Bristol. He is the author of *Economic Strategy and the Labour Party* (Macmillan, 1996).

Dominic Wring is a Lecturer in Communication and Media Studies, and a member of the Communication Research Centre, Loughborough University. He is completing a book, *Marketing the Labour Party*, for Macmillan.

Acknowledgements

The editors would like to thank the authors of each chapter for the prompt and accurate submissions of contributions. Production of this book has incurred a number of debts. Thanks are due to the following: Bill Jones for his help in setting up the project; Nicola Viinikka, Rebecca Crum and Pippa Kenyon at Manchester University Press for commissioning the book and helping throughout its production; Jo-Ann Cundill for proof-reading; David Williams and Steven Fielding, Lecturer in the Department of Politics and Contemporary History at the University of Salford, for helpful comments on draft chapters and Kath Capper, secretary in that department, for her help in production. Naturally, as editors, we accept responsibility for any errors within the text.

Finally on a personal note, Jon Tonge thanks Anita and Connell for their forbearance and dedicates this book to his parents, Stanley and Brenda Tonge.

List of abbreviations

APNI	Alliance Party of Northern Ireland
BES	British Election Study
CAP	Common Agricultural Policy
CBI	Confederation of British Industry
DSD	Downing Street Declaration
DUP	(Ulster) Democratic Unionist Party
EC	European Community
EDM	Early Day Motion
EMU	economic and monetary union
ERM	Exchange Rate Mechanism
EU	European Union
GDP	gross domestic product
IRA	Irish Republican Army
OBV	Operation Black Vote
PC	Plaid Cymru
PTA	Prevention of Terrorism Act
SDLP	Social Democratic and Labour Party
SEA	Single European Act
SF	Sinn Fein
SNP	Scottish National Party
TEU	Treaty on European Union
TUC	Trades Union Congress
UUP	Ulster Unionist Party
VAT	value added tax

Introduction

Andrew Geddes and Jonathan Tonge

Labour's landslide

Prior to polling day Tony Blair stated that Britain is not a landslide country. Mr Blair may have been warning his supporters against complacency, but was wrong: on Thursday 1 May 1997 Britain *was* a landslide country, at least in terms of seats won in the House of Commons. With 44 per cent of the vote and 65 per cent of the seats Labour proved this point at the 1997 general election. Britain's first past the post electoral system is capable of delivering landslides that are not reflected in the share of the vote. But, even though a Labour victory was widely expected, its scale surprised or even amazed. Labour returned to government after eighteen years in opposition with a majority of 179. On the Richter scale of political earthquakes, the 1997 general election ranks alongside Asquith's victory in 1906 and Attlee's triumph in 1945. This book tells the story of Labour's landslide.

To describe the scale of Labour's victory, and the Conservative defeat, as a landslide may not actually capture the sheer magnitude of events. One BBC election expert perhaps overstated the inter-galactic significance of the election when he said that the appropriate analogy was an asteroid hitting the Earth and destroying practically all life. Former cabinet minister David Mellor was more down to earth when he likened the defeat to a tidal wave sweeping away Conservative candidates. Lord Parkinson greeted the second Conservative seat of the night by remarking that at least there was now a rival for the Party leadership.

Hyperbole and gallows humour aside, the scale of the Conservative defeat was devastating. The Conservative Party's share of the vote collapsed to 31 per cent, its lowest since 1832. A mere 165 Conservative MPs were returned to the House of Commons, their smallest number since the Liberal victory of 1906.[1] Seven cabinet ministers lost their seats, including Foreign Secretary Malcolm Rifkind and Defence Secretary Michael Portillo. Worse still, the self-proclaimed defenders of the Union had no representation in Scotland and Wales. Michael Forsyth, the Thatcherite Secretary of State for Scotland, lost his Stirling seat to Labour, whilst the President of the Board of Trade, Ian Lang, saw his Galloway and Upper Nithsdale seat fall to the Scottish National Party (SNP). Even true-blue Eastwood abandoned the Conservatives and fell to Labour.

Conservative desolation was matched by Labour euphoria. The exit polls predicted a crushing majority and early results showed large swings to Labour in its urban heartlands. As night turned into early morning the declaration of results achieved a slightly surreal quality as 'Sittingbourne: Labour gain', 'Hove: Labour gain', 'Wimbledon: Labour gain' and so on were beamed onto television screens across the nation. The swing in the South of England was truly calamitous for the Conservatives. Labour had not, for instance, held a seat in Kent since 1979; by the morning of 2 May 1997 it held eight of the seventeen seats in the county. Astonished Labour victors had to hurriedly re-arrange their lives to take account of their new status as MPs. The look of delight and amazement on Labour candidate Stephen Twigg's face as he won Enfield Southgate from Michael Portillo encapsulated the drama of the night.

The Liberal Democrats too enjoyed a breakthrough as middle Britain took its revenge on the Conservatives. Even though the Party's share of the vote fell from the 18 per cent it won in 1992 to 17 per cent, it increased its number of seats by twenty-seven to hold forty-six in the new Commons – the largest number of Liberals since 1929. The Liberal Democrats profited from anti-Conservative sentiment to make particularly significant gains in its South West of England heartland where it won twelve seats. For the Liberal Democrats health and education were the top priorities and, unlike Labour, they made it clear that they were prepared to increase income tax to boost education funding. The Conservative wipe-out in Scotland and Wales helped the nationalist parties. The Scottish National Party saw a slight dip in support, but increased its representation from three in the 1992 contest to six seats. Plaid Cymru held its four seats but did not match the share of the vote attained during its peak years in the 1970s.

Prevailing assumptions about British electoral politics had been turned on their heads. Labour's front-bench politicians, inured to the toil of opposition, merrily clambered into ministerial limousines. In contrast, former Conservative ministers faced the prospect of spending rather more time with their families than with their red boxes. For the electorate too, old certainties were shattered. Millions of younger voters had little or no recollection of Labour's last spell in government all of eighteen years ago.

As well as the decisive shift in the balance of the political parties, the 1997 general election also altered the gender imbalance in the House of Commons. Prior to dissolution the House of Commons had only sixty-two women MPs, less than 10 per cent of the total. Women politicians played little part in the national campaign, but the election of 120 women MPs, almost one-fifth of the total, may help prompt reform of some of the Commons' more antiquated procedures. Even so, the number of women MPs still needs to more than double again if the gender balance in the Commons is to reflect that amongst the population as a whole.

The long goodbye

John Major invested his hopes of victory in a six-week campaign, the longest in British electoral history. The aim was to highlight Labour's supposed policy weaknesses, but Labour's overwhelming poll lead barely dwindled and Conservative support stayed at around 30 per cent. Labour's claim that it was 'time for a change' triumphed over the rival assertion that 'you can only be sure with the Conservatives'. The British people decided that, to borrow another Labour slogan, 'enough was enough'.

Throughout the campaign, and in fact for over four years, the opinion polls indicated an impending Conservative defeat, but the failure of the polls to predict the outcome of the 1992 general election prompted a reluctance to accept forecasts of the 1997 outcome: Labour dared not believe the polls, whilst the Conservatives spoke of the positive reception they claimed to receive on the doorstep. This, they said, belied polling evidence.

The Conservative campaign was blown off-course as first 'sleaze' and then Europe dominated the news agenda. The first two weeks of the campaign were a waste for the Conservatives as a number of their candidates were enmired by allegations of sexual and financial sleaze. The sleaze issue refused to go away and was personified by the campaign of former BBC television journalist Martin Bell who stood as an Independent against Conservative candidate Neil Hamilton in the Cheshire constituency of Tatton. Bell comfortably captured what had been one of the safest Conservative seats in the country. When the sleaze issue died down it was replaced by Conservative divisions over the European single currency. Even Conservative ministers dissociated themselves from John Major's 'negotiate and decide' (or 'wait and see') stance by issuing personal manifestos distancing themselves from the Government's policy.

The seeds of defeat were, though, actually sown far earlier, on Wednesday 16 September 1992 to be precise, when the Conservatives suffered their own double whammy. First, the centrepiece of the Government's economic strategy fell to pieces when sterling was unceremoniously ejected from the European Community's Exchange Rate Mechanism (ERM). The Conservatives' reputation for economic competence, a key factor in the 1992 general election victory, was wrecked. The events of 'Black Wednesday' then ignited a Euro-war within the Conservative Party. Once the blue touch paper was lit, the opposition parties could stand safely back and watch the Conservatives fight themselves to a standstill during the ratification process of the Treaty on European Union (more commonly known as the Maastricht Treaty). Sir James Goldsmith's lavishly funded and anti-EU Referendum Party sniped at the Conservatives and added to John Major's woes. The Referendum Party secured less than a million votes, but in nineteen seats lost by the Conservatives the Referendum Party's vote exceeded the majority of the winning candidate.

Despite the Conservatives' determined assertion that 'Britain is booming' the electorate gave the governing party little credit for economic recovery. Noises-off drowned out good news.

The election defeat was a shattering blow for the Conservative Party. The challenge for William Hague is to heal rifts that run so deep that they threaten to provoke divisions as far-reaching and long-lasting as those that afflicted the Party in the nineteenth century over reform of the Corn Laws and in the early twentieth century over free trade and imperial preference. For most of its dwindling and ageing band of supporters the Conservative Party is, if it is anything, a party of government. In the 1980s and 1990s debates within the Conservative Party assumed a quasi-ideological flavour, particularly on the Party's Thatcherite wing. Once internal Party debates were cast in such fundamental terms it became far more difficult to heal Party divisions. One reason John Major was elected Conservative leader was that it was thought he could hold the Party together. If anything, though, the Conservative ideologues loathed him for his pragmatism. Major had led the Conservatives to unexpected success in the 1992 general election and by so doing secured the largest popular vote for any British Prime Minister; but by 1997 the divisions within the Conservative Party were so deep and the Party had fallen so precipitously in public esteem that it was unelectable. New Labour won the election but, just as assuredly, the Conservative Party lost it.

Another reason why the Conservative campaign flopped so disastrously was the abandonment of the Party by many of its former supporters in the press. The issue that agitated the right-wing newspapers was European integration. For instance, the *Daily Mail* and the *Sunday Telegraph* became vitriolic critics of the Major Government's EU policy. *The Times* even went so far as to refuse to endorse the Conservative Party, calling instead for a vote for Euro-scepticism. In one of the most symbolically significant shifts of the campaign Britain's biggest selling daily newspaper, the *Sun*, which had been a bitter critic of what it saw as the Major Government's incompetence, proclaimed that 'The *Sun* backs Blair. Give change a chance'.

For the Labour Party the road to victory in 1997 had been long and hard. The disastrous defeats of 1979 and 1983 impelled the Party on a programme of change and modernisation that culminated with the election to the leadership of Tony Blair in 1994 following the death of John Smith. Labour's campaign managers ensconced in Millbank Tower close to Parliament had learnt the lessons of previous campaigns. In 1992, Labour had been hit by Conservative allegations that they would deliver a tax-and-spend double whammy to the electorate. In 1997 Labour was determined to neutralise this tax-and-spend weakness. It did so, by developing a cautious and carefully costed manifesto that outlined five key pledges on income tax, young offenders, the health service, education and employment. It was also the first election since Labour became a national party in which public ownership or control of industry was not an issue.

Even in its moment of triumph the Labour Party remained cautious. There was none of the triumphalism that greeted the 1945 landslide and prompted Sir Hartley Shawcross to proclaim that 'we are the masters now'. At his declaration in Sedgefield Tony Blair stated that 'we have been elected as new Labour and we will govern as new Labour'. This was no mere tautology: Labour had based its electoral appeal on modernisation of its organisation and policy. Labour offered the British people a series of pledges that were modest, but also provided a benchmark by which Labour's success or failure in government could be judged. The eyes of Labour's leadership are fixed on a more distant horizon: a second term.

Plan of the book

In the chapters that follow the terrain upon which the 1997 general election was fought is sketched. The results are carefully analysed, as too are the performances of the political parties. The role of the media is evaluated in the light of an election that was seen as representing a continued shift to soundbite politics. The politicians took centre-stage, but never too far away were the ubiquitous spin doctors.

The campaign was hard fought: an allegation would elicit a rapid rebuttal to be followed by a rejoinder and counter-allegation. But only a relatively small number of issues were the focus of these partisan exchanges. In this book, we organise these issues under the following headings: the management of the economy, the provision of services, Europe and the constitution. It was heat rather than light that was generated by many of these debates and the campaign appeared curiously bereft of politics. Labour's obsession with electability meant that the issues were 'trust' and 'management'. The electorate was asked which party and, in particular, which leader could be trusted to manage the economy, run the welfare state and lead the country. Arguably, therefore, this was the first post-war British election not to be fought by the two main parties competing on the basis of rival ideologies.

On other important issues campaign skirmishes were few and far between. It may be that the questions associated with environmental protection are too difficult or that the solutions are too radical for them to be easily articulated and debated during an election campaign, but equivalent drawbacks did not prevent prolonged and arcane debates on the advantages and disadvantages of Britain joining a single European currency at some unspecified point in the future. The Conservative Secretary of State for the Environment, John Gummer, had a campaign profile so low as to be non-existent. His Labour shadow, Michael Meacher, spent most of the campaign in his Oldham constituency. So, whilst the environmental protester Swampy and his friends burrowed ever deeper into the Cheshire countryside in their attempt to thwart Manchester

Airport's second runway, the issues that so concern those hundreds of thousands of British citizens who belong to environmental pressure groups were scarcely mentioned.

Other issues have faded in electoral salience. Immigration, for example, no longer has the power to whip up racist hostility towards Britain's black and Asian population, although the focus of debate has turned to the under-representation of Britain's ethnic minorities in elected institutions. Defence, too, was not a central issue in the 1997 campaign. In the early 1980s it had been a defining issue as Labour embraced unilateralism. The issue's principal legacy was its capacity to embarrass the current Labour leadership when confronted by their support for the party policies of the 1980s which had since been so comprehensively abandoned.

In Northern Ireland a rather different election was being fought. On the mainland it has become fashionable to speak of the fluidity of modern politics as old left–right divisions seem less relevant. Notions of dealignment have little part to play in Northern Irish politics. Of more significance were shifts in voting within the two main traditions. These saw the Ulster Unionists gain at the expense of the Democratic Unionists and Sinn Fein win two seats: West Belfast from the Social Democratic and Labour Party (SDLP) and Mid-Ulster from the Democratic Unionist Party (DUP).

The politicians, pundits and pollsters dominated the campaign but British general elections are still fought on a constituency basis. As well as outlining the principal features of the national campaign this book provides snapshots of some of the most interesting contests of the 1997 general election. The 1997 general election will be remembered for Tony Blair's overwhelming victory, but it was at a constituency level that the campaign touched the lives of millions of British people.

Note

1 This number fell by one shortly after the general election following the death of Sir Michael Shersby, the MP for Uxbridge.

1

The results: how Britain voted

David Denver

Introduction

The Conservative Party entered the 1992 general election campaign in a weaker electoral position than any governing party since Labour in 1931. In the five years from 1992 they had plumbed new depths of unpopularity in the opinion polls, lost thousands of council seats in local elections, lost all eight seats that they defended in parliamentary by-elections and achieved their worst ever national result in the European elections held in June 1994. At the end of February 1997, less than three weeks before the election date was announced, the final by-election of the Parliament (Wirral South) was lost to Labour in spectacular fashion. It is well established that the modern British electorate is, potentially at least, much more volatile than it used to be, but, even so, the chances of the Conservatives recovering by enough during the six-week campaign to snatch a surprise victory appeared remote. None the less, few anticipated the scale of the rout that was to come. The first Conservative general election defeat in more than twenty years was a humiliation and their eighteen years in office came to an ignominious end. With hindsight, commentators should have had more faith in the opinion polls, which were unwavering in their predictions of a Labour landslide.

Opinion polls

The second most nervous group of people on election night must have been the opinion pollsters. The final campaign polls during the 1992 election had been seriously wrong in their estimates of the eventual distribution of votes and even exit polls carried out on polling day significantly under-estimated the Conservative lead. As a result, the polls came in for much criticism and even derision.

In response to their perceived failure in 1992, however, the five main polling firms changed their methods in various ways. Alterations were made to how respondents were selected, how voting intentions were elicited and how 'Don't Knows' were treated. In two cases (ICM and NOP) the pollsters began to make significant adjustments to the raw data to produce their 'headline' figures for voting intention. These changes, it was hoped, would reduce the chances of embarrassment in 1997. None the less, had their predictions been significantly out of line with the election result the future of political polling in Britain might have been called into question.

Table 1.1 Summary of campaign poll results

Fieldwork dates	*Con*	*Lab*	*Lib Dem*	*Other*	*Number of polls*
17–23 March	29	53	12	6	3
24–30 March	30	50	15	6	3
31 March–6 April	30	53	11	6	7
7–13 April	32	49	13	6	7
14–20 April	31	47	16	6	6
21–7 April	31	47	14	8	6
28–30 April	31	47	15	7	5
Exit polls	30	47	18	6	2
GB result	31	44	17	7	

Note: The calculations – the simple mean in each case – are based on the 'headline' figures reported by the polls, whether these were adjusted or unadjusted. Panel and 'rolling' polls are excluded. Each poll is assigned to the week in which the majority of the fieldwork was carried out.

Source: Author's calculations.

The results of national polls conducted by the five major polling companies during the campaign are summarised in Table 1.1. As can be seen, the polls were gloomy for the Conservatives. Although some, in particular one by ICM for the *Guardian*, suggested a glimmer of light, the overall story is that the level of Conservative support hardly moved from the 30 per cent mark throughout the campaign. There was some slight slippage in Labour's fortunes – having had 50 per cent or more of voting intentions in the first three weeks they eased down to 49 per cent and then settled at 47 per cent of voting intentions. Support for the Liberal Democrats ebbed and flowed a little more, but there is a suggestion that it was on an upward trend from the middle of the campaign. Comparing the final polls with the election result in Great Britain (Northern Ireland is not covered by the national pollsters) shows that, although there was a slight over-estimation of the Labour share of the vote, the polls gave a good prediction of the result. After the disaster of 1992 the polls regained credibility, especially since during the campaign many experts and commentators simply refused to believe that Labour was so far ahead. The pollsters stuck to their guns, however, and in the end, much to their relief, no doubt, their faith in their results was largely vindicated.

Party support

The national result

The distribution of votes at the general election in Great Britain, as compared with the 1992 election, is shown in Table 1.2.[1] By any standard the result was dramatic. The swing from Conservative to Labour of 10.3 per cent was a post-war record; the Government lost more than half of their seats, including all that they held in Scotland and Wales and those of seven current cabinet ministers; the number of Conservative MPs elected was the smallest since the 'Liberal landslide' of 1906. Labour's vote share was its highest since 1966 and they took many seats that would normally have been considered as certain wins for the Conservatives. Labour's overall majority in the House of Commons (179) was bigger even than that achieved in their 1945 triumph (146). The Liberal Democrats too made a surprising advance. Although their vote share in 1997 was slightly down on that achieved in 1992, their support was more effectively distributed across constituencies so that they more than doubled their number of seats from a 'notional' eighteen to forty-six – the largest number for a third party in the post-1945 era. The SNP in Scotland (included amongst 'others' in Table 1.2) also benefited from the Conservative disaster, doubling their seats from three to six, whilst Plaid Cymru in Wales retained their four seats. The remaining 'other' seat was won by Martin Bell standing as an Independent in the formerly solid Conservative seat of Tatton against Neil Hamilton. Bell was the first Independent, with no ties to any political party, to be elected to Parliament in a general election since 1945. Apart from the nationalists, the most significant of the plethora of other parties and candidates standing for election (the number of candidates was another new record set in 1997) was the Referendum Party. Financed by the millionaire Sir James Goldsmith, the Party put forward 547 candidates and won 2.7 per cent of the votes. There were nineteen constituencies in which Referendum Party candidates won more votes than the number by which the Conservatives were defeated.

Table 1.2 The national result (Great Britain)

Party	*Share of vote*	*Change*	*Number of seats*	*Change*
Conservative	31.4	−11.4	165	−178
Labour	44.4	+9.2	419	+145
Lib Dem	17.2	−1.1	46	+28
Others	7.0	+3.3	11	+5

Note: Change in the number of seats won is based on the 'notional' number of seats that each party would have won in 1992 had the new constituency boundaries been in operation. The Speaker is counted as a Labour candidate although she was not opposed by the other major parties.

Measuring electoral change by means of 'swing' figures is a useful shorthand. However, it indicates only the net change in the positions of two parties relative to one another and, as the British party system has become more complicated, the usefulness of swing has declined. In addition, the net figure tells us nothing about the behaviour of the voters which brought about the change – how many switched between the major parties, how many switched from abstention to voting, and so on. For this we need a 'flow-of-the-vote' table based on survey data. Table 1.3, which is derived from the BBC/NOP exit poll, shows the flow of the vote between 1992 and 1997.[2]

Table 1.3 The flow of the vote 1992–1997 (%)

	1992 vote				
	Too young	*Did not vote*	*Con*	*Lab*	*Lib Dem*
1997 vote					
Con	20	20	71	1	6
Lab	57	55	14	90	23
Lib Dem	18	20	10	7	66
Other	5	5	4	2	6
(N)	116	148	863	729	268

Source: NOP/BBC exit poll.

Being based on an exit poll, Table 1.3 is incomplete since, by definition, non-voters in 1997 are excluded. In addition, the data on the 1992 vote depend on voters accurately recollecting what they did five years previously, which is certainly not the ideal way to analyse behaviour at two separate points in time. None the less, the table shows some striking patterns.

First, amongst those who voted there were massive defections from the Conservatives. Almost 30 per cent of 1992 Conservatives switched parties. Most went directly to Labour although a substantial minority (10 per cent) moved to the Liberal Democrats. Second, the only significant defections from Labour were to the Liberal Democrats and it is likely that these mostly occurred in constituencies in which Labour appeared to stand little chance of winning. Switching from the Liberal Democrats to Labour may also in part reflect tactical considerations, but it is likely that the much larger scale of defection (23 per cent of 1992 Liberal Democrats) is indicative of the general tide towards Labour. Third, amongst those who did not vote in 1992 or were first-time voters in 1997 the Conservatives did very badly. They were roughly on a par with the Liberal Democrats and trailed well behind Labour. Taken together with the pattern of non-voting in 1992 – to which I return below – these movements to and fro underlie the large net swing to Labour.

Regional patterns in party support

A major feature of general elections in the 1980s was a sharp widening of the North–South electoral divide. In broad terms, voters in Scotland, Wales and the North of England moved very sharply away from the Conservative Party whilst voters in the South swung heavily away from Labour. In the 1992 general election there had been a slight reversal of this trend but, even so, the North–South divide remained an important and obvious feature of the British electoral landscape.

Table 1.4 Party shares of votes and changes in vote shares in standard regions (%)

						Change 1992–97		
Region	*Con*	*Lab*	*Lib Dem*	*Nat*	*Oth*	*Con*	*Lab*	*Lib Dem*
Scotland	17.5	45.6	13.0	22.1	1.9	−8.2	+6.6	−0.1
Wales	19.6	54.7	12.4	9.9	3.4	−9.0	+11.4	0
North	22.2	60.9	13.3		3.7	−11.2	+10.3	−2.2
North West	27.1	54.2	14.3		4.5	−10.7	+9.3	−1.5
Yorks & Humbs	28.0	52.0	16.0		4.1	−9.9	+7.6	−0.8
West Midlands	33.7	47.8	13.8		4.7	−11.1	+9.0	−1.2
East Midlands	34.9	47.8	13.6		3.7	−11.7	+10.4	−1.6
East Anglia	38.7	38.3	17.9		5.1	−12.3	+10.3	−1.6
South East	41.4	31.9	21.4		5.4	−13.1	+11.1	−2.0
Gtr London	31.2	49.5	14.6		4.7	−14.1	+12.5	−0.6
South West	36.7	26.4	31.3		5.6	−10.9	+7.2	−0.1

Note: 'Nat' means the Scottish National Party or Plaid Cymru.

Table 1.4 shows the distribution of votes in the eleven British standard regions in 1997 and the change in vote shares since 1992. The North–South divide still exists. The Conservatives generally had a smaller share of the vote and Labour a larger share in the 'northern' regions (Scotland, Wales, North, North West and Yorkshire and Humberside) than in the Midlands or South. The poorest Conservative performances were in Scotland and Wales where they fell below 20 per cent, but the figures for change in vote share show that the electoral divide narrowed further. Although the swing from Conservative to Labour was nation-wide, the Conservatives generally lost votes more heavily and Labour gained more substantially in the South than in the North, with Greater London producing the largest swing of all. The smaller scale of Conservative losses in the 'North' is largely explained by the fact that there were simply many fewer Conservatives available in these regions for the other parties to recruit, but the effect, none the less, was to bring the regions of Britain more closely into line with one another so far as party support is concerned.

The concentration of Liberal Democrat support in the South West of England is also apparent from the figures and it is worth noting that their share of the vote here did not change very much whilst Labour's increase was smaller than in any other English region. This is another indication that there was significant tactical voting against the Conservatives. In Scotland and Wales the nationalist parties increased their vote shares slightly – the SNP by 0.6

per cent and Plaid by 1.1 per cent. The operation of the first-past-the-post electoral system means that differences between regions in terms of seats won are more stark than those in terms of votes. As Table 1.5 shows, the Conservatives won no seats (out of 112) in Scotland and Wales and only seventeen (out of 161) in the North of England.

Table 1.5 Distribution of seats within regions

Region	*Con*	*Lab*	*Lib Dem*	*Nat*
Scotland	0	56	10	6
Wales	0	34	2	4
North	3	32	1	
North West	7	60	2	
Yorks & Humberside	7	46	2	
West Midlands	14	44	1	
East Midlands	14	31	0	
East Anglia	14	8	0	
South East	73	36	8	
Greater London	11	57	6	
South West	22	15	14	

Note: The 'other' seat won by the Independent, Martin Bell, in the North West is not shown.

It is something of an irony that it was the Conservatives – the party most implacably opposed to electoral reform – who suffered most from the electoral system. In both Scotland and Wales they had more votes than the Liberal Democrats, but the latter ended up with twelve seats. In the five northern regions combined, the Conservatives got 6.2 per cent of the seats for 23.3 per cent of the votes whilst the Liberal Democrats had the same proportion of seats with only 13.9 per cent of the votes. Labour was, of course, massively over-represented, winning 83.5 per cent of the seats with 52.7 per cent of the votes.

Constituency variations

Analysing changes in party support between 1992 and 1997 at constituency level is inhibited by the fact that new constituency boundaries came into effect in 1997. Only 238 British constituencies were unchanged or were minimally altered (involving less than 5 per cent of the electorate). We can measure changes in party support in individual constituencies, however, by using a set of 'notional' 1992 results which were calculated for the new constituencies.[3] These have been, and will be, widely used in analysing the 1997 election. It should be remembered, however, that they are *estimates* of how 1992 votes would have been distributed under the new boundaries, and this is bound to make the measurement of change more problematical than usual.

On the basis of these figures there were, of course, large variations across constituencies in the extent to which the major parties' vote shares changed.

Thus, for example, the Labour share increased by more than 20 per cent in five constituencies, but actually declined in twelve; the Conservatives increased their share in two seats but declined by more than 18 per cent in eight. The Liberal Democrat performance was mixed – a decreased share in 431 seats, virtually no change in fourteen and an increased share in 194.[4] Although some of the extreme cases may be due to errors in estimating 1992 votes, the existence of substantial variation in change from 1992 is undeniable.

As we have already seen, these variations were partly regional. Scotland, for example, had a smaller decrease in the Conservative vote and a smaller increase in the Labour vote than other regions. Two other possible sources of variation have already been alluded to – the level of pre-existing support for the Conservatives and the tactical situation in the constituency concerned.

Table 1.6 Changes in party shares of votes according to the Conservative share of vote in 1992 (%)

	53+	44–53	32–44	*Less than 32*
Change in:				
Con	–13.1	–12.2	–12.0	–8.3
Lab	+10.6	+10.8	+9.4	+7.5
Lib Dem	–1.2	–1.5	–0.6	–1.7
Constituencies	151	172	154	162

Note: Figures shown are means in the constituencies concerned.

Tables 1.6 and 1.7 present some evidence on these suggestions. It can be seen in Table 1.6 that the stronger the previous position of the Conservatives the greater was their decline in vote share and, conversely, the bigger the Labour increase. We can measure these relationships more precisely. The correlation coefficient measuring the association between notional Conservative share of the vote in 1992 and change in their share between 1992 and 1997 is –0.589 whilst for change in Labour share it is +0.306.[5] Both coefficients are significant and that for Conservative change is especially strong. The negative sign indicates that the larger the previous Conservative share of the vote, the smaller (more strongly negative) was their increase in vote share. Put simply, the more Conservatives there were around the greater their decline.

Changes in the vote shares of Labour and the Liberal Democrats were related to the tactical situation, as indicated by the estimated 1992 constituency results. Table 1.7 shows that, in constituencies in which the notional 1992 results put Labour and the Conservatives in the first two places, Labour increased by 10.6 per cent on average whilst the Liberal Democrats fell by 1.8 per cent. Where the Conservatives and Liberal Democrats shared the two top spots Labour's increase was smaller and the Liberal Democrats increased their average share by 0.4 per cent. This clearly implies tactical voting and helps to explain why the Liberal Democrats won so many seats when their overall share of the vote fell. Where it mattered they at least held their own and, with Conservative support evaporating, that was enough to see the Liberal Democrats home.

Table 1.7 Changes in party shares of votes according to tactical situation in constituency (%)

	Con/Lab	*Con/Lib Dem*	*Lab/Lib Dem*
Change in:			
Con	−11.7	−12.2	−4.1
Lab	+10.6	+8.0	+8.6
Lib Dem	−1.8	+0.4	−7.1
Constituencies	410	173	13

Note: Figures shown are means. Constituencies are grouped according to the parties which were in first and second places in the notional 1992 results.

Source: Author's calculations.

Turning to variations in party support across constituencies in the 1997 election itself, it is apparent that these are associated with variations in the social composition of constituencies. Table 1.8 shows correlations between various aspects of the social and economic structure of constituencies and the shares of the vote gained by the major parties.

Table 1.8 Correlations between social composition of constituencies and party shares of vote (%)

Social group	*Con*	*Lab*	*Lib Dem*
Professional and managerial	0.67	−0.64	0.41
Manual workers	−0.53	0.56	−0.34
Owner occupiers	0.67	−0.50	0.30
Private tenants	−0.04 [a]	−0.14	0.14
Local authority tenants	−0.73	0.58	−0.39
People aged 18–29	−0.34	0.46	−0.32
People aged 75+	0.26	−0.42	0.39
Employed in agriculture	0.24	−0.52	0.36
Persons per hectare [b]	−0.29	0.39	−0.22
Households with no car	−0.77	0.70	−0.41
Ethnic minority	−0.16	0.29	−0.20

Note: N = 639. All coefficients, except that marked [a], are significant ($p < 0.001$); [b] denotes *number* of persons per hectare.

Sources: Social composition variables are derived from the 1991 Census.

Despite the fact that Conservative support is, overall, at a significantly lower level than before, variations across constituencies are related to the social characteristics of constituencies much as would be anticipated. The more middle-class a constituency, indicated by the percentage of professional and managerial workers, the bigger the Conservative vote and the more working-class a constituency, indicated by the percentage of manual workers, the smaller their vote. Housing patterns – the percentages of owner occupiers and of council tenants – are even more strongly related to Conservative support, although the percentage of private tenants has no effect. Conservative support is also stronger where there are more older people and weakens the more young people there are.

A simple perusal of election results shows that the Conservatives are generally stronger in rural areas and weaker in more urban areas, being especially weak in inner cities. This is reflected in the coefficients for the percentage of the population employed in agriculture and persons per hectare, the latter being a good measure of the position of constituencies on a rural–urban dimension. The percentage of households with no car is an indicator of the general level of prosperity or poverty in a constituency and, as can be seen, has a strongly negative association with the size of the Conservative vote (the strongest of all shown here). The proportion of the population belonging to ethnic minorities does not correlate very strongly with Conservative vote share – or, indeed, with the level of support for any of the parties. This is because ethnic minority voters tend to be concentrated in a relatively small number of seats.

The pattern of support for Labour is almost a mirror image of that for the Conservatives, whilst that for the Liberal Democrats is more of a pale reflection in that the coefficients for the two parties almost all have the same sign, although those for the Liberal Democrats are mostly weaker. In general, Liberal Democrats and Conservatives tend to do better or worse in the same sorts of constituencies. The data suggest, however, that the distinction between rural and urban areas (percentage employed in agriculture) makes an even bigger difference to the level of Liberal Democrat support than it does to the Conservatives and that the Liberal Democrats have a special appeal in areas with larger proportions privately renting their homes. In addition, the strong correlation with the percentage of old people probably reflects the strong Liberal Democrat performance in retirement areas in the South of England.

Three cautionary points need to be made about the interpretation of these correlation coefficients. First, they are derived from aggregate data and refer to the characteristics of constituencies, not individuals. We cannot infer from these data that people with no car do not vote Conservative, or that agricultural workers vote Liberal Democrat. Rather, the figures tell us that the greater the proportion of households with no car in a constituency the lower, usually, is the Conservative vote and the more agricultural workers there are in a constituency the better the Liberal Democrat vote. Second, the social composition variables are based on the 1991 Census so that, although the data would have given an accurate picture of the social make-up of constituencies at the time of the 1992 election, they were six years out of date by the 1997 election. Third, the various measures of social composition are themselves highly inter-correlated. Thus constituencies in which a large proportion of households have no car tend also to have larger proportions of ethnic minority voters, council tenants, manual workers and young people than average, as well as higher population density.

Sorting out which variables are the most important influences on levels of party support requires multivariate analysis, which indicates whether a particular variable still exerts a significant influence when all others are held constant and also enables us to assess the extent to which combinations of factors can explain variations.[6] Such an analysis reveals that, in the case of the Conservative vote, five variables remain significant (no car, professional and managerial occupation, persons per hectare, old people and council tenants) and together they explain 73.8 per cent of the variation in the Conservative vote across constituencies. For Labour, all variables are significant except three (council tenants, ethnic minority and persons per hectare) but together the remaining eight account for 76.5 per cent of the variation in the Labour vote. The more diffuse nature of Liberal Democrat support is indicated by the fact that only 35.2 per cent of variation across constituencies is explained by four significant factors (no car, age, owner occupiers and council tenants).

It is worth emphasising again that these data relate to the make-up of constituencies and not to individuals. They tell us how different kinds of constituencies voted, not how particular groups of electors voted. To get information about the latter we need to turn again to survey data. Table 1.9 shows voting patterns on the basis of age, sex, occupational class and housing tenure.

The data suggest that Tony Blair's strategy of appealing to 'middle England' paid off handsomely. Confirming the analysis of constituency data, the biggest Conservative losses were amongst groups which have normally given them large majorities – the middle class (non-manual workers) and owner occupiers. In contrast, Labour's advance amongst manual workers and council tenants was relatively modest. There were also very large swings amongst younger voters whilst those in the most senior age group showed little change. The party choice of men and women was virtually identical so that there was no 'gender gap' in 1997. Indeed, more detailed analysis shows that younger women were more strongly Labour than younger men. Amongst eighteen-to-twenty-nine-year-olds, the Labour lead over the Conservatives was 25 per cent amongst men but a huge 45 per cent amongst women.

Turnout

In the euphoria on the one hand, and consternation on the other, which greeted Labour's landslide victory in the election, little attention was paid by

Table 1.9 Vote by social group (%)

				Change 1992–97		
Social group	*Con*	*Lab*	*Lib Dem*	*Con*	*Lab*	*Lib Dem*
Non-manual	37	37	20	–18	+15	0
Manual	24	58	13	–10	+8	0
Aged:						
18–29	22	57	17	–21	+20	–1
30–44	26	50	17	–17	+17	–4
45–64	33	43	18	–15	+10	–2
65+	44	34	17	–5	–2	+3
Men	31	46	17	–13	+10	0
Women	32	45	17	–15	+12	–1
Owner occupiers	35	41	17	–18	+14	–1
Council tenants	13	66	15	–5	+1	+2
Private tenants	24	54	16	–18	+15	+2

Notes: The rows do not total 100 because votes for 'others' are not shown. The figures for change compare the 1997 exit poll with the 1992 BES cross-section survey.

Source: BBC/NOP exit poll 1997; British Election Study (BES) survey 1992.

media commentators to another significant feature of the results – the sharp fall in the turnout of electors. During the campaign, fears were expressed that the electorate might be 'turned off' by the length of the campaign and by the saturation media coverage, and the fact that there was a dramatic decline in audiences for television news programmes during the campaign is persuasive circumstantial evidence in support of this view.

Such fears proved to be well founded, for the election saw the lowest turnout in any modern general election (71.6 per cent) and the decline compared with 1992 (–6.3 per cent) was the largest recorded between any pair of elections in the post-war period. As Table 1.10 shows, the South West had the highest turnout in 1997 (75.1 per cent) as it had in 1992 (81.1 per cent), but three regions (North, Yorkshire and Humberside, Greater London) fell below 70 per cent. In terms of change, Scotland had much the smallest decline (–4.0 per cent) whilst the North West and East and West Midlands had the largest (–7.3 per cent).

The changes in constituency boundaries already referred to mean that a full analysis of variations in the change in turnout across constituencies is not possible.[7] We can, however, explore the topic to some extent by focusing on the 238 constituencies in which there were no boundary changes or in which the changes involved 5 per cent or less of the electorate.

It has been suggested that the main reason for the fall in turnout was that many former Conservatives decided not to vote.[8] This is certainly a plausible

Table 1.10 Overall turnout 1992–1997 (%)

Region	*1992*	*1997*	*Change*
Scotland	75.4	71.4	–4.0
Wales	79.7	73.5	–6.2
North	76.5	69.5	–7.0
Yorks & Humberside	75.4	68.4	–7.0
North West	77.3	70.0	–7.3
West Midlands	78.2	70.9	–7.3
East Midlands	80.6	73.3	–7.3
East Anglia	80.0	74.6	–5.4
South East	80.2	73.8	–6.4
Greater London	73.8	67.8	–6.0
South West	81.1	75.1	–6.0
Great Britain	77.9	71.6	–6.3

Source: Author's calculations.

hypothesis, given the sharp drop in the Conservative share of the vote, but it finds no support in an analysis of the results. Where we can make meaningful comparisons with 1992, the fall in turnout was smaller in Conservative-held seats (–5.8 per cent, N=107) than in those that were Labour-held (–7.9 per cent, N=103). The correlation between the change in turnout and previous Conservative share of the vote was 0.258, whilst with previous Labour share it was –0.356. The more 1992 Conservative voters there were in a constituency, the smaller (less negative) was the decline; the more Labour voters there were, the steeper the decline. Moreover, correlation analysis shows no significant relationship between change in turnout and change in any of the parties' share of the vote.[9] This suggests that the Conservative defeat is not to be ascribed to 'stay-at-home' supporters, but (as seen in Table 1.3) to large-scale switching by former Conservatives to the other parties.

Previous research has established that variations in constituency turnout in general elections can largely be explained by two main sorts of factors – the electoral context and the social composition of constituencies. In broad terms, turnout tends to be lower in safe seats and in poorer, urban areas and in those in which a large proportion of the electorate live in privately rented accommodation (which is associated with a relatively transient population). More marginal seats and those in more affluent, rural and suburban areas tend to have higher turnouts. These patterns were confirmed in 1997 as the correlation coefficients in Table 1.11 indicate.

The figures show that, as anticipated, turnout was positively related to previous marginality, despite the fact that boundary changes made estimating the marginality or safeness of seats difficult both for the parties and the voters. In terms of social composition, turnout was lower the more manual workers

Table 1.11 Correlations with constituency turnout (%)

Previous marginality	0.258
Social group:	
Professional and managerial	0.502
In agriculture	0.378
Manual workers	–0.332
Persons per hectare [a]	–0.649
Owner occupiers	0.690
Aged 18–29	–0.595
Private tenants	–0.298
Aged 75+	0.152
Local authority tenants	–0.554
Households with no car	–0.809
Ethnic minority	–0.488

Note: All coefficients are significant, $p < 0.001$, N = 639.
[a] denotes *number* of persons.

Source: Author's calculations.

there were in a constituency, the more private and council tenants, the more persons per hectare, young people, ethnic minority voters and (especially) the more households without a car. It was higher where there were more professional and managerial workers, owner occupiers, people employed in agriculture and older people.

As before, multivariate analysis gives a better indication of the determinants of turnout levels than simple correlations and a combination of seven significant variables (marginality, no car, manual workers, persons per hectare, young people, private tenants and ethnic minority households) accounts for 78.8 per cent of the variation in constituency turnout in 1997. Indeed, the first three of these account for 69.6 per cent of the turnout variation.

This analysis of turnout patterns provides a sobering counter to the euphoria generated by Labour's landslide victory. The landslide was won on the lowest turnout since the war and it was lowest of all and fell most sharply in Labour areas. There was clearly an across-the-board decline, but, although we cannot properly infer it from the constituency data, the evidence suggests that past and potential Labour supporters stayed away from the polls in larger numbers. A large section of the electorate – largest of all in poor, inner-city areas – were not sufficiently moved by the issues at stake in the election, or the personalities involved, to turn up at the polling stations. This may have been due to a belief that the election was already won, or to disillusion as a consequence of Labour's abandoning traditional policy stances and ideology. Whatever the reason, the turnout figures for 1997 suggest that, although the election results were humiliating for the Conservatives, there are some (admittedly relatively minor) disturbing messages for Labour strategists.

Conclusion

The concern in this chapter has been to describe what happened in the general election. The question of why it happened is considered at length elsewhere in the book. Certainly there is nothing in the six-week campaign that can account for the rout of the Conservatives. Explanations must focus on the events of the previous five years. A review of the popularity of the parties between 1992 and 1997 suggests that the electorate's deep and enduring disaffection from the Conservatives was due to the Government's poor handling of the ERM crisis in September 1992, which lost the Party its reputation for economic competence; the succeeding budgets which destroyed its credibility on taxation; the image of sleaziness; divisions over European policy; the various events which changed the once popular policy of privatisation into an electoral albatross and the accession of Tony Blair to the Labour leadership in July 1994.[10] All of these find echoes in the NOP/BBC election-day exit poll.

Amongst voters who had a view, Labour led the Conservatives as the party most trusted on the economy (45 per cent to 42 per cent), on tax (44 per cent to 36 per cent) and on sleaze (49 per cent to 22 per cent). Whilst 69 per cent thought that the Labour Party was united only 16 per cent thought the same of the Conservatives. More than three-quarters of respondents (78 per cent) believed that there should be no more privatisations. When asked about the party leaders, 79 per cent described Blair as a strong leader compared with 33 per cent who said the same of Major. Blair was also clearly first choice as the leader who would make the best Prime Minister, being preferred by 47 per cent of respondents compared with 33 per cent for Major and 20 per cent for Ashdown.

In the end, the events of the previous five years made most voters simply weary of the Conservatives and they were duly cast out into the electoral wilderness. Whether they will wander there as long as Labour did after 1979, or even for as long as Moses and the Israelites, remains to be seen. Blair played the role of Joshua for Labour, but, as yet, there does not appear to be a Moses in the Conservative ranks.

Notes

1 For reasons of space, Northern Ireland is excluded from consideration in this chapter. The party system and the issues at stake are unique to that part of the United Kingdom and normally all votes cast and all seats won (eighteen) are assigned to 'others' in the UK context.

2 I am grateful to Nick Moon of NOP and Brian Horrocks of the BBC for the early

release of the exit poll and for their permission allowing academic commentators to use the results.

3 The 'notional' 1992 results are to be found in C. Rallings and M. Thrasher, *Media Guide to the New Constituencies* (Local Government Chronicle Election Centre, University of Plymouth, 1995).

4 Here and in all subsequent analyses of constituencies, Tatton (which was not contested by Labour and the Liberal Democrats) and West Bromwich West (where the Speaker was not opposed by the Conservatives or Liberal Democrats) are excluded.

5 Correlation coefficients measure the strength of association between two variables. Values range from +1 through zero to –1. A positive sign indicates that as scores on one variable increase, so do scores on the other; a negative sign means that as scores on one variable increase, so scores on the other decrease. The closer a coefficient is to +1 or –1 the stronger is the relationship. Coefficients close to zero mean that the variables concerned are not related. For further explantion see D. Denver, *Elections and Voting Behaviour in Britain*, second edition (Hemel Hempstead: Harvester Wheatsheaf, 1994), pp. 14–19.

6 'Multivariate analysis' here refers to multiple regression analysis. This is a statistical technique in which scores on a number of variables are used to 'predict' scores on a dependent variable (such as a party's share of the vote). Such analysis tells us which factors are statistically most important in explaining the dependent variable and also the proportion of variation in the dependent variable that can be explained by various combinations of other variables. For further explanation see Denver, *Elections and Voting Behaviour in Britain*, pp. 14–19.

7 The Boundary Commission for England did not use 1992 electorates to define the new constituencies. The 'notional' 1992 results found in Rallings and Thrasher's *Media Guide to the New Constituencies* are intended only as estimates of the distribution of votes in the new constituencies and should not be used to estimate 1992 constituency turnouts.

8 Garret Fitzgerald argues in *The Times* (12 May 1997) that 'the whole of the two million fall in the total poll was accounted for simply by Tories staying at home'.

9 The analysis of change in turnout at constituency level is restricted to England and Wales. Scotland is excluded because the decline in turnout is much smaller and there is a heavy preponderance of Labour seats amongst the unchanged constituencies. Within Scotland the patterns described in the text also apply.

10 See D. Denver 'The perils of government' in A. King (ed.), *Britain at the Polls 1997* (Chatham, New Jersey: Chatham House, forthcoming).

Wirral South

Before the 1997 general election each gain by the opposition at a by-election elicited a two-fold response from whichever government minister had been deputed to defend the government: the result was a protest vote and the Conservatives would win the seat back at the next general election. The Conservatives could take comfort in the fact that they had in fact regained all the seats they lost in by-elections prior to the 1992 general election. Moreover, Labour had not managed to hold a by-election gain since it won the Rutherglen seat in Lanarkshire at a 1964 by-election and held it in that year's general election.

The familiar litany of Government excuses were on parade when the Conservatives lost their previously safe seat of Wirral South in a March 1997 by-election. Labour won the by-election with a massive 17 per cent swing which converted a Conservative majority of 8,183 in 1992 into a Labour majority of 7,888. The Conservatives expressed confidence that they would win the seat back. Health Secretary Stephen Dorrell dismissed the vote as a 'demo'; but an element of doubt was also apparent when he added: 'I accept that it's not an easy voter reaction to explain.'

Labour's successful by-election candidate was Ben Chapman, a former diplomat and North West regional director of the Department of Trade and Industry. Chapman had been a member of the Labour Party for less than a year and had been hurriedly selected for the seat when the original candidate stood down following allegations about his private life. Chapman's pinstripe suited sobriety was ideal in a previously Tory seat. Labour's slogan: 'Ben Chapman means business', captured the candidate's appeal and was emblematic of New Labour's attempt to portray itself as a party with which business could work. The Conservative candidate at the by-election and general election was Les Byrom, an estate agent from nearby Southport.

Labour's retention of Wirral South at the general election elicited little surprise amidst the avalanche of anti-Conservative results on election night; but it showed that the writing had been on the wall for the Conservatives for some time prior to the 1997 general election. The Wirral South by-election had not been a blip or a protest: it showed the abandonment of the Conservatives by 'Middle England', a fact the general election confirmed.

Result

Wirral South			
Ben Chapman	Lab	24,499	
Les Byrom	Con	17,495	
Phil Gilchrist	Lib Dem	5,018	
	Others	1,083	
Total vote		48,095	Turnout 81.01%
Lab majority		7,004	
Lab gain from Con			
Swing Con to Lab 15.4%			

2

Labour's path to power

Steven Fielding

Introduction

On 1 May 1997 the Labour Party won 419 constituencies, giving it a Commons majority of 179. Gaining a 44.4 per cent share of votes cast, this was Labour's best result since 1966, the product of a national swing of 10 per cent, the biggest shift of support from one party to another this century. The Party had added 2 million votes to its 1992 tally; the 13.55 million total being Labour's biggest ever popular vote, apart from 1951. Moreover, the Party did well across society: it was supported by three-fifths of the unskilled, over half of the skilled, almost half of office workers and nearly one-third of the professional middle class. Tony Blair had made Labour into a 'people's party', something it had not been since the 1940s. To some, 'landslide' hardly described what had occurred.

Modernisation

If landslide it was, the 1997 result was a long time in the making: fourteen years, in fact. As Blair has acknowledged, without Neil Kinnock, Labour's revival would have been impossible. Kinnock became Party leader in October 1983, a few months after Labour slumped to 27.6 per cent at that year's general election. Commentators speculated that Labour was fated to become a party of the 'excluded', that is, inner-city ethnic minorities and the declining unskilled manual working class. Kinnock rejected this prospect. Arguing that Labour's programme was too extreme, he stated that the Party would recover only when it could articulate the 'aspirations of the majority' and 'share their values'. Policies and the Party itself had to change.[1]

There were few enthusiasts for Kinnock's programme. Amongst the minority were the newly elected MPs Gordon Brown and Tony Blair: they and others who supported Kinnock became known as 'modernisers'. Yet, even Kinnock under-estimated the scale by which Labour had to transform itself. Thus, the Party only slightly improved its position in 1987, winning 30.8 per cent of votes. This disappointment led Kinnock and others – like Peter Mandelson, the Party's communications director – to press for more fundamental change. Labour's Policy Review of 1987–89 was the result. During this reappraisal, the modernisers tried to reconcile Labour's traditional commitment to state economic intervention and the redistribution of wealth with the preoccupations of an increasingly affluent and individualistic society. Many analysts considered they had reached the right balance and believed Labour would win the 1992 election. This conviction was underpinned by the fact that Britain was enduring a depression which particularly hurt the Conservative South East. Yet Labour still lost, only marginally bettering its 1987 performance by winning a 34.4 per cent share of the vote.

Tony Blair

As Labour came to terms with this fourth defeat in a row, Kinnock was succeeded by John Smith, the Shadow Chancellor. Smith had supported Kinnock's changes, but had not been a prominent advocate. Indeed, Smith accommodated the likes of John Prescott, who doubted the merits of Kinnock's modernisation of the Party. Such figures believed that in 1992 Labour had been the victim of contingent factors – such as Kinnock's own unpopularity. Thus, policy could be left alone: to win next time, Labour merely had to make 'one more heave'. This view appeared convincing after the collapse of Conservative economic strategy in the autumn of 1992: from that point Labour enjoyed a commanding opinion poll lead. Whilst not as complacent as some, Smith none the less pursued a policy of benign inactivity. In June 1994 Labour won 44 per cent of votes in elections for the European Parliament. Immediately prior to these elections, however, Smith died. The Party had to choose another leader and selected one whose analysis of Labour's position was radically different from that of his predecessor.

Party members elected Tony Blair with an overwhelming majority, largely because they supposed he appealed to those who had not favoured Labour in 1992. Like other modernisers, but in contrast to many of those who voted for him, Blair believed Kinnock's failure proved Labour had to press on with change. He thought it needed to abandon redistributing incomes through tax as well as direct state intervention in the economy. This would, he imagined, help Labour increase support amongst white-collar and skilled manual workers, described by sociologists as the C1s and C2s and by journalists as 'middle Britain'. Forming half the electorate, they were especially numerous in what Party officials referred to as 'key seats' which were themselves concentrated in England. As Blair told the Party's 1996 conference:

> I can recall vividly the exact moment that I knew the last election was lost. I was canvassing in the Midlands, on an ordinary, suburban estate. I met a man polishing his Ford Sierra. He was a self-employed electrician. His dad always voted Labour, he said. He used to vote Labour, too. But he'd bought his own house now. He'd set up his own business. He was doing quite nicely. 'So I've become a Tory,' he said ... In that moment he crystallised for me the basis of our failure ... People judge us on their

> instincts about what they believe our instincts to be. And that man polishing his car was clear. His instincts were to get on in life. And he thought our instincts were to stop him.[2]

The opinions of such people were analysed by Labour's pollsters; they gathered 'focus groups' to discuss the Party in detail. Kinnock and Smith had both been interested in such work: under Blair, however, it came to dictate Labour's electoral strategy to an unprecedented extent.

Most of Labour's research was kept secret. Fortunately, between 1992 and 1994, the Fabian Society published three detailed studies of C1 and C2 Conservative 'waverers', that is, people who considered voting Labour in 1992 but remained loyal to John Major.[3] According to these investigations, the waverers were not entirely persuaded by the Conservatives' faith in unregulated markets. Whilst sceptical about the merits of higher taxation, they wanted the state to remain in charge of education and health care. These waverers did not vote Labour in 1992 because they considered it would ruin the economy and were persuaded that its proposed tax increases would hurt them to no general benefit. However bad things were, they feared Labour would make them worse. Such concerns derived from the impression that the Party was too closely tied to the unions and the poor. More worryingly, for Labour, such views did not change after 1992. The Party's opinion poll lead under Smith was based on disillusion with the Conservatives more than faith in Labour. Thus, according to this analysis, once economic circumstances improved, Labour's lead would disappear. To prevent this, the authors concluded that Labour needed to become more sympathetic to the waverers' aspirations. The Party also had to persuade them it could manage the economy without hitting their pockets. Significantly, one conclusion was: 'we have to become a new Labour Party'.

New Labour

Blair accepted the Fabian evaluation of Labour's predicament which, in any case, echoed Party research undertaken since the later 1980s. Consequently, to signify that Labour had changed with his leadership, Blair referred to the Party as 'New Labour'. This simple conceit was so insidious, even Conservatives talked of New Labour. Blair knew he had to go further than this cosmetic device: at Labour's 1994 conference he demanded that Clause Four of the Party's constitution be revised. First drafted in 1918, this formally committed the Party to extend the 'common ownership of the means of production, distribution and exchange'. It had long since ceased to have any impact on policy, but was a link with what Blair vaguely but damningly described as 'Old Labour'. Thus, it was the clause's symbolic – rather than actual – significance which led him to want its replacement with a form of words pledging the Party to fostering, amongst other things, a 'dynamic economy'. Where

Hugh Gaitskell had failed in 1960 and other leaders had feared to tread, Blair was successful in securing an overhaul of the clause.

Whilst words and symbols were important, Blair knew that substance was also required. Like Kinnock and even Smith, Blair appreciated Labour had to alter its relationship with the unions if the Party was to improve its image with the waverers. Thus, by 1997, the unions controlled only half the votes cast at Labour's conference, down from about 90 per cent in the 1980s. They also contributed proportionately less to Party income: from 90 per cent in 1990 to about half. By the time of the election it was exceptionally difficult for the Conservatives to persuade voters that Labour was dominated by union 'barons'. This assertion was even less tenable as Blair repeatedly stated that, if elected, he would treat unions on the basis of 'fairness not favours'.

Blair and his Shadow Chancellor Gordon Brown appreciated that middle Britons would be most impressed if Labour changed its position on 'tax and spend'. They believed Labour's 1992 proposals to increase tax on higher earners to pay for spending on pensions, education and health had been the key to its defeat. Thus, in January 1997 Brown made a speech which the *Economist* considered 'altered the course of the election campaign'.[4] Brown promised that a Labour government would not increase the basic rate of direct tax, nor increase its top limit, nor raise VAT. Indeed, he committed Labour to cutting VAT on heating and fuel, thereby reversing one of the Major Government's most resented tax increases. Brown also said he would follow existing Conservative spending plans for his first two years in office. The rationale for these commitments was clear: by making them, Peter Mandelson stated, Labour could nail 'Tory lies about us on tax and spending' well in advance of the election.[5] Significantly, the only tax-raising measure included in Labour's programme was one to be levied on privatised companies to pay for schemes to reduce youth unemployment. It was no accident: this 'windfall tax' was popular with middle Britons because they bitterly resented 'fat cat' directors and chief executives who prospered as a result of leaving the public sector.

Just as Labour moved closer to Conservative policies on 'tax and spend', the Party also appeared seemingly to adopt Conservative postures on a wide range of other issues: in particular, education, crime and Europe. Thus, the education spokesperson David Blunkett talked of improving 'standards' in schools, even endorsing the reintroduction of uniforms; Jack Straw, who shadowed the Home Secretary, promoted curfews for the young and criticised 'squeegee merchants' and beggars; and, in foreign affairs, Robin Cook suggested a Labour government would be unlikely to enter the single currency during its first term. Thus, waverers' preferences for 'traditional' schooling, obsession with law and order and scepticism about Europe were all assuaged.

The pursuit of middle Britons would have been less effective had the Party's relationship with the Conservative-inclined popular press not been transformed. Blair's press officer Alastair Campbell was particularly aware of the extent to which the tabloids' treatment of Labour had distorted perceptions of the Party in 1992. He sought to improve relations with them, especially the *Sun* which had more C1 and C2 readers than any other paper. This was done with the full knowledge that, as Campbell put it, they were still dealing with a press that 'basically wants to do us in if it can'.[6] Blair most famously courted Rupert Murdoch, owner of the *Sun*, *The Times*, *Sunday Times* and *News of the World*: he finessed Labour's position on cross-media ownership to suit Murdoch's interest. To the surprise of many, in the first week of the campaign, the *Sun* went so far as to call on its readers to support Blair. Of the other Murdoch titles, Labour was later endorsed by the mass circulation Sunday *News of the World*, whilst *The Times* remained effectively neutral; only the *Sunday Times* still backed the Conservatives.

Blair, therefore, entered the campaign, offering wavering voters 'a degree of continuity as well as change', reassuring them that Labour was 'safe' on the unions, tax and the economy.[7] This emphasis had already proved itself. Labour had won the safe Conservative seat of Wirral South with a 17 per cent swing in a by-election held weeks before the general election. Whilst this strategy appeared to work, it none the less disturbed many in the Party. Robin Cook reportedly stated in the autumn of 1996 that there was 'a very real danger' that whilst reaching out for Conservative waverers, Labour would ignore the needs of the poor.[8] Some also claimed the Party was no longer interested in black voters or 'women's issues'. In traditional Labour areas, a few MPs claimed it was hard to motivate activists to work for a Labour victory. Members in Scotland were especially hostile: they suspected Blair's commitment to devolution was weak due to his fear that it troubled English voters. Blair countered such criticism by referring to the 'radical centre'. Thus: if 'you want to push through the kind of radical changes we're talking about, you have to drive it from the centre'. By this he meant: Labour had to appeal to Conservative waverers because without them the Party could not win office. According to Blair, this meant rejecting the notion that radicalism had to be measured by increasing tax. In any case, he stated, Labour's new policies were 'not just the route to power', they were 'right'.[9]

Millbank

A crucial element of Blair's approach was his unprecedented emphasis on Party image: hence 'New Labour'. This involved the Party hierarchy – mainly himself, Brown, Mandelson and their minions – managing how the Party presented itself through the media. Such control increased as election day approached. Thus, during the campaign efforts were focused on ensuring that all stayed 'on message'. Faxes, electronic mail, mobile phones and pagers were used to make Party spokespeople and candidates aware of the approved responses to issues as they developed. The principal object was to avoid inconsistencies, which would be inflated by the Conservatives and the media into 'splits'. Such a stress on image and message was partly the result of the experience of previous elections, particularly in 1987 and 1992. Labour also learnt from Bill Clinton's presidential campaigns of 1992 and 1996. Much of this wisdom was, however, hardly new. In the late 1950s Labour leaders recognised how party image could influence voters' affiliations. During its move leftwards, culminating in the public relations disaster that was the 1983 campaign, the Party had decided to ignore such insights.[10]

Labour's efforts were directed from Millbank Tower in Westminster where it had taken a lease on two floors during the autumn of 1995. At Millbank, about eighty staff under Mandelson's supervision had, months prior to the campaign, concentrated 'on one thing: how to get our positive message across'.[11] Whilst Mandelson acted as general election campaign manager, Gordon Brown was in charge of campaign strategy. Ironically, for such a well-organised operation, the exact division of these two men's responsibilities was never clear. Moreover, as they allegedly disliked each other, the potential for conflict was ever-present. Two million pounds were spent installing equipment for the 250 or so staff who would work at Millbank during the campaign. Once in place, they were arranged into a dozen task-forces specialising in particularly crucial tasks. The rapid rebuttal unit was the most prominent of these and benefited from a £300,000 database system grandly named 'Excalibur'. This allowed the Party to respond quickly to Conservative claims and expose their inconsistencies. It meant that, unlike in 1992, the Party could neutralise any attack within minutes of it being launched. This capability was vitally important in the era of 'rolling news'.

The media made much of what some called the 'Millbank Tendency'. There were also numerous Labour critics who worried about the influence Millbank's image-makers exerted over strategy. Even deputy leader John Prescott dismissively described some Millbank staff as 'political smart arses'. To such traditionalists, Millbank represented all that was dubious about New Labour. In their eyes it was composed of a small clique, ignorant of the labour movement and willing to say almost anything to win votes.

However centralised and elitist, Labour's campaign strategy still relied heavily upon the work of the Party's established organisation and the efforts of ordinary members. First, under John Smith, the Party ensured that the 1993–94 Boundary Commission review of constituency borders did not harm Labour as much as many had predicted. This was principally because, unlike the Conservatives, Labour officials had focused their efforts on maximising the Party's overall advantage rather than allowing individual constituency parties to dispute the redrawing of boundaries amongst themselves.

Second, without the commitment of Labour's activists, many of whom questioned Blair's moderation, the Party's campaign would have been less effective. In 1992 the targeting of key seats had won Labour more seats than its national vote merited. In 1997 Labour's national resources – both money and personnel – were concentrated in ninety seats which could be won on a swing of 6 per cent or less. A year or so before the poll, activists in these seats were encouraged to identify potential Labour voters. This information was passed to Millbank which then assumed responsibility for bombarding such waverers with telephone calls, letters from Blair and even videos.[12] Activists worked especially hard once the campaign had begun, in particular ensuring Labour's supporters actually voted. Surveys in key seats also revealed they were posting far more leaflets through doors and making a much greater number of personal calls than their Conservative counterparts.

The campaign

Labour's leaders were confident they had constructed a bomb-proof programme able to survive the campaign unscathed. Possible controversies had been defused months before. Thus, aware of the danger posed by Conservative claims of a 'tartan tax', Blair had forced his Scottish members to accept an additional question on the tax-raising powers of a devolved Parliament. This matter resurfaced during the campaign when Blair compared the powers of a future Parliament to those of a parish council. However, it is possible Blair deliberately made this provocative comment to further reassure English voters, calculating Scots would vote Labour whatever he said. Issues which could not be resolved were left to future referendums, committees, commissions and reviews. Blair, thereby, side-stepped many difficult questions by stating that pensions, the minimum wage, the care of the elderly, the single currency and electoral reform were all matters 'for government, not opposition'.[13]

Indeed, Labour had effectively published its manifesto nearly a year before the election with *New Labour: New Life for Britain*. This was distributed free to voters, accompanied by an explanatory election broadcast and supplemented by a mass phone link to the leader. *New Life* contained five 'early pledges': to cut class sizes for young schoolchildren; to halve the time between arrest and punishment for young criminals; to cut NHS waiting lists; to get 250,000 young unemployed into work; and to 'set tough rules' for government spending and borrowing. These pledges formed the basis of Labour's final manifesto. In fact, so familiar had the Party's programme become, it was decided to delay announcing the proposal that funds raised by the National Lottery should be spent on health and education. This popular initiative, one of Labour's few policy novelties of the campaign, was put back until the vital final week.[14]

In the first few days of the campaign, Labour's leading figures were surprisingly jittery. This was because, whilst the election was Labour's to lose, it could still be lost by silly mistakes. They were particularly haunted by the belief that Kinnock's triumphalist 1992 Sheffield rally had contributed to his defeat. Eighteen years out of power also added to the sense that, as Blair declared at the manifesto launch, 1997 was Labour's 'historic opportunity', adding, if the

Party blew 'this opportunity, we blow our place in history'. Blair was especially nervous early on, conscious that the 'whole weight of the thing' was on his shoulders. Yet, as he stated, 'this is the big moment we've been preparing for. If you can't get through this, you shouldn't be doing the job.'[15]

Union recognition

Fortunately for Labour, 'sleaze' initially dominated the campaign. The Party was content to see news headlines demanding the Conservative MP Neil Hamilton stand down in Tatton. Indeed, later in March, Labour kept the controversy going by withdrawing its own prospective candidate in Tatton in favour of the former television journalist Martin Bell. When media attention shifted to policy at the start of the second week, Labour found matters more problematic. The Conservatives highlighted Labour's long-standing proposal that workers could legally force employers to recognise their representation by a trade union if more than half those in a designated 'bargaining unit' voted for it. This was supported by unions who saw it as the means of recruiting up to 5 million more members. Yet Blair claimed to be the 'entrepreneur's champion' and had won the endorsement of numerous business leaders. Indeed, the Party's first campaign broadcast featured prominent business people describing Labour as the 'Party of business'. Such recommendations reassured Conservative waverers that Labour could be trusted with the economy. Unfortunately, union recognition was opposed by the Confederation of British Industry (CBI) and Federation of Small Employers, the very people whose approval Blair sought.

Unable to change the policy but realising the damage it could do, Labour strategists had drawn a veil over it. Thus, they had not briefed journalists or even advised Labour spokespeople about how best to stay 'on message'. The Conservatives were, then, attacking one of Labour's weak spots. They gleefully presented the policy as an 'imposition' by unions wanting to claw back powers enjoyed before 1979. This measure would, they stated, increase industrial inefficiency and ruin the economy. Over and above such hyperbole, there were unresolved details which the Conservatives gnawed at, such as how a 'bargaining unit' was defined and whether workers opposing recognition would be forced to join a union.[16] Labour eventually found answers but looked flustered and uncertain: the Millbank machine was bruised in one of its first skirmishes. Fortunately, by the end of the week, sleaze had reasserted itself and the media caravan moved on.

On 3 April Labour launched its manifesto, *New Labour: Because Britain Deserves Better*, which endorsed Blair's belief that the election was about 'trust'. It expanded Labour's earlier five pledges into a ten-point personal 'contract with the British people', the central aim being to improve education. In introducing the programme, Blair wanted to 'make a virtue of the fact that our manifesto does not promise the earth. It does not say it can do everything.

There are no magic wands or instant solutions.' This confident modesty of ambition was based on the knowledge that Labour's focus groups showed a lack of trust in parties making grandiose promises. As the research of the Fabians and others had shown, Labour would only be believed if it made concrete proposals which would have a clear impact on people's lives. This is what the five early pledges had been: these were reinforced during the campaign when the Party issued posters which stated simply that 'Class sizes will be smaller', 'Income tax will not rise', 'Young offenders will be punished', 'More jobs for young people' and 'NHS waiting lists will be shorter'. This approach paid handsome dividends: according to the opinion pollsters, Harris, even 45 per cent of those intending to vote Conservative trusted Labour more.

Privatisation

Having placed Labour in this enviable position, Millbank experienced an awkward few days after the manifesto launch. It had been known for some time that the Major Government's spending plans were based on the assumption it would raise £1.5 billion from privatisation receipts. Thus, when Gordon Brown said the Party would follow these plans, he knew he was probably committing Labour to selling off some state assets. Brown was not bothered by this likelihood. Nor was Blair, who considered the Shadow Chancellor's flexibility exemplified Labour's economic pragmatism. New Labour, he told a City audience, had no dogmatic belief in either the public or the private sector.[17] Whilst this might have been the case for some at the top, it was unacceptable to others. Many members had only reluctantly accepted that a Labour government could not renationalise any of those concerns sold off since 1979. For Labour to pursue its own privatisation programme was beyond the pale.

The Conservatives asked how Labour would fill the funding gap: increase borrowing, raise taxes or continue to privatise? The first two alternatives would offend waverers; the third would result in Labour uproar. Brown let it be known, through the press, that he would draw up an inventory of state assets to determine what could be sold off: this would include the air traffic control service. Yet, at Labour's 1996 conference Andrew Smith, the Party's transport spokesperson, described the privatisation of air traffic control as 'crazy'. Whilst this line had been changed in February 1997, it had not been shouted from the rooftops. Once again, the real gap was one of information: because it was a sensitive issue, Party managers had tried to avoid discussing it and so had not briefed journalists in advance of the campaign. Indeed, many Labour candidates had inadvertently issued personal manifestos which condemned further privatisations. Moreover, the story in the press was 'over-spun'. Brown wished to reassure waverers that Labour would look at the matter sensibly and pragmatically: but some journalists wrote that Labour had abandoned its principles in a scramble for votes. This raised questions about the Party's competence on the key issue of economic management and exposed hidden Labour divisions.

Focus on fear

Millbank's problems with union recognition and privatisation had no clear impact on Labour's poll standing. None the less, some argued that the Party was losing the campaign. Brown favoured protecting Labour's poll lead by responding to Conservative claims with a detailed rebuttal. Mandelson, on the other hand, wanted to attack the Conservatives, thereby reducing their capacity to mount their own assaults on Labour's programme. However, the 'wobble' over privatisation was the last time Labour came under pressure. Even the publication on 22 April of an ICM poll which put the Party's lead at five points was of no great moment: it was soon shown to be a rogue result.

Labour strategists, none the less, decided that it was now time to go on the offensive. It had long been their plan to do so, and they saw no need to hold back. Their object was to exploit fears about what the Conservatives would do if re-elected. Labour used pensions to focus wavering voters' anxieties in a way which echoed the Conservatives' use of tax in previous elections. Whilst Party spokespeople did not exactly lie, the substance of their claims was, at best, dubious. Thus, Labour stated that the Conservatives wanted to 'abolish' state pensions without indicating that another system would be put in their place. The problem for the Conservatives was that many believed Labour. This was especially the case with the key C1 and C2 voters, in particular those in early middle age who, unlike existing pensioners, would be affected by Conservative plans. Labour's opponents consequently spent vital days explaining what their plans really were. It was the nastiest but most effective moment of Millbank's campaign.

Millbank's last five days unit co-ordinated the work of similar bodies formed in every key seat to ensure those who said they backed Labour actually voted for the Party. Not daring to believe that Labour's opinion poll lead would be translated into real votes, this work dominated Party members' attention for most of the last week of the campaign. After pursuing fickle 'middle Britons', Labour's efforts now concentrated on its traditional supporters, who tended to have an abstention rate higher than that of core Conservatives. Thus, core Labour voters were exhorted to exercise their franchise through numerous means: Millbank despatched thousands of stickers, flags, hats, balloons, posters, leaflets and even branded rain ponchos to 'encourage and enthuse'.

In the end, Labour survived six weeks of campaigning mainly because it had closed down most of the avenues of Conservative attack months, if not years, before. There had, none the less, been one or two 'wobbles' which showed that Millbank was not as omnicompetent as some believed. Moreover, had the Conservatives not been so preoccupied with their own internal difficulties or burdened with such a bad record, things might have been less easy.

Some considered that because of this, Labour's campaign could have been less cautious and, perhaps, even taken a few risks by challenging, not confirming, the waverers' prejudices.[18] To such critics, Blair asked: 'How was I to know the Tory campaign would be such a shambles?'[19] Millbank did what it thought had to be done to guarantee Labour's victory: until 1 May, ensuring this was all that mattered.

The 'landslide'

Some on the left saw Labour's victory in almost apocalyptic terms. The Blair-friendly *Guardian* considered it showed that the electorate wanted 'big, systematic and thorough-going change'.[20] Tony Benn, a long-standing Labour left-winger, even thought it 'represented the wholesale rejection of the crude capitalist philosophy associated with Margaret Thatcher which put profit before people'.[21] The evidence, however, suggests Labour's success should be seen in more prosaic terms. The most obvious point is that the Party's huge Commons majority was the product of a skewed system of representation: in return for 44.4 per cent of votes, Labour was given 65.2 per cent of seats.

More consequentially, Labour's victory was principally based on Blair's disciplined focus on the concerns of C1 and C2 voters. Thus, whilst Labour's mandate was for change, it was 'safe' change. The Party had promised not to threaten the interests of suburban dwellers, most of whom had done well out of the Thatcher years. This was the key to Labour's increase in support in the South East, from 21 per cent in 1992 to 32 per cent in 1997, which brought an additional thirty-one seats.

Yet, whilst winning their votes, Labour had won few hearts amongst the waverers of middle Britain. Focus groups convened by numerous national newspapers in key seats during the campaign revealed the shallow nature of the Party's support. More generally, NOP discovered that 46 per cent of those polled agreed with the statement 'I'm not enthusiastic about them [Labour] but they can't be worse than the Tories'. The waverers were, as ever, critical of the Major Government but, whilst inclined towards Labour, remained sceptical about the Party's merits. The thoughts of one 1992 Conservative voter from Stevenage who chose Labour in 1997 must stand for many. A married local government worker with three children, a 'nice home' and, along with her husband, a 'nice job', this voter was asked why she had changed allegiance. She replied: 'I thought I would take the chance. I don't know what convinced me, but when it came down to it I thought I would like better health and education. Whilst things are OK under the Conservatives, I just thought they could be better.'[22] Unconsciously echoing Labour's campaign theme, D:Ream's 'Things can only get better', she believed Labour was worth the risk. On the basis of such fragile support, Labour won Stevenage for the first time since 1974 with a 14 per cent swing.

Conclusion

In 1997 Tony Blair did what Neil Kinnock had wanted, but proved unable, to do: he made Labour reflect the 'aspirations of the majority' – or at least 44.4 per cent of voters. Yet, that number was composed of many 'middle Britons' whose party affiliations were weak even in the midst of a 'landslide'. In government, Blair aims to strengthen the bond of 'trust' between Labour and these voters tentatively established in the campaign. He proposes to do this by keeping the few and limited promises made in his manifesto 'contract'. Having proved that New Labour remains true to its word, Blair proposes to turn to the voters and say: 'Look, this is the direction, and we want to go further.'[23] Is this 'trust' a chimera, impossible to obtain? If Labour is to make things 'better', some in middle Britain – described by one commentator as 'feckless and selfish' – might have to pay the price, be it through direct or indirect tax increases. They may not like this. Labour won in 1997 as a result of the biggest shift of support from one party to another this century. In this movement, the C1s and C2s played a crucial part. Despite appearances, the 1997 election did not indicate that Britain was a landslide country. It did, however, demonstrate that, in middle Britain at least, the electoral ground can shift quickly underfoot when the narrow interests of the suburbs are not upheld.

Notes

1 *Report of the Annual Conference of the Labour Party, 1983* (London: Labour Party, 1983), p. 30.
2 *Daily Telegraph*, 2 October 1996.
3 G. Radice, *Southern Discomfort*, Fabian Pamphlet, 555 (London: Fabian Society, 1992); G. Radice and S. Pollard, *More Southern Discomfort*, Fabian Pamphlet, 560 (London: Fabian Society, 1993); G. Radice and S. Pollard, *Any Southern Comfort?*, Fabian Pamphlet, 568 (London: Fabian Society, 1994).
4 *Economist*, 25 January 1997.
5 *New Statesman*, 24 January 1997.
6 *Guardian*, 17 February 1997.
7 *Daily Telegraph*, 18 March 1997.
8 *Sunday Times*, 29 September 1996.
9 *Guardian*, 29 September 1996 and 25 April 1997.
10 D. Kavanagh, *Election Campaigning* (Oxford: Blackwell, 1995), pp. 77–109.
11 *Guardian*, 28 September 1996.
12 *Guardian*, 22 February 1997; *Independent*, 3 May 1997.
13 *New Statesman*, 21 March 1997.
14 *New Statesman*, special edition, May 1997.
15 *Guardian*, 15 April 1997.
16 *Guardian*, 25 March 1997; *Daily Telegraph*, 26 March 1997.
17 *Guardian*, 8 April 1997.
18 *New Statesman*, 18 April 1997.

19 *Sunday Times*, 4 May 1997.
20 *Guardian*, 3 May 1997.
21 *Tribune*, 9 May 1997.
22 *Guardian*, 28 and 30 April 1997.
23 *Guardian*, 1 May 1997.

Enfield Southgate

The defeat of Defence Secretary Michael Portillo was perhaps the most sensational of a host of extraordinary results. If the millions watching on television were amazed, so too, judging by the expression on his face, was the Labour candidate, Stephen Twigg. Early in the BBC's election night coverage, the Defence Secretary had been asked by Jeremy Paxman whether he would 'miss the ministerial limo'. Now Portillo, a Euro-sceptic seen by many as the next leader of the Conservative Party, found his political career wrecked.

Yet the warnings preceded the earlier results and exit polls that evening. On 27 April, an ICM poll in the *Observer* suggested that Portillo was in trouble, particularly if Liberal Democrats voted tactically for Labour. In the event the poll, which still showed Labour trailing by four points, actually *overstated* the extent of Conservative Party support. Portillo lost due to the huge Conservative to Labour swing, embracing a collapse in the Conservative vote, features particularly acute in London and the South East.

Reflecting upon his fate in the *Sunday Telegraph* (4 May) Portillo blamed the 'combined forces of the Referendum Party and a candidate called Mal the Warrior'. True, their combined votes exceeded the Labour victor's majority. Portillo had already acknowledged wider reasons, however, as early as 10.15 p.m. on election night, commenting that the Conservative Party had 'done itself no good by showing its divisions ... we need a happy medium between the discipline required to keep a party credible and attractive to the electorate and the Maoist imposition of thought and deed'.

Twigg, one of six former presidents of the National Union of Students to be elected to Parliament, could meanwhile reflect on the capture of a famous scalp and its wider implications. Labour had moved into the middle-class outer suburbs of the metropolis, gains beyond the fantasies of even its most optimistic adherents. Portillo considered Paxman's offer to 'drink hemlock'.

Result

Enfield Southgate			
Stephen Twigg	Lab	20,570	
Michael Portillo	Con	19,137	
Jeremy Browne	Lib Dem	4,966	
Nicholas Luard	Ref	1,342	
	Others	518	
Total vote		46,533	Turnout 70.72%
Lab majority		1,433	
Lab gain from Con			
Swing Con to Lab 17.40%			

3

The Conservative Party: decline and fall

Philip Cowley

Introduction

The morning of 10 April 1992 *seemed* a good time to be a Conservative. Against the odds the Party had pulled off a record-breaking fourth consecutive election victory, securing the largest ever vote for a British political party. With the benefit of hindsight, victory in 1992 is now viewed slightly differently by Conservatives. At best, it masked other signs of Conservative decline: the party's grassroots membership had fallen from around 1.5 million members in 1979 to just 500,000 by 1992. Those members who were left were no spring chickens: almost half were over sixty-five, with only one in twenty aged under thirty-five. The average age was sixty-two.[1] The local council base of the Party was also shrinking, down from over 12,000 councillors in 1979 to just over 8,000 by 1992. Defeat would have forced the Party to face up to its decline, just as it is now doing. At worst, victory came to be seen as harmful to the Party; it would, people argued, have been better if the Party had lost in 1992: being in opposition would have saved it the humiliation of the exit from the Exchange Rate Mechanism (ERM) and the ensuing in-fighting. That, though, is not how it seemed at the time. The Conservatives appeared unstoppable. The consequences of Britain having become a one-party state were seriously discussed.[2] Five years later, Conservatives waking up on the morning of 2 May 1997 had fewer reasons to be cheerful. The Party was left with just 165 MPs and the support of less than a third of the electorate. On 1 May, as William Hague admitted, 'the Conservative Party was not merely defeated. It was humiliated.'[3]

To have moved from dominant party to English-based rump in just five years is quite an achievement. It is one for which the Conservatives cannot take all the credit. It was not all their own work. The transformation of the Labour Party and the changed attitude of the media were important. But 1997 was largely an election that the Conservatives lost: the most striking feature about the results was not the rise in Labour's vote – because, impressive as it was, Labour had polled better in the past – but the collapse in the Conservative vote. It was that, above all else, which delivered the Labour landslide; and so it is to the Conservative Party – and in particular, to the public's perceptions of the Conservative Party – that we must look for explanations.

The record

By May 1997 the achievements of the Major Government were not prominent in the minds of the electorate. Yet despite the smallest Conservative parliamentary majority since 1951 the Government had enacted a substantial legislative programme. For the most part, it was a programme which demonstrated a high degree of continuity with the policies of Major's predecessor. The beating of inflation remained central to economic policy. The importance of the market continued to be stressed. The coal industry, the nuclear industry and the rail network were all sold. Finance for public projects was sought via the Private Finance Inititative. If areas of the state, such as parts of the health or civil services, could not be sold and private finance was not an option, then they were at least made to perform in a more 'market orientated' way. Deregulation of business was encouraged. A Trade Union and Employment Rights Act introduced yet more curbs on the powers of unions and a Jobseekers Act tightened social security payments. There were also elements of what Ivor Crewe terms 'popular authoritarianism', another central component of Thatcherism.[4] Penal policy was tightened; the police were given new powers and immigration was restricted.[5]

To be sure, Major's style was different from that of his predecessor, as were the circumstances (a smaller parliamentary majority: twenty-one at the start of the Parliament), but the main thrust of the Government's policy continued, advanced and consolidated what had gone before.[6] There were, though, some policy differences. Lady Thatcher was to say that she would not have signed the Maastricht Treaty and she advocated a referendum before its ratification. The much-ridiculed Citizen's Charter was a distinctly Majorite policy, as was the emphasis placed on the problem of Northern Ireland.

These achievements, though, were overshadowed by the many difficulties into which the Government ran almost as soon as it was elected. The recession, which Major had promised would end the day after a Conservative government was returned, instead proved both deep and long. Just five months after the election Britain was ignominiously driven out of the ERM, leaving the Government's economic policy in tatters. Tax rises followed, including the imposition of VAT on domestic fuel, despite promises made to the contrary during the 1992 election.

The Government became embroiled in a series of conflicts with the European Union (EU): over the extension of qualified majority voting; over the appointment of a successor to Jacques Delors as the Commission's president and over the world-wide ban on British beef imposed by the EU. On both the first and the last issue, the Government was, after much posturing, humiliatingly forced to back down. The bill to give effect to the Maastricht Treaty which Major had brought back in triumph before the election came under concerted attack from a group of the Government's own backbenchers. The Government suffered one defeat during the bill's passage, avoided others only by a series of embarrassing retreats and required a vote of confidence to achieve ratification, after suffering another defeat on the issue of the Social Chapter.

The proposal to close thirty-one coal mines caused protest from Conservative backbenchers in October 1992, forcing the Government to promise a 'review' before any closures. The funding of the EU caused further unrest on the Conservative benches, only overcome by yet another vote of confidence. A group of eight MPs refused to support the Government over the issue and as a result had the party whip withdrawn.[7] Many of the same group of eight MPs then voted against the second stage of the imposition of VAT on domestic fuel, inflicting a further defeat. In 1994 the privatisation of the Post Office had to be abandoned in the face of threatened rebellions from Conservative backbenchers. There were also large-scale rebellions against the Government's planned divorce reforms and the proposals to ban certain types of hand guns, following the massacre at Dunblane. In the course of the Parliament four Conservative MPs changed parties, making highly derogatory comments about the Party they were leaving.[8] In June 1995, continuing unrest on the back benches led John Major to the unprecedented step of calling a contest for his own job, urging his rivals to 'put up or shut up'.

The Government was also swamped by the emergence of what became known as sleaze. A series of ministers were forced to resign, after a wide variety of sexual or financial misconduct was revealed. Allegations that Conservative MPs were prepared to take money to ask parliamentary questions and wider claims about the links between MPs and organised interests led to the establishment by the Prime Minister of the Committee on Standards in Public Life, chaired by a judge, Lord Nolan. Concern over the behaviour of ministers over the issue of arms sales to Iraq prompted an inquiry under Lord Justice Scott.

These events resulted in three common and damaging perceptions of the Party and Government: that they were incompetent; that they were disunited; and that they were 'sleazy'.

Competence

Since 1964 the polling company Gallup has periodically asked the following question: 'With Britain in economic difficulties, which party do you think will handle the problem best – the Conservatives under [Leader X] or Labour under [Leader Y]?' Only once between 1964 and September 1992 did the public place Labour ahead of the Conservatives. Even when Labour was popular, people still saw the Conservatives as more competent.

After September 1992 – when Britain was driven out of the ERM – the public *never* put the Conservatives ahead.[9] At times the gap between the parties was huge. In December 1993 the Gallup 9000 poll – an aggregate of all the polls Gallup conducted that month – showed that just 19 per cent of the public thought the Conservatives could better handle the economy compared with 51 per cent who chose Labour, a gap of 32 percentage points. Throughout 1994 and 1995 the gap averaged at least 25 percentage points. For the Conservatives, the party of 'business', which prided itself on its links with the City, this was a remarkable state of affairs.

If the management of the economy was a normal political issue it would have been both embarrassing and damaging enough. But the economy has attained near mythical status as *the* issue which decides elections. It was possible to demonstrate a link between the economy and support for the governing party. More accurately, what mattered was not the objective economy (what is happening) but the subjective economy (what people *think* is happening). The two are linked – if the economy *is* faltering people are more likely to think that it is – but there can be a divergence between reality and perception. This subjective economy has become known as 'the feel-good factor', but David Sanders showed that what mattered most was people's economic *expectations* – whether people thought that they were going to feel better in the coming year – rather than whether they felt good at present. Sanders showed how levels of support for the government rose (or fell) as people's economic expectations rose (or fell).[10] In 1992, as in 1987 and 1983, this relationship worked for the Conservatives. Despite the recession, by the end of the 1992 campaign net economic expectations were positive. People expected a better future and trusted the Conservatives to deliver that future.

Two factors explain why the relationship did not work in 1997. The first was the nature of the recovery: export-driven, with no accompanying rise in consumer confidence. That, combined with the growth in job insecurity, dampened economic expectations. The second factor is more important and it shows why the loss of the Conservatives' reputation for economic competence was so damaging. Put simply, following Britain's exit from the ERM, the link between economic expectations and government support ceased to exist. Economic expectations rose from their nadir in April 1994, but there was no accompanying rise in Conservative support. Even when the improvements in the objective economy filtered into people's subjective economy, the Conservatives failed to benefit. Once they no longer trusted them to run the economy, the public saw no reason to reward the Conservatives for the performance of the economy.

Unity

A similarly dramatic transformation occurred with the public's views on the unity of the Conservative Party. By October 1992 those who thought the Conservatives were *dis*united outnumbered those who thought they were united by sixty-five points. By the middle of 1996, the percentage of people who thought that the Conservatives were united had fallen into single figures. The public saw the Conservatives as riven.

It was Lord Kilmuir who propounded the often-cited dictum that the Conservatives' secret weapon was loyalty. As Arthur Aughey has pointed out, the events of recent years make that dictum look a little ridiculous.[11] It is, however, best to be clear what these events were. It is frequently claimed that under John Major Conservative parliamentarians were especially rebellious. In its 1997 Election Guide the *Guardian* claimed that the 1992 Parliament had seen 'unprecedented' levels of rebellion.[12] They were not, and it did not.[13]

Conservative MPs broke ranks in 13 per cent of parliamentary divisions between 1992 and 1997. In absolute terms this is not high: only one out of every eight divisions in the Parliament saw any Conservative dissent. The other seven saw complete Conservative cohesion. More importantly, in relative terms the figures are no higher than for other recent Parliaments. Table 3.1 shows the levels of dissent by government backbenchers for every Parliament since 1945.

Table 3.1 Dissent by government backbenchers 1945–1997

Rank	*Date*	*Party*	*% of divisions seeing dissenting votes by government MPs*
1	1974–79	Lab	20
2	1970–74	Con	19
3	1983–87	Con	17
jnt 4	1992–97	Con	13
jnt 4	1987–92	Con	13
jnt 4	1979–83	Con	13
7	1959–64	Con	12
8	1966–70	Lab	8
9	1974	Lab	7
10	1945–50	Lab	6
11	1950–51	Lab	2
jnt 12	1955–59	Con	1
jnt 12	1951–55	Con	1
14	1964–66	Lab	0.25

Source: Updated from P. Cowley and P. Norton, *Are Conservative MPs Revolting?* (Hull: University of Hull, Centre for Legislative Studies, 1996).

At 13 per cent the 1992 Parliament ranks joint fourth, equal with Mrs Thatcher's first and third Parliaments and less troublesome than her middle Parliament. And it was noticeably less troublesome than two of the Parliaments of the 1970s: Heath saw his backbenchers defy the Party whips in 19 per cent of divisions and between October 1974 and 1979 Wilson and

Callaghan saw their MPs revolt in 21 per cent of divisions. The 1992 Parliament, then, did *not* see particularly high levels of dissent from Conservative MPs: cohesion remained the norm, dissent the exception.

There was, therefore, no collapse in Party discipline. More than four out of every five divisions saw all the Conservative MPs present enter the same lobby. When they did dissent, the number of Conservative MPs breaking ranks was usually fewer than ten. Even the most rebellious MP was loyal in more than nine out of ten votes. In this, the behaviour of the Conservative Party in the 1992 Parliament was of a type seen since 1970.

Indeed, these overall figures mask the consensus that existed on most issues. Between 1970 and 1990 the Conservative Party saw conflict between the economic left (the 'wets') and the economic right (the 'drys') with the drys largely victorious by the late 1980s.[14] The main fault line in the Conservative Party is now the issue of Europe. That is evident both from surveys of Conservative MPs and from the levels of dissent seen on other issues in the Commons.[15] The majority of Conservative dissent in the 1992 Parliament occurred on just one bill: the European Communities (Amendment) Bill to give effect to the Maastricht Treaty. Over 60 per cent of all Conservative dissenting acts took place on that one bill. Not only that, but these were the larger of the rebellions. With Maastricht excluded, no Conservative MP broke ranks on more than eighteen occasions and only four MPs did so on more than ten occasions.[16]

To be sure, there were large rebellions on other issues. The largest came over the issue of firearms control, when up to ninety-five Conservative MPs defied their whips in eight separate rebellions. Yet compared with the Maastricht rebellions, the other rebellions were either limited (over half consisted of just one MP) or extremely sporadic (as with firearms). Other than Europe these large rebellions were on socio-moral issues (such as firearms, Sunday trading and divorce) rather than on economic matters. The overall level of dissent, itself nothing out of the ordinary, masked the unity that existed on most issues other than Europe.

The first part of the explanation for the divergence between these data and the public's perception of the Party as hopelessly divided is to accept the inadequacy of using dissenting votes as the *sole* measure of a party's divisions. On some occasions (as with the privatisation of the Post Office) the Government backed down before any dissenting votes were cast, or announced concessions to limit the number of such votes (as with the coal mines). On other issues – as with Sunday trading, corporal punishment and divorce – it permitted a free vote, knowing that it would not be able to contain the dissent. In other cases, especially in much of its European policy, the Government only managed to limit rebellions by extensive use of patronage or threats, or by making the issue a vote of confidence.

Analysis of Early Day Motions (EDMs) found far greater levels of division amongst the Party than was shown in the division lobbies. For example, when the 'no' vote in the Danish referendum on Maastricht led to the suspension of the Maastricht bill, eighty-four Conservative MPs signed an EDM calling on the Government to make a 'fresh start' to European policy. Yet only twenty-six of these went on to vote against the later 'paving motion' enabling the bill's passage,[17] and forty-one did not cast a single dissenting vote against *any* part of the treaty. Similarly, we know from the work carried out during the Parliament by David Baker and his colleagues that the splits in the Conservative Parliamentary Party over the European issue were more serious than indicated by the levels of dissent in the division lobbies.[18]

The real level of division and dissent on the Conservative benches was higher than might be suggested by an analysis – like that above – of dissenting votes. However, whilst an important cautionary note, it does not vitiate the analysis. Even if we take into account those occasions when the Government did back down in order to lessen the rebellions, the levels of discontent on the back benches were still not greatly higher than in other recent Parliaments. Similarly, it may be that surveys or EDMs revealed wider splits amongst the Party, but whilst these academic findings were widely disseminated, it is unlikely that we can explain the perception of division either from EDMs or from academic papers alone.

The expansion of political coverage has made dissent more noticeable than in the past. Yet this is clearly not the full explanation. During the 1992 Parliament, under exactly the same conditions, Labour MPs voted in greater numbers against their Party on a greater number of issues than did their Conservative counterparts.[19] They too signed EDMs and participated in surveys revealing division. Yet the Labour Party came to be seen as united by the public, largely because Labour rebels took a near Trappist vow of silence outside the Commons. Most important of all, therefore, was not the actual rebellions by Conservative MPs, but the suicidal willingness of Conservative MPs to utilise the expanded media facilities to broadcast their differences. This extended far beyond the European rebels, and came to include almost any Conservative MP who had a difference with the Government. Some rebels were embarrassed by their notoriety; others revelled in fame, or notoriety.[20]

By concentrating on the doctrinal splits in the Party over Europe, therefore, it is possible to miss two other important points. First, that on many other issues there was almost complete doctrinal harmony. Second, that there was a change in what Drucker, in his seminal work on the Labour Party, called the Party's 'ethos' ('its traditions and habits, its feel').[21] At the 1993 Conservative conference Major appealed to the Party's more traditional ethos, claiming 'we have our agreements in public and our disagreements in private'. Unfortunately for the Conservatives the reverse was true.

The biggest rebellion

The impression of disunity was confirmed on 22 June 1995 when, after yet another depressingly bad series of local election results, a bruising (and disrespectful) encounter with the 'Fresh Start' group and amid talk of a challenge to his leadership in the coming November, John Major resigned as Conservative Party leader – but not as Prime Minister – to precipitate a leadership contest. He urged his detractors to 'put up or shut up'.

They put up. John Redwood resigned from the Cabinet and stood against Mr Major for the leadership of the Party. The result on 4 July was:

John Major	218
John Redwood	89
Abstained/spoilt/did not vote	22

To win on the first ballot a candidate in a Conservative leadership contest needs to clear two hurdles. He or she must gain *both*: (i) an overall majority of the votes of those entitled to vote *and* (ii) 15 per cent more of the votes of those entitled to vote than any other candidate. Major cleared both these hurdles comfortably. Because he was Prime Minister it was claimed that he also had to clear a third, informal, hurdle: he had to win 'convincingly'.[22] Leading up to the contest the press and media had been setting this third hurdle at 100 defections (that is, votes against and abstentions, or what one journalist called 'acts of non-love'). Yet despite the total number of defections reaching 111, the press hailed the result as a great triumph for Major.[23]

This clash between prediction and outcome owed much to the media skills of the Prime Minister's campaign team. There was a concerted and well-planned effort to get Major-supporting MPs – and especially ministers – on to the television screens in the first half-hour after the election result was announced in order to win the battle of perception. MPs were given pre-prepared lists of favourable comparisons and told to avoid the press and head towards microphones and television cameras.[24] It worked superbly and was to be one of the few times when perceptions were to work to Major's advantage.

Yet even on the raw figures, the result meant that one-third of Conservative MPs felt unable to back their own Party's incumbent Premier. If all of the MPs in Mr Major's Government stayed loyal to him (which they did not)[25] a total of 111 defections meant that half of his backbenchers had rejected him. Either way, it was far from a vote of confidence.[26]

The European divide explains most but not all of the result. At their core the 111 comprised the Maastricht rebels. Around 80 per cent of those MPs who broke ranks over the Maastricht bill either abstained or backed Redwood (more usually the latter). This was particularly true of the bill's more dedicated opponents: of those who voted against the Maastricht bill on eleven or more occasions nearly 90 per cent did not support the Prime Minister. Yet the

Maastricht rebels accounted for only around one-third of those who failed to back the Prime Minister. Around them, however, was a wider Euro-sceptic element. Some 60 per cent of the signatories to the Fresh Start EDM, for example, either voted for Redwood or abstained. Of the 111 who did not back the Prime Minister over 60 per cent could be classed as Euro-sceptic; of those who voted for Redwood the figure was nearer 85 per cent. In addition, as well as a scattering of those who felt that they could not win under Major, or who felt personally aggrieved towards him, there was also a small group – no more than ten, most of whom abstained – who wanted to depose Mr Major in order to install Michael Heseltine.

When he called the contest, Mr Major had claimed that he was being opposed by a 'small minority' of MPs. The result showed that this was not so. Paradoxically, whilst it secured his position and ensured that the Conservative Party would fight the next election under his stewardship, the 1995 leadership contest demonstrated the weakness of Mr Major's position. In 1990 he had been supported by those on the centre and right of the Party, especially those on the Euro-sceptic right.[27] In 1995, by contrast, much of his support came from the centre and left of the Party, whilst much of the Euro-sceptic right eschewed him. By 1995, then, much of his support came by default: it came from people who had rejected him in 1990 but feared the alternative(s) in 1995. Mr Major stood on ever-shifting sands, a difficult and uncomfortable position.

Sleaze

The third factor to damage the Conservatives was 'sleaze'. The term used to refer to 'disorderly houses, illicit liquor or drug dens, low dives, questionable night clubs and other disreputable premises'.[28] It is now used about politicians, especially Conservative politicians. The rise in its use was phenomenal: by 1994–95 the term was used in the press forty times more frequently than a decade earlier.[29] However, its all-encompassing use hides important differences in the actual offence. The term broadly encompassed three main concerns:

(i) Financial wrongdoing by MPs and ministers, including the taking of money to ask parliamentary questions ('cash for questions'), excessive links with lobbying firms and the movement of former ministers into the boardrooms of companies with which they had dealt in government. The sources of party funding also caused concern.

(ii) Sexual wrongdoing by MPs and ministers, most commonly adultery.

(iii) Wrongdoing by and within government. This is the broadest category of the three, and includes the alleged packing of quasi-non-governmental organisations (quangos) with Conservative supporters, the overturning of ministerial decisions by the courts, allegations that the Government was prepared to send innocent men to jail to hide its own actions (the so-called 'Arms to Iraq' affair), and concern about the linking of overseas aid to British arms sales (the 'Pergau Dam' affair).

The belief in sleaze was widespread. In 1994 almost two-thirds of the public thought that 'most members of Parliament make a lot of money by using public office improperly' and fewer than one in five thought that appointments to public bodies were made on merit.[30] Three factors made the issue of sleaze damaging for the Conservatives. First, most of the MPs shown to be committing offences (i) or (ii) happened to be Conservatives. Just concentrating on these two offences it is possible to identify almost thirty Conservative MPs – just under one in ten of the Parliamentary Party – who had some allegation made about them during the Parliament. Many were ministers, and as a result the rate of resignations in the Major Government was the highest of any post-war Conservative administration.[31]

Second, since only the Conservatives had been in government since 1979 they also got the blame for all types of offence (iii). This led to allegations that the longevity of Conservative rule had itself led to arrogance: it is a widespread belief that one-party rule – at local or national level – leads inevitably to corruption.[32]

The third factor was self-inflicted. Major's speech to the 1993 Conservative conference included a call for a return to core Conservative values, to 'get back to basics'. It was later claimed that by this he did not mean individual morality. However, the briefings that journalists were given at the time made it clear that personal morality *was* central to the policy.[33] As a result journalists claimed that they had a justification for investigating the personal lives of all Conservative MPs. Not all survived such investigation.

The impact of the sleaze allegations, therefore, was not neutral. It worked to the Conservatives' disadvantage. Opinion polls regularly found that between two-thirds and three-quarters of the public believed that the Conservatives were 'sleazy and disreputable', whereas around just a quarter of the public thought the same about Labour. This reinforced negative images of the Government and strengthened the argument that it was time for a change; it made Major appear as if he could not control his own MPs and it dominated the headlines for much of the Parliament.

John Major

In the 1992 election Major had been an asset to his Party. On his election as Prime Minister he had overnight transformed the Conservatives' standing in the opinion polls. His personal approval rating was high and he trumped Neil Kinnock on almost all measures. In 1997, however, Tony Blair trumped John Major. Not only was Blair the clear winner when the public was asked who would make the better Premier, but, as Table 3.2 shows, he also led Major on every attribute about which the pollsters asked. In part this was caused by

Table 3.2 Image of party leaders 1997 (%)

Attribute	*Blair's rating*	*Major's rating*	*Blair lead over Major*
Concerned for country as whole	+35	+4	31
Caring	+71	+34	37
Can be trusted	+37	−1	38
Competent	+73	+8	65
A winner	+65	−18	83
Firmly in charge	+51	−43	94
Decisive	+61	−19	80
Likable as a person	+54	+33	21
Listens to reason	+57	+20	37
Able to unite the nation	+31	−42	73

Note: Ratings calculated by subtracting the percentage who would claim an opposite statement best applies (for example, 'concerned only for himself and his Party') from the percentage who would choose the phrase in the table.

Source: Gallup Political and Economic Index, 440, April 1997.

Blair being seen as better than Kinnock. As the table shows, in 1997 Blair had positive net scores on all attributes, ranging from +31 to +73, and averaging +54. In 1992 Kinnock's ratings ranged from −23 to +55, and averaged just +11. There was also a dramatic slump in the public's view of Major during the intervening five years. In 1993 his monthly 'satisfaction rating' averaged 23, the lowest for any Premier since records began. In 1994 he broke his own record, averaging 21. Similarly, in 1992 John Major had positive scores on all but one attribute, ranging from −8 ('able to unite the nation') to +60 ('likable as a person'). The intervening five years saw every score fall by between 9 ('caring') and 47 ('firmly in charge') percentage points.

An exercise in 'fantasy politics' demonstrates the effect of this clearly. Whereas in 1992 Major had led Kinnock on seven of the ten characteristics, by margins of up to 53 percentage points, the hypothetical contest five years later would have seen Kinnock lead Major on all but two areas, and by margins of up to 49 percentage points.

Ivor Crewe has convincingly argued that Mr Major's loss of popularity was more 'consequence than cause' of his Government's unpopularity.[34] Despite his poor ratings Mr Major polled better than his Party; disillusioned Conservatives did not place him high on their list of reasons for deserting the Party and polls did not indicate – as they had done at times with Mrs Thatcher – that under another leader the Conservatives would poll better. The events of the five years of his Government, however, had taken their toll: by May 1997 he was no longer the asset he once was.

The campaign

Despite Major's impressive campaign itinerary, covering over 10,000 miles and fifty-six constituencies, it is unlikely that *any* election campaign could have rescued the Conservatives. As one Conservative official said after the election: 'We were too far behind from the beginning. You cannot overturn people's image of the last five years with a six-week campaign. This is not about whether a load of posters worked or didn't.'[35]

The campaign, though, did not help. First, there was sleaze, both sexual and financial. A series of revelations dominated the early stages of the campaign, and the candidature of Neil Hamilton, one of the MPs against whom 'cash for questions' allegations had been made, dogged Mr Major throughout the campaign. Then, second, there was disunity: hundreds of Conservative candidates rejected the idea of a European single currency in their personal election addresses, defying Mr Major's carefully stitched together 'wait and see'/'negotiate and decide' policy.[36] Despite assurances that ministers would accept collective responsibility, these rebels included a number of ministers. None was dismissed. Third, despite a series of good economic announcements during the campaign, the level of Conservative support throughout stayed resolutely low.

Sleaze and splits dominated the headlines, preventing the Party talking about the areas in which it felt it was strong. When it did manage to raise the economy as an issue, the loss of reputation for competence meant a loss of impact. In short, the campaign was the previous five years in microcosm.

Conclusion

The transformation of the Conservative Party from dominant party to English-based rump has its roots in three perceptions of the Party: that it was incompetent; that it was disunited; and that it was sleazy. These three perceptions damaged both its own standing and that of John Major. All three perceptions had some validity, but all were exaggerations. The perception of incompetence masked economic recovery. The evident disunity on the issue of Europe and the willingness of Conservative MPs to broadcast their differences hid the unity that existed in many policy areas. The sleaze allegations, as the Nolan Committee noted, were vastly overstated. However, perception is more important than reality and as a result by May 1997 the British public had decided that it was time for a change.

Notes

I am very grateful to Matthew Bailey and Mark Stuart, who helped with the research on which parts of this chapter are based, and to Philip Norton for his perceptive comments on a draft.

1 P. Whiteley, P. Seyd and J. Richardson, *True Blues: The Politics of Conservative Party Membership* (Oxford: Clarendon, 1994), p. 42.

2 See, for example, A. King, 'The implications of one party government', in A. King, I. Crewe, D. Denver, K. Newton, P. Norton, D. Sanders and P. Seyd, *Britain at the Polls 1992* (Chatham, New Jersey: Chatham House Publishers, 1993).
3 W. Hague, 'Energy, enthusiasm, beliefs – these I offer', *The Spectator*, 10 May 1997.
4 I. Crewe, '1979–96', in A. Seldon (ed.), *How Tory Governments Fall* (London: Fontana, 1996), p. 430.
5 See D. Kavanagh and A. Seldon (eds) , *The Major Effect* (London: Macmillan, 1994); S. Ludlam and M. J. Smith (eds), *Contemporary British Conservatism* (London: Macmillan, 1996) and P. Norton (ed.), *The Conservative Party* (London: Prentice Hall, 1996).
6 Whether by design or default is a moot point. See P. Norton, 'The Conservative Party', in A. King (ed.), *Britain at the Polls 1997* (Chatham, New Jersey: Chatham House Publishers, forthcoming).
7 A ninth, Sir Richard Body, resigned the whip in sympathy. The previous year Rupert Allason had also had the whip withdrawn after he failed to support the Government in the earlier vote of confidence.
8 See E. Nicholson, *Secret Society* (London: Indigo, 1996). In addition, Sir John Gorst at one stage announced that he was withdrawing co-operation from the Government, but he did not resign the whip. See P. Cowley, 'Crossing the floor: representative theory and practice in Britain', *Public Law* (summer 1996): 214–24.
9 However, no causal link should be assumed. 'Whether it was the trauma of the crisis itself that provoked the step shift in perceptions, or whether the crisis merely triggered a change in perceptions that, as a result of three years of recession, was "waiting to happen", is impossible to say.' D. Sanders, 'Economic performance, management competence and the outcome of the next general election', *Political Studies*, 44 (1996): 203–31, at p. 207.
10 Sanders modelled levels of net economic expectations by subtracting those who said that they thought their family circumstances were going to get worse in the next twelve months from those who thought they would get better. See D. Sanders, '"It's the economy, stupid": the economy and support for the Conservative Party, 1979–1994', *Talking Politics*, 7 (1995): 158–67.
11 A. Aughey, 'Philosophy and faction', in Norton, *The Conservative Party*, p. 83.
12 L. Neville, 'Rebellions', in M. Linton (ed.), *The Election* (London: Fourth Estate, 1997), p. 32.
13 This section is based on a larger ESRC project examining parliamentary behaviour since 1979, co-ordinated by Philip Norton. Findings up to June 1996 were reported in P. Cowley, 'Men (and women) behaving badly? The Conservative Parliamentary Party since 1992', *Talking Politics*, 9 (1997): 94–9. The findings presented here report data for the full Parliament.
14 See P. Riddell, 'The Conservatives after 1992', *Political Quarterly*, 63 (1992): 422–31.
15 See, for example, J. Garry, 'The British Conservative Party: divisions over European policy', *West European Politics* 18 (1995): 170–89.
16 See P. Cowley and P. Norton, *Are Conservative MPs Revolting?* (Hull: University of Hull, Centre for Legislative Studies, 1996), esp. pp. 20–44.
17 D. Baker, A. Gamble and S. Ludlam, 'Whips or scorpions? The Maastricht vote and the Conservative Party', *Parliamentary Affairs*, 46 (1993): 151–66.
18 D. Baker, I. Fountain, A. Gamble and S. Ludlam, 'The blue map of Europe', in

C. Rallings, D. M. Farrell, D. Denver and D. Broughton (eds), *British Elections and Parties Yearbook 1995* (London: Frank Cass, 1996), p. 66.

19 See P. Cowley and P. Norton with M. Stuart and M. Bailey, *Blair's Bastards: Discontent within the Parliamentary Labour Party* (Hull: University of Hull, Centre for Legislative Studies, 1996).

20 One trick used by rebels was to appear at BBC reception and claim that they had been invited to appear on a programme; once they had arrived many producers used them, whether invited or not. Private information.

21 H. Drucker, *Doctrine and Ethos in the Labour Party* (London: Allen and Unwin, 1979).

22 The phrase was Michael Heseltine's. For a sceptical discussion of the third hurdle see P. Cowley, 'The mystery of the third hurdle', *Politics*, 16 (1996): 79–86.

23 See P. Cowley, '111 not out: the press and the 1995 Conservative leadership contest', *Talking Politics*, 8 (1996): 187–90.

24 Private information.

25 More than ten ministers withheld their support. This and the following analysis are based on a poll of all Conservative MPs undertaken at the time by a national Sunday newspaper. I am very grateful for being allowed sight of the unpublished canvass returns and to the journalists and campaign workers who discussed the subject with me. The Nuffield Foundation's Small Grants Scheme funded the research involved.

26 According to one account, Mr Major thought the result bad enough briefly to consider resigning. Private information.

27 P. Cowley, 'How did he do that? The second round of the 1990 Conservative leadership election', in D. M. Farrell, D. Broughton, D. Denver and J. Fisher (eds), *British Elections and Parties Yearbook 1996* (London: Frank Cass, 1996); P. Cowley and J. Garry 'The British Conservative Party and Europe: the choosing of John Major', *British Journal of Political Science* (forthcoming).

28 T. Smith, 'Causes, concerns and cures', in F. F. Ridley and A. Doig (eds), *Sleaze: Politicians, Private Interests and Public Reaction* (Oxford: Oxford University Press, 1995), p. 3.

29 P. Dunleavy and S. Weir, 'Media, opinion and the constitution', in Ridley and Doig, *Sleaze*, p. 57.

30 R. Mortimore, 'Politics and public perceptions', in Ridley and Doig, *Sleaze*, pp. 31–3.

31 Measuring the rate – that is, the number of resignations per year – takes into account the different lengths of administration. K. Dowding and W. T. Kang, 'Ministerial resignations 1945–95', *Public Administration* (forthcoming).

32 P. Cowley, 'The promise of reform', in L. Robins and B. Jones (eds), *Half a Century of British Politics* (Manchester: Manchester University Press, 1997), p. 123.

33 N. Jones, *Soundbites and Spindoctors* (London: Indigo, 1996), pp. 197–8.

34 Crewe, '1979–96', p. 433.

35 *Guardian*, 2 May 1997.

36 The government preferred the latter; everyone else used the former.

Tatton

'Sleaze' dogged the dying days of the Major administration. The sexual peccadilloes of Conservative MPs had shamed a party that after its 1992 victory had proclaimed its enthusiasm for assuming the moral high ground and getting 'back to basics'. Perhaps more seriously, financial sleaze and allegations of corruption tarnished the reputation of the Conservative Government, and of politics and politicians more generally.

Some of the most serious allegations were levelled by the *Guardian* newspaper against former Trade Minister Neil Hamilton, the MP for the prosperous Cheshire constituency of Tatton. These allegations included the claim that Hamilton had strayed beyond the remit of legitimate consultancy work, for the lobbying company Ian Greer Associates, by accepting cash for asking parliamentary questions on behalf of the owner of Harrods, Mohammed Al Fayed. Hamilton rejected the allegations, but in 1996 withdrew at the last moment from a libel action against the *Guardian*. The *Guardian* renewed its onslaught against Hamilton and other (mainly) Conservative MPs whom it accused of corrupt activities. Hamilton's position was weakened when one of his co-accused, Tim Smith, the MP for Beaconsfield, resigned as parliamentary candidate after admitting receiving cash from Al Fayed for asking parliamentary questions.

Hamilton's position in his constituency was undermined still further when the Labour and Liberal Democrat candidates agreed to stand down and make way for an Independent anti-sleaze candidate. The BBC war correspondent Martin Bell stepped somewhat reluctantly into the limelight with the initial hope that his mooted candidacy would prompt Hamilton's resignation. But Hamilton and his formidable wife, Christine, vowed to fight on. Bell had no campaign experience and neither did many of his election team – the so-called 'Bell's belles' – but he did receive surreptitious organisational assistance from Labour and the Liberal Democrats. Bell's candidacy received a hostile response from some right-wing pundits who were quick to denounce the 'media candidate' and the over-arching pretension of what they saw as the attempt by some sections of the media to act as moral arbiters.

Bell was swiftly introduced to the rough and tumble of politics when he was confronted by the Hamiltons on Knutsford Common following his first press conference. His seeming tentativeness on this occasion led some to express concern about his stomach for the fight, but these fears were misplaced: Bell was a tenacious campaigner and there was a groundswell of support for his stand against Hamilton, including from within the ranks of the local Conservative Party. Support for Hamilton haemorrhaged as the campaign progressed. On election night it became clear that the Conservative vote in Tatton – previously the Conservatives' fourth safest seat – had collapsed. Hamilton's defiant speech made in his moment of defeat summed up for many the condition of the Conservative Party at the time of the 1997 general election: weakened and discredited, yet apparently unable to accept the magnitude of rejection.

Result

Tatton			
Martin Bell	Ind	29,354	
Neil Hamilton	Con	18,277	
	Others	1,161	
Total vote		48,792	Turnout 76.5%
Ind majority		11,077	
Ind gain from Con			
Swing not measurable			

4

Third and minor party breakthrough?

Justin Fisher

Introduction

Discussion of the outcome of the 1997 general election was highlighted by two themes: the change of government and the size of Labour's majority. However, the performance and post-election position of the smaller parties was also a critical aspect. The Liberal Democrats doubled their seat representation in the House of Commons. This was achieved with a lower aggregate vote share than in 1992. It seemed that whilst the electoral system might still be said to discriminate against smaller parties, the Liberal Democrats were in some seats benefiting from the effects of the first-past-the-post system.

The election also presented a new scenario for the nationalist parties of Scotland and Wales. First, with the Conservatives losing all their seats in both countries, the nationalist parties assumed an enhanced status. Second, the victory of the Labour Party made the future establishment of a Scottish Parliament and a Welsh Assembly much more likely. Whilst both nationalist parties were critical of the extent of Labour's plans, the likely outcome of the establishment of any such chambers would be the effective institutionalisation of these parties as well as enhanced party status within them, particularly since there was the prospect of these chambers being elected by proportional representation.

The Liberal Democrats

Campaign background

Whilst the Liberal Democrats achieved remarkable success in the general election, it was not necessarily clear that they would do so prior to the event. Though the 1992 general election had been the first fought by the new Party, its performance was seen as disappointing, being the second lowest third party vote share since 1970 (1979 was the lowest). That said, it had been a remarkable recovery after the disaster of the 1989 European elections when the Party was famously beaten into fourth place by the Greens. However, there was conflicting suggestive evidence as to how the Liberal Democrats would fare in 1997. Certainly, at local level the Party had been performing so well that it was now Britain's second party (behind Labour). In 1995, it gained 23.6 per cent of the English vote, 9.2 per cent in Scotland and 10.2 per cent in Wales.[1] In 1996, it won 22.5 per cent in England.[2]

Projected nationally, this suggested vote shares of 23 per cent in both years.[3] At European level, the 1994 elections had also provided something of a breakthrough, the Party gaining the second highest vote share for a third party (16.7 per cent). Significantly, the Party also won seats, a feat not previously achieved by the Liberal Democrats or their electoral predecessors. At parliamentary by-elections, however, the Party had performed less well in the preceding two years. Whilst it had gained the seat of Littleborough and Saddleworth from the Conservatives in 1995, it had only marginally increased its vote share. In the 1996 by-elections, the vote share had always declined and in one (Staffordshire South East) the party lost its deposit. The one by-election of 1997 had produced a decline in vote share of 4.5 per cent, though given the dramatic swing to Labour, which was clearly the second-placed party in 1992, one cannot rule out an element of tactical voting depressing the Liberal Democrat poll.

However, whilst the Party generally fared well at local and European elections, national opinion polls gave less cause for optimism. Unadjusted polls for 1995 and 1996 gave mean ratings of 15 per cent in both years, and although Paddy Ashdown was very popular as a party leader he was consistently ranked behind John Major as the person considered best suited to be Prime Minister. The picture in the months prior to the election was similarly discouraging. From January to March, the Party's mean poll rating was 13 per cent whilst in the final month of the campaign it rose to 14 per cent – still four points adrift of its 1992 vote share. Paddy Ashdown's personal ratings also remained very similar. Whilst his popularity as Liberal Democrat leader continued to rise, his standing as best person to be Prime Minister was rooted at around 13 per cent. All of these indicators gave rise to the impression that the Party might be squeezed in the election, particularly since Labour's apparent ideological shift towards a more centrist position made it a less threatening electoral prospect for disenchanted Conservative voters.

The manifesto and campaign

The Liberal Democrat manifesto was divided into eight policy sections: education, jobs and the economy, the environment, secure communities, health and community care, political reform, equal opportunities and Britain in the world. Policy priorities might be measured in terms of word counts.[4]

Health and welfare were given priority (32 per cent of the manifesto), with education registering 16 per cent. The economy, employment and taxation registered 14 per cent whilst rights and democracy accounted for 13 per cent. All other areas registered in single figures. Using the same technique as for Topf's previous analyses of party manifestos, the manifesto indicated a slight overall shift to the right, though Labour's shift using this reductionist technique was more dramatic.

Whilst the manifesto may have prioritised health and welfare, the Liberal

Democrats pursued education as a critical issue and, as in 1992, pledged an increase of one penny in the basic rate of income tax to fund further spending in that domain. Policy was prioritised towards schools. Nursery education was to be provided on demand and primary school class sizes were to be cut. There were also pledges to increase funding for books and equipment and to tackle a backlog of building maintenance. Non-school education policy was largely concerned with further education and workplace training. Like other parties, the question of higher education was largely left to the Dearing Committee.

In terms of the economy, the manifesto confirmed the Party's increasing distance from its liberal economic heritage. Whilst the manifesto pledged support for the market economy as the best way to deliver prosperity and distribute economic benefits, there was recognition that market mechanisms alone were insufficient. Specifically, the Party was concerned with providing economic stability through low inflation and interest rates. Critically this was to be achieved within the single European currency, though membership of this was conditional upon popular support in a referendum. In terms of taxation, apart from the pledge to raise the basic rate of tax, there were also plans to introduce a tax rate of fifty pence in the pound for those with salaries in excess of £100,000 as well as a commitment in the long term to shift the burden of taxation away from income and consumer products and on to goods and industries that were polluters or which involved the depletion of natural resources.

This commitment to shift the burden of taxation was a principal plank of Liberal Democrat environmental policy. Tied to this principle was the idea of setting new targets for the reduction of pollution as well as investment in public transport, especially rail and a commitment to retain London Underground within the public sector, opposing the pre-election Conservative proposals to privatise this utility. There were also to be tax incentives to reduce car engine size and use as well as a commitment to invest in home insulation, designed to aid poorer households as well as reduce energy waste. In terms of power generation, there was a commitment to support research into non-nuclear sources, such as renewable energy. There was also an indication that nuclear power stations would not be replaced at the end of their design life.

Law and order policies were based around local community concerns. To that end, there was a priority commitment to put an additional 3,000 police officers on the beat as well as a pledge to make the police more responsive to local communities as a means of strengthening public confidence. Like other parties, the Liberal Democrats saw youth crime as a particular problem and sought to ensure that offenders would compensate victims. In keeping with the idea of strengthening local communities, there was a pledge to build more houses and foster partnerships between local authorities and private capital. Moreover, in a bid to build more affordable housing, there was also an ambitious target of ending homelessness (defined as sleeping rough) by the year 2000.

Health policy was largely directed towards a commitment to the maintenance of a comprehensive National Health Service, free at the point of need and funded primarily from general taxation. There were commitments to halt all 'finance-driven' closures for six months pending an audit of needs and facilities, the restoration of free eye and dental checks and an end to what was seen as a two-tier system derived from the fundholder status held by a considerable number of GPs. Like Labour, the Liberal Democrats envisaged moving money away from what was seen as wasteful bureaucracy. There were also some plans to promote preventative medicine through a ban on tobacco advertising, an increase in tobacco duty and the creation of an independent Food Commission.

One of the policy areas that has given the Liberal Democrats a distinctive character has been their commitment to political reform. Despite this, it has not been the dominant feature of third-party manifestos and since 1983 has apparently declined in importance.[5] Nevertheless, the 1997 manifesto still gave such issues some prominence. The priorities for the Liberal Democrats centred around three themes: a guarantee of rights and freedoms; reform of Parliament and the electoral system and decentralisation.

Specifically, the Party proposed to establish a Bill of Rights and incorporate the European Convention on Human Rights into British law. In addition, there was support for both national and local referendums, the introduction of a system of proportional representation, the reduction of the number of MPs by 200 and the creation of an elected second chamber. In terms of devolution, there were proposals for the creation of a Scottish Parliament and a Welsh Assembly (though with the predetermined ability to raise taxation), as well as the development of regional Assemblies in England.

The Party did not give prominence to all policies. For example, whilst a strong commitment to electoral reform remained, Liberal Democrats chose not to campaign upon the issue since it was judged to be one that confused voters. The Party played down talk of strategy in the event of a hung Parliament for similar reasons. In the light of the experience of the 1992 election, this may have been considered a wise move. During the 1992 campaign, the Labour leadership appeared to flirt with the idea of electoral reform and hung Parliaments. This provided the Conservative Party with ammunition to claim that a vote for the Liberal Democrats was a 'Trojan horse' for a Labour government. As a result, the Liberal Democrats concentrated their 1997 campaign largely upon the areas of education, health and crime.

A final feature of the Liberal Democrats' policy and campaigning stance was the fact that this election was not fought under the principle of the Party adopting equidistance between the Labour and Conservative Parties. That policy was officially abandoned in 1995, the Party now leaning more closely towards Labour. Indeed the Liberal Democrats had already co-operated with

Labour on political reform and pledged a constructive relationship with a Labour government, although this did not prevent the Party attacking Labour on occasion for having lost conviction in its beliefs.

The Liberal Democrat campaign also displayed other new strategic characteristics. First and most critically, whilst the Party fielded candidates in 639 constituencies, resources and national efforts were concentrated in fifty key seats either being defended or where the Party was seen as having a good chance of victory. A second was that media appearances were dominated by Paddy Ashdown. In an analysis of television and newspaper appearances during the campaign, Ashdown made many appearances but no other Liberal Democrat politician appeared in the top twenty.[6]

Campaign success?

The Liberal Democrats ended the election with forty-six seats – the highest number of Liberal, Alliance or Liberal Democrat seats won since 1929. In one sense, this was a major success for the Party. It now had a considerably enhanced presence in the House of Commons and, in terms of targeted seats, a 92 per cent success rate is clearly remarkable, eclipsed only by Labour's astonishing performance. However, the Party received a lower total vote (5,243,440) and average vote share (17.2 per cent) than in 1992 (5,999,384 and 18.3 per cent respectively). Second, the Party performed much better in the South than in the North. In the South West, it polled 31.3 per cent of the vote and in the South East 21.4 per cent, whilst in the northern part of England, it polled an average of 14.5 per cent. In Scotland, though it became the second largest party in terms of seats, it was fourth in terms of vote share, behind the Conservatives. The Party polled worst in Wales (12.4 per cent of the vote – third in terms of vote share, and behind the seatless Conservative Party) but still won two seats. Third, three of the Liberal Democrat gains were the most marginal results in the election with majorities of fifty-six in Kingston and Surbiton, twelve in Torbay and two in Winchester. Finally, whilst the Party made many gains, it lost Rochdale to Labour and Christchurch (a 1993 by-election gain) to the Conservatives, whilst also failing to win the notionally Liberal Democrat seat of Inverness East, Nairn and Lochaber). Yet, for all these points, it is clear that the Party's campaign and policy of targeting seats were a success and leave the Liberal Democrats in a much stronger position.

The Scottish National Party

Campaign background

The recent electoral history of the SNP had been a mixture of trauma and success. The Party had not reached the heights that it did in October 1974 when it scored 30.4 per cent of the Scottish vote, but the 1992 election did see it improve significantly upon its 1987 vote share. Nevertheless, it still managed to secure only three seats. In the 1994 European elections, the Party managed to gain a second seat, having attained its highest vote share in these elections. In terms of opinion polls, the SNP averaged around 24 per cent throughout the campaign, higher than during the 1992 election, but in line with its averages for 1995 and 1996.[7] The most recent local elections for the new unitary authorities were held in 1995. Here, the Party's vote share was slightly higher at 26.2 per cent.

The manifesto and campaign

The SNP manifesto proclaimed a confident message of 'Yes we can!' Much of the manifesto was concerned with the virtues of political independence from the United Kingdom and a commitment to full membership of the EU. The Party also presented many proposals to be implemented under an SNP government. This was defined as a situation when the SNP had a majority of the MPs in Scotland, at which point the Party would initiate negotiations for independence from the UK. The basic premise of the manifesto was that Scotland was not a financial burden on the United Kingdom, the claim being that an independent Scotland would be the eighth richest nation in the developed world.

The SNP promoted a wide-ranging manifesto reflecting a social democratic ideological position. A written constitution was proposed, including a Bill of Rights. This was to codify not only rights such as freedom of expression but also the right to housing, education, decent working conditions, a minimum wage and free health care. The European Convention on Human Rights was also to be incorporated into Scottish law. Other constitutional proposals included the establishment of a single-chamber Parliament elected by proportional representation which resembled Scottish society in terms of sex, ethnicity and geography. The franchise for this chamber was to be extended to those aged sixteen years and over. Proportional representation was also to be extended to local government. The Queen was to remain head of state, but only whilst in Scotland. During her absence, the Chancellor (the Speaker) of the Parliament would assume that role.

The economic platform of the Party was left-wing. A central aim was full employment. This was to be assisted by government intervention to create new jobs in addition to the creation of a National Apprenticeship Scheme. There were also pledges of government investment in industrial expansion, agricultural diversification as well as full support for the EU Social Chapter and a minimum wage. Trade union rights were to be protected by an SNP Charter. The economic platform was not wholly directed at employees, however. The SNP was also committed to a reduction in business taxation. Personal taxation would start at fifteen pence in the pound.

In terms of social policy, there were pledges to increase child benefit as well as the restoration of benefits for sixteen- and seventeen-year-olds as a counter to youth crime. In housing, there were pledges to expand the Scottish stock of affordable housing. In law and order, following the Dunblane tragedy, there was a commitment to a ban on hand guns. In education, local authorities were to be required to ring-fence dedicated funds for Gaelic education.

Environmentally, the SNP was committed to a ban on nuclear reprocessing with an immediate end to any currently undertaken. Instead energy policy was to be focused upon oil. In transport, there were pledges to improve Scotland's infrastructure, particularly for outlying areas. This was to be achieved by both road and rail, with the Scottish parts of Railtrack to be returned to public ownership.

Foreign policy committed Scotland to membership of the EU, Commonwealth and United Nations. Defence was to be established through a Scottish army, navy and air force, though with support for an EU Common Foreign and Security Policy. However, there were proposals for a phased withdrawal from NATO due to opposition to nuclear weapons, though military co-operation was to be maintained.

The SNP campaign took the idea of independence as its core which was in keeping with its manifesto whereby most pledges were made within the context of an independent Scotland. It rejected Labour's proposals for a Scottish Parliament as inadequate, as Westminster would still be sovereign. Campaigning was sophisticated, spurred on by improvements in political communications and an impressive Internet site.[8] Nevertheless, it was by no means dominated by positive calls for independence. In fact, the SNP fought a surprisingly negative campaign. In the period between 17 March 1997 and the election, the party issued 104 press releases. Of these, 41 per cent were negative attacks upon its political rivals, particularly the Labour Party, its main electoral competitor.

The Party stood in all seventy-two Scottish seats, though only sixteen seats could be captured with a swing below 10 per cent. That said, a further twenty-four seats were within 15 per cent and fifty-seven required under a 20 per cent swing. Given that both the Labour and Liberal Democrat Parties were proposing at least a Scottish Parliament, it was always unlikely that the SNP would gain the national swing of 13.96 per cent required to produce a majority of SNP MPs.

Campaign success?

The results for the SNP represented both success and disappointment. First, the Party doubled its Members of Parliament from three to six, holding its existing three seats and gaining three (Galloway and Upper Nithsdale, Tayside North and Perth) from the Conservatives. This is the highest number of MPs the party has had in recent years but still lower than the seven victories in February 1974 and eleven in October 1974. Second, the Party received 22 per cent of the Scottish vote. This was only half a per cent higher than in 1992 and yielded a lower total number of votes – 622,260 in 1997 as opposed to 629,552 in 1992. This left the SNP as Scotland's third party (behind Labour and the Liberal Democrats) in terms of seats, but Scotland's second in terms of vote share. However, the seat that it needed the least swing to gain (0.8 per cent in Inverness, Nairn and Lochaber), was won by Labour despite a swing to the SNP of 9.9 per cent. Indeed, the SNP's principal electoral dilemma (as ever) was the electoral strength of the Labour Party, since most of the sixteen seats that required less than a 10 per cent SNP swing for victory were held by Labour. In a situation where the Conservatives were demoralised and Labour was not only in the ascendant but offering a referendum on a Scottish Parliament, the SNP's task was always going to be difficult. Against this background, the SNP performance appears more impressive. On the other hand, of course, it was still thirty-one seats short of achieving a Scottish majority.

Plaid Cymru

Campaign background

Like the SNP, Plaid Cymru (PC) enjoyed its greatest electoral successes in the mid-1970s and its share of the vote had been in gradual decline prior to a slight surge in 1992. The Party entered the 1997 election with more MPs than ever (four) but showed little sign of extending its appeal beyond the core areas of its support. Traditionally, this has been partly due to the resilience of the Labour Party in Wales. Furthermore, Wales is not homogeneous and can be divided into three distinct groups: Welsh Wales in the industrial South, where English is spoken but identity is Welsh rather than British; *Y Fro Gymraeg* in the Welsh-speaking West and North West, where again Welsh identity is paramount; and British Wales, in the east and south-west, where identities are British rather than Welsh.[9]

Plaid Cymru has only generally scored well in *Y Fro Gymraeg*. Nevertheless, Plaid has enjoyed some notable though sporadic successes at local level. Indeed, in Welsh local elections in 1995, PC came second to Labour in terms of seats, though again its support was heavily concentrated and PC won only one seat (out of a possible 187) in the three main urban areas in the south of Cardiff, Newport and Swansea.

The manifesto and campaign

The Plaid Cymru manifesto had three principal pillars: a Welsh Parliament; social justice (in terms of education, health care and taxation); and sustainability (in terms of economic stability, community and the environment). However, where the SNP saw independence as a prerequisite for enacting much of its programme, PC proposed policies to be achieved under a Welsh Parliament, with a secondary commitment to full self-government.

An Assembly was proposed by Labour, but PC wanted a Parliament with enhanced powers similar to that which was proposed by Labour for Scotland.

Plaid Cymru envisaged that such a Parliament would take over full responsibility for education, housing, health care, jobs, agriculture, transport and environmental policy in Wales. This stage was referred to as Phase I – a prelude to possible self-government. The manifesto offered two perspectives on policy – that which could be achieved under the auspices of a Welsh Parliament and that which would be proposed under self-government – Phase II. It was suggested that full self-government could follow Phase I after a minimum period of five years. Such a Parliament could debate and decide upon self-government, the constitution of which would be put for approval by a referendum to the people of Wales. If this was achieved, Wales would take an independent place within the EU, Commonwealth and United Nations.

It was proposed that the Parliament of Wales would have two chambers. The lower chamber (known as the House of Representatives) was to be the legislative house directly elected by proportional representation, whilst the upper chamber (known as the Congress of Wales) was to be chosen by Welsh local authorities. In both houses, it was planned to have equal numbers of men and women. If Phase II (self-government) was enacted, there were proposals for a written constitution and Bill of Rights including rights of freedom of expression, assembly, demonstration, the right to join peaceful pressure groups or political parties, the right to join a trade union, freedom from discrimination and the right to trial by jury.

Plaid Cymru viewed local authorities as key actors in Phase I. Many of the manifesto pledges were to be delivered by them, reflecting the Party's constitutional commitment to community socialism. Local authority funding was also to be reformed. Proposals included the abolition of the Council Tax. This was to be replaced with a local income tax reflecting the ability to pay as well as levying taxes on second homes. Uniform business rates would be replaced by an incorporation tax linked with profits. Finally, local authorities were to be given the choice as to whether to use direct provision of services or put them out to competitive tender.

In terms of social welfare, there were two principal targets: discrimination and poverty. Anti-discrimination proposals included codified acts to counter sexual, racial, age and disability discrimination. There was also to be an integrated national policy for sexual equality in education and training. In terms of poverty, there were commitments to tackle long-term unemployment, enact a minimum wage of £4 per hour, restructure child benefit to include older children and a restoration of benefit entitlements for 16–25-year-olds.

In housing, there was a commitment to developing a national strategy for house building, both by local authorities and in partnership with the private and voluntary sectors. This strategy included the building of hostels to reduce homelessness. In education, there were plans to devise a distinct Welsh system. In health there was a commitment for the community GP to be at the heart of Welsh medicine, backed up by a network of extended community hospitals.

To that end, PC proposed the abolition of GP fundholding and NHS Trusts. Prescription charges were to be abolished, as were charges for eye and dental care.

Under the heading of a sustainable economy and society, there were proposals for job creation, transport and the environment. Like the SNP, there was a commitment to full employment as being both desirable and achievable. Underlying this was a willingness to increase public expenditure, partly by taxation and partly by borrowing, with a National Development Authority for Wales established. Environmental policy pledged enhanced public transport designed to cut car use.

The preservation of the Welsh language had been one of the cornerstones of the early nationalist movement. This issue became less central in the early 1960s when PC began to focus more on social and economic issues and the Welsh Language Society was formed, thus defusing the issue to an extent within PC.[10] Yet, whilst the language was not central to PC's manifesto pledges, there were still a number of key proposals. First, both Welsh and English were to be official languages. Second, all public bodies were to provide a comprehensive service in Welsh. Third, all defendants were to have the right to have their cases heard in Welsh and finally all children were to have the right to an education in Welsh. These measures were to be overseen by a Welsh Language Authority.

The Party stood in all forty Welsh seats under the slogan 'Best for Wales'. Whilst it was openly hostile to the Conservatives, the Party was also critical of Labour's proposals for a Welsh Assembly, which it was claimed offered insufficient autonomy. There was criticism that proposals for Scottish devolution, though themselves criticised by the SNP, had considerably more teeth. For all that, however, the Party was realistic about its electoral prospects and sought modest gains, targeting specific seats like Carmarthen East and Dinefwr where it needed a swing of 6.23 per cent to seize the seat from Labour.

Campaign success?

Like the SNP, Plaid Cymru had a mixed result. On the positive side, the party retained all four of its seats, consolidating the one constituency gain from 1992 (Ceredigion). Second, it held three of the four seats with impressive majorities. Only in Ynys Mon was the percentage majority in single figures. Third, the party secured its highest vote share (9.9 per cent) since 1974, 1.1 per cent more than it had received in 1992 and higher as well in terms of votes received – 161,030 as opposed to 154,439.

However, there was also a less positive side. First, whilst securing a higher vote share than in 1992, this was still lower than the Party's electoral high-point in the early 1970s. Second, whilst most of the majorities in PC seats were impressive (the lowest was still over 2,000) there was a swing from PC to Labour in all PC-held seats except Meirionnydd Nant Conwy. Third, PC seats remained confined to areas of traditional support. Indeed, nearly 40 per cent of the total PC vote was cast in these four seats. In a country with forty seats, it was difficult to claim that PC was truly the party for Wales, especially when Labour not only now held thirty-four seats, but also secured nearly 55 per cent of the vote. Moreover, whilst PC became the second party in Wales in terms of seats, it was the fourth in terms of vote share, nearly 10 per cent behind the Conservatives, who were left with no seats. Like the SNP, the task of Plaid Cymru was always going to be difficult with Labour so much in the ascendant and offering a Welsh Assembly, albeit with limited powers. Plaid Cymru appears to have arrested its falling vote share and in a Welsh Assembly is likely to be a significant force.

Other parties

A feature of the 1997 campaign was the large number of small parties contesting a significant number of seats. All of the parties discussed below fielded more than fifty candidates.

The Referendum Party

The Referendum Party was formed in 1994 by Sir James Goldsmith. It campaigned on a single issue, demanding a referendum on Britain's future relationship with the European Union. In the event of an election victory, the Party pledged to pass a Referendum Act and then call a fresh election. The Party would then dissolve itself. In the interim, a national government would be formed with members drawn from all political parties. In the event of the Party not forming a majority, it pledged to form an *ad hoc* coalition with pro-referendum MPs from other parties and would vote tactically to best ensure the passing of a Referendum Act. The Party argued that the question asked of the British people in such a referendum should be: *Do you want the United Kingdom to be part of a Federal Europe?* or *Do you want the United Kingdom to return to an association of sovereign nations that are part of a common trading market?* Notes were provided detailing the Party's interpretation of the meaning of a 'Federal Europe' as well as its definition of a 'common trading market'. The Party pledged to stand in parliamentary constituencies in which 'the principal candidates of the major parties have not proven their commitment to a fair referendum on the Maastricht Treaty and its proposed amendments'. In the end, it contested 547 seats.

In the run-up to the election, there was a perception that the existence of the Referendum Party might harm Conservative interests. The former Conservative treasurer, Lord McAlpine, supported the new Party as did Mrs Thatcher's former economic adviser, Sir Alan Walters, whilst the deselected Conservative MP Sir George Gardiner became, briefly, the Party's representative in the House of Commons. Moreover, Goldsmith pledged £20 million to fund the Party's campaign. For all that, however, the party polled 811,829 votes. This meant an average of 1,484 votes per seat contested, a mean of 3.1 per cent per seat and 2.7 per cent of the British vote. It saved forty-three deposits.

UK Independence Party

This party was formed from the Anti-Federalist League in 1993. It was led by the academic Alan Sked and advocates total withdrawal from the EU, claiming that it is highly wasteful. The UK Independence Party claimed in its manifesto that withdrawal would save Britain £19 billion per year. This money would be used to reduce taxation and help fund the NHS and British defence. Whilst the Party had received tiny vote shares in recent by-elections, it did at least enter the election with three local councillors and a claimed membership of 16,000. In this election, it contested 194 seats and saved only one deposit.

Natural Law Party

The Natural Law Party first appeared in the 1992 election, fielding 309 candidates. In 1997 it fielded 195. No deposits were saved. The Party advocates yogic flying and claims as 'scientific fact' that natural policies such as collective thought are a cure for society's ills. Originally boasting the former Beatle, George Harrison, amongst its supporters, Tony Blair will have been immensely relieved at the Party's offer of help for the new Government.

Green Party

At the end of the 1980s, the Green Party appeared poised for something of a political breakthrough after securing 15 per cent of the vote in the 1989 European elections. Indeed, in 1992 the Party fielded a record number of candidates (253) as well as entering into three electoral pacts with Plaid Cymru, one of which produced a gain for the Welsh Nationalists. Yet the Party only received a mean of 1.3 per cent of the vote in 1992, although in the 1994 European elections, standing in all constituencies, it did gain 3.2 per cent of the vote. At local level, the Party had been more successful and had around 125 councillors. In 1997, it fielded only ninety-seven candidates, partly through lack of resources. No deposits were saved, but in two London seats the Party did gain over 4 per cent of the vote. It continued to stand on its traditional ecological platform and argued that economic success should not be measured by indicators like gross domestic product (GDP) but by quality of life – how well people's needs are met and how well resources are protected.

Socialist Labour Party

Arthur Scargill's SLP was formally launched on 1 May 1996. Whilst Scargill had long been a critic of the Labour leadership, the ditching of Clause Four was the final straw. In by-elections prior to the 1997 election the electoral performance had been poor, even on home territory like Barnsley, though in local government there were more encouraging electoral signs as well as the defection of over twenty Labour councillors to the Party. It pledged policies such as renationalisation, full employment and wealth redistribution and fielded sixty-three candidates. Three deposits were saved.

The Liberal Party

The Liberal Party was reborn after the creation of the Liberal Democrats and consisted of those Liberals opposed to the merger. It had the distinction of being the only 'minor minor' party to save a deposit in the 1992 election and entered the 1997 election with thirty-three councillors. The Party fielded fifty-five candidates who secured 45,166 votes, a mean of 821 votes per contested seat (1.7 per cent of the vote). It saved two deposits and scored a remarkable second place in the constituency of Liverpool West Derby with 9.6 per cent of the vote, beating the Liberal Democrat into third and the Conservative candidate into fourth. It stood on a wide platform of policies, opposing the Liberal Democrats in many, including opposition to the single European currency, nuclear weapons and the proposed alternative electoral system – the Liberal Party favours the single transferable vote.

British National Party

The electoral profile of the far-right British National Party was raised when it won a council seat in east London in 1993. Though the seat was soon lost, it was feared that the prospect of a far-right electoral threat might re-surface, especially in the light of experience in continental Europe. In 1997, the BNP fielded fifty-five candidates and saved three deposits. Its main policies included the ending of non-white immigration, 'repatriation' of non-white Britons, withdrawal from the EU, restoration of the death penalty, protectionist economics and the rebuilding of Britain's manufacturing base.

Pro-Life Alliance

The Pro-Life Alliance was founded in 1996. It stood on the issues of opposition to abortion, euthanasia and the destruction of human embryos. To that end, the Alliance sought the repeal of the 1967 Abortion Act and the Human Fertilisation and Embryology Act of 1990 as well as the outlawing of voluntary or involuntary euthanasia and an end to overseas programmes of sterilisation. It fielded fifty-five candidates and as such qualified for a party election broadcast, from which scenes were cut in the 'interests of public decency'. No deposits were saved.

Conclusion

In one sense, the 1997 general election was one where the term 'minor party' may need examination. First, the Liberal Democrats showed that third-party politics was not a diminishing force and since the Party now has nearly 30 per cent of the total of Conservative members, it is clearly not only an electoral force but a parliamentary one. Nationalist parties cannot be considered minor in the countries in which they operate. In 1997, the SNP doubled its number of MPs whilst Plaid Cymru maintained its level of parliamentary representation. In both countries, with the absence of any Conservative MPs, these parties have a more important role.

However, perhaps the key change for the nationalists is that when Labour's proposals for a Scottish Parliament and a Welsh Assembly become reality, the likelihood is that both will assume even more important roles in their countries' politics. In that sense, the election of a Labour government in the United Kingdom was very significant for Plaid Cymru and the SNP.

On the negative side for the nationalists and Liberal Democrats is the fact that their vote share was not especially impressive. However, the context of 1997 is significant. Whilst the Conservatives were in disarray everywhere, Labour was in the ascendant. Labour did not lose a single seat and was the victor in many where the smaller parties might have hoped to make some gains. Set against the avalanche of Labour support, the performance of all three 'major minor' parties seems respectable.

The message for the genuinely minor parties, however, is to reiterate that under a first-past-the-post system, their chances of electoral success are very small, no matter how much is spent. Although the Referendum Party may claim that it succeeded in putting the idea of a referendum on the political agenda, its electoral performance was a failure. That said, 1,308,378 [11] electors cast their votes for parties and independents other than the main British and nationalist ones, amounting to 4.3 per cent of voters clearly not wishing to support the main parties. In conclusion, the 1997 general election was marked not only by Labour's landslide, but by the growth of the Liberal Democrats as a political force, consolidation for the nationalists and the failure of the genuine minor parties to do anything but offer a little more electoral choice and swell the Treasury's coffers with lost deposits.

Notes

I am most grateful to Richard Topf for supplying preliminary findings from his study of the 1997 manifestos.

1 D. M. Farrell, D. Broughton, D. Denver and J. Fisher, *British Elections and Parties Yearbook 1996* (London: Frank Cass, 1996).
2 C. Pattie, D. Denver, J. Fisher and S. Ludlam, *British Elections and Parties 7* (London: Frank Cass, 1997).
3 Ibid.
4 R. Topf, 'Party manifestos' in A. Heath, R. Jowell and J. Curtice (eds), *Labour's Last Chance?* (Aldershot: Dartmouth, 1994).
5 Ibid.
6 *Guardian*, 28 April 1997.

7 Farrell, Broughton, Denver and Fisher, *British Elections and Parties Yearbook 1996*; Pattie, Denver, Fisher and Ludlam, *British Elections and Parties 7*.
8 P. Lynch, 'Professionalization, new technology and change in a small party', in Farrell, Broughton, Denver and Fisher, *British Elections and Parties Yearbook 1996*.
9 D. Broughton, 'Plaid Cymru and Welsh nationalism', paper presented to the American Political Science Association Annual Conference, Chicago, 1995. R. Levy, 'Nationalist parties in Scotland and Wales', in L. Robins, H. Blackmore and R. Pyper (eds), *Britain's Changing Party System* (London: Leicester University Press, 1994), p. 149.
10 J. Fisher, *British Political Parties* (Hemel Hempstead: Prentice Hall, 1996), p. 126.
11 This total does not include the 29,354 votes for Martin Bell in Tatton since the circumstances in that constituency were unique.

Glasgow Govan

Govan is a name associated with contemporary Scottish nationalism. In November 1973, Margo MacDonald won the Govan by-election for the SNP, starting a bandwagon which saw the Party advance in the two general elections in 1974. Though MacDonald lost the seat in the first of those elections, Govan had become part of SNP folklore. In November 1988, Jim Sillars, MacDonald's husband, recaptured the seat for the SNP in another dramatic by-election. The capture again only lasted until the general election, but, as in the 1970s, it heralded a significant increase in the SNP vote in the national contest.

The first signs of nationalist advance thus surface in this variable constituency, which Labour none the less regards as its territory. Predominantly working-class, the constituency has some of the worst housing in Glasgow. It contains Ibrox Stadium, home of wealthy Rangers football club. Affluent Pollokshields makes up a geographically large part of the constituency, although small in population terms. It has the highest proportion of ethnic minorities in Glasgow, although it is predominantly white.

Sillars having stood down after his 1992 defeat, the SNP chose Nicola Sturgeon, a twenty-six-year-old lawyer, as its candidate for the 1997 contest. One of the most able Scottish politicians of her generation, Sturgeon proved a formidable opponent for Labour's candidate, Mohammed Sarwar. Sarwar's nomination followed the redrawing of boundaries which reduced by one the number of seats in Glasgow. An unedifying scramble for nominations ensued with Mike Watson, MP for Glasgow Central, fighting Sarwar in the most bitter selection battle in Scotland. Amidst accusations of racism, duplicity and vote-rigging, the Labour selection battle proved far more bitter than the general election contest in the constituency. A re-run of the selection battle was ordered by Labour headquarters after Watson narrowly won. Sarwar won the re-run. The local Party was deeply divided.

Problems emerged for Labour during the election campaign when it was reported that there had been an exceptionally large number of late registrations from the part of the constituency represented by Sarwar on the city council. Sturgeon was widely credited with having defeated Sarwar in a public debate. Labour shielded their candidate, even using veteran trade unionist Jimmy Reid as a replacement on the hustings. More serious problems emerged at the conclusion of the campaign. There were accusations that Sarwar had attempted to bribe one of the fringe candidates, Badar Islam, to sign an affidavit claiming that there had been a dirty tricks campaign against Sarwar. The victorious Labour candidate admitted paying a 'loan'. As allegations of sleaze now troubled Labour, the national Party instigated an inquiry, removing the whip from Sarwar pending its deliberations.

Result

Glasgow Govan			
Mohammad Sarwar	Lab	14,216	
Nicola Sturgeon	SNP	11,302	
William Thomas	Con	2,839	
Robert Thomas	Lib Dem	1,915	
	Others	1,970	
Total vote		32,242	Turnout 64.7%
Lab majority		2,914	
Lab gain from SNP			
Swing Lab to SNP 3.19%			

5

The media and the election

Dominic Wring

Introduction

Perhaps conscious of Marshall McLuhan's famous phrase 'the medium is the message', many commentators view modern elections as media-dominated events.[1] During the 1997 election this view was publicly aired by Tony Blair and Michael Portillo, both of whom expressed their unhappiness with the coverage. Adverse comments of this sort are nothing new, especially when made by defeated politicians. But concern about the role of journalism in electoral matters is a legitimate issue and people of various persuasions are voicing concern about the influence of those who control the mass media in Britain.

For many years researchers assumed the media had a limited effect on voters during campaigns. More recently this assumption has been challenged by scholars, particularly those in Britain interested in the power of the press.[2] This preoccupation with audiences often obscures discussion of other important effects, notably the influence the media have on the way in which politicians perceive the issues. Arguably journalistic interest in the European question during the 1997 election damaged the Conservatives by making the Party focus on a subject which was not uppermost in the minds of the electorate.

When analysing campaigns, commentators divide media coverage into two categories. First there are 'free' media, the exposure parties or candidates are given by newspapers, television or radio during an election. Though frequently sought by the politician, this coverage provides a journalistic perspective. By contrast, 'paid' or 'controlled' media give the candidate or party the opportunity to directly address voters. Typically this is done through advertising in the press, on poster hoardings, television or, as is the case more recently, the Internet.

This chapter will assess the contribution made by free and paid media to the 1997 general election. Sections will analyse the most controversial form of free media, the national press, and the role of television and radio broadcasting. Mention will also be made of how parties used advertising in its various guises to generate publicity for themselves and their policies.

Television

Television is regarded as the most important political medium because of its perceived mass appeal and persuasive potential. Voters otherwise suspicious about politics tend to regard broadcast news as an important source of information, particularly during campaigns.[3] The credibility of the medium derives in part from legal regulations which compel it to cover party political matters in a neutral way. This impartiality extends to elections, in which competitors jealously guard against any perceived infringement in the quantity or quality of treatment they are given by broadcasters.

Though John Major called the election in mid-March, reporting of the campaign did not start in earnest until after the Easter holiday two weeks later. Thereafter, saturation coverage was provided by the five terrestrial broadcasters (BBC1, BBC2, ITV, Channel 4 and Channel 5) and satellite station Sky. Ironically for a service which marketed itself on a largely politics-free diet of sport and entertainment, it was *Sky News* which offered subscribers round-the-clock electoral analysis designed to go 'beyond the soundbites'. Of the main news programmes, only BBC1's *Nine o'clock News* was extended by thirty minutes. The most novel bulletins were provided by Channel 5 which began broadcasting on 30 March.

BBC2's *Newsnight* and *Channel 4 News* explored the campaign in greater depth, courtesy of discussions with politicians and policy specialists. Cross-examination of experts featured in the programmes' weekend counterparts, Channel 4's *A Week in Politics* and the special editions of *Newsnight* shown each Saturday.[4] Broadcast every weekday, Channel 4's *Midnight Special* invited an expert panel to explore a major policy area. Elite opinion was also sought by BBC economics editor Peter Jay for his Sunday evening series *Vote Now, Pay Later*. On BBC1's *Breakfast News* Sir Robin Day hosted a regular panel discussion between three ex-cabinet ministers entitled 'The Elder Statesmen'.

There was a concerted attempt by broadcasters to involve the public in debates, the assumption being that the not-so-gentle voters would enliven a programme with unpredictable and irreverent questioning of politicians. With its established telephone interrogation format, the BBC had long allowed the public to harass party spokespeople. This tradition continued with the phone-in programme *Election Call* broadcast simultaneously on BBC1 and Radio 4 every weekday morning. Most guests coped well, with some, like Robin Cook, even suggesting hostile questioners might be opponents' stooges. The programme did, however, provide some uncomfortable moments for politicians such as John Major and John Prescott.

Cross-examination of politicians by voters was a central feature of other programming. Regional audiences questioned party spokespeople on *Breakfast News* and BBC2's thrice-weekly *Campaign Roadshow*. Public participation added to the established BBC and ITV Sunday lunchtime outputs *On the Record* and *Dimbleby*. In the absence of the anticipated first-ever televised leaders' debate,[5] *On the Record* hosted a confrontation between the deputies. The leaders did not escape scrutiny and a BBC1 series of *Question Time* was devoted to this task. The three major party leaders were also billed to make their traditional, separate appearances on the final programme in the series *ITV 500: The People's Choice*. Even before the first question there was controversy when John Major opted to send deputy Michael Heseltine in his place.

Ironically at the time he was due to appear on *ITV 500* Major was being interviewed by David Dimbleby on BBC1. Part of a pre-recorded *Panorama* series, the programme was shown after *Eastenders* in the hope of attracting a large audience. Viewing figures were reportedly poor and, a rarity for BBC1, even lower than those for *The Antiques Show*, screened simultaneously on BBC2.[6] This, and the sharp decline in audiences for the extended *Nine o'clock News*, suggested millions were consciously avoiding the coverage. It was a trend borne out by the large increase in video rentals during the campaign.

Perhaps conscious of the public antipathy towards politics, the smaller networks experimented with different formats. In its first major electoral venture, Channel 5's *Tell the Truth* allowed activists and the undecided to question politicians whilst on Channel 4 *Voters can't be Choosers* enabled disillusioned voters to challenge spokespeople over their parties' apparent consensus on the need for lower taxation, further European integration and more draconian law and order policies. This theme was picked up in Channel 4's *Spot the Difference*, a programme which asked if the main parties were now indistinguishable.

Broadcasters' commitment to public access manifested itself in other ways. In BBC2's *Video Nation* people recorded their own viewpoints. Channel 4 used a similar format in *Thatcher's Children*, a slot which allowed twenty-two-year-olds born on the day the former Premier became Conservative leader to discuss politics. Many did so with a clarity lacking in some professionals. Probably the most experimental form of access programme, Channel 4's *Power to the People*, offered undecided guests the opportunity to evaluate the manifestos over a weekend: following intensive deliberations, there was a marked swing from the Conservatives towards the Liberal Democrats amongst the group.

Other means were used to encourage voter interest. For the older viewer Channel 4's *1964 and All That* took a nostalgic look at another Labour leader's first general election. For the very young, BBC1's *Newsround* ran mock school elections in which Labour were just short of a majority, the SNP won Scotland and the Conservatives did poorly everywhere except Northern Ireland. Youth interest was courted by BBC2's *The Enormous Election*. Making jokes at the expense of various public figures, host Dennis Pennis acted as the link between features on unemployment, drugs, morality and less formal leader interviews conducted by celebrities like David Baddiel and Ulrika Jonsson. Humour featured in Channel 4's *Long Johns Election Specials* and *Three Men and a Vote* programmes. One of those involved, Rory Bremner, also supplied light-hearted interludes on BBC1's *Breakfast with Frost* whilst Harry Enfield did the same on Saturday *Newsnight*. On polling day BBC2's *Have I Got News for You* and the sketch-based *Election Night Armistice* offered a comedy alternative to the high-tech results services.

There were few documentaries but, just prior to the campaign, a couple were shown featuring two groups alienated by the prevailing political climate. These were Channel 4's *Cutting Edge: The Dinner Party* about a group of opinionated Conservatives, and a BBC1 *Heart of the Matter* on environmental protesters. During the campaign itself, Channel 4's *Dispatches* investigated media reporting of the 1992 election whilst Channel 5 broadcast a film about the leaders' childhoods called *Two Little Boys* on its launch night.

Radio

Like television, radio is subject to the same stringent legislation prohibiting biased coverage. Though now secondary to television, radio has proved to be a durable medium: five national BBC plus numerous other stations continue to command large audiences. Given this and that, by comparison with television, different networks tend to cater for more select groups, radio remains an important outlet for politicians.

With its news remit, BBC Radio 5 Live offered the most in-depth coverage. Besides regular updates, Radio 5 offered a mid-morning campaign report. Unencumbered by the need to relay photo-opportunities, those involved were able to explore issues in some detail. This allowed the station, like *Sky News*, to follow breaking stories such as John Major's dramatic plea for Conservative unity during the campaign. The passion of Major's live message was somewhat dissipated in edited bulletins and a tame party election broadcast later that day. No politician, not even a Prime Minister, can escape being reported in soundbites, whatever the message.

Radio 5's coverage continued with discussion on Sybil Ruscoe's afternoon show and *Brian Hayes' Election Night*. Though primarily entertainment stations, Radio 1 and Radio 2 offered their respective, electorally important middle-aged and youth audiences a limited but tailored diet of politics. It was on Radio 2's *Jimmy Young Show* that the host embarrassed Tony Blair over rail privatisation policy whilst Radio 1's current affairs strand *Newsbeat* allowed listeners to question politicians themselves. The same programme commissioned a poll of youth which provided analysis for the whole BBC. The station also allowed parties to advertise in *Minute Manifesto* broadcasts on the popular morning show.

Of the culturally 'highbrow' BBC services, classical music station Radio 3 featured little of the campaign. With its expert discussion formats, Radio 4 provided coverage for the politically engaged listener. Besides the news programmes, Radio 4's *Analysis* and series *Election Agenda* offered in-depth commentary. Apart from *Election Call*, Radio 4 continued to allow listener access courtesy of its regional debating programme *Any Questions?* In contrast to the public service-orientated BBC, a multitude of commercial stations gave audiences a break from politics. Inevitably there were exceptions like Talk Radio and it should not be forgotten that local BBC stations provided their own coverage. Table 5.1 shows the issues that preoccupied these.

Table 5.1 The issues in the news

Issue	*% of selected media coverage*
Conduct of the campaign	32
Europe	15
Sleaze	10
Education	7
Taxation	6
Constitution	5
Privatisation	4
Health	3
Other	18

Note: 'Other' includes Environment, Employment, Northern Ireland, Housing, Defence, Social Security, etc.

Source: Loughborough University Communication Research Centre.[7]

Newspapers

Over the past two decades the political importance of the press has been the subject of considerable public interest. Many believe the overwhelmingly pro-Conservative press helped secure election victories for Margaret Thatcher and John Major.[8] Since 1992, however, the so-called 'Tory press' has begun to reappraise its relationship with the Party in light of Major's perceived incompetence and weakness.

In contrast to the legal regulations governing broadcasters' coverage of party politics, no restrictions apply to press reporting beyond the general laws concerning libellous journalism. Consequently newspapers offer an alternative, more opinionated view of elections. Besides determining *how* events are covered, the press plays an important so-called 'agenda-setting' role by determining *what* is reported. Whilst this can condition readers' understanding of a given issue it may also influence broadcasters' interpretations of what is news.[9]

Besides issues like health and education, the press covered every aspect of the campaign from keynote speeches to the cuisine available to journalists on the leaders' tour buses. More significantly newspapers reported on subjects hardly mentioned in the previous campaign.[10] Foremost amongst these were the controversies over European integration and so-called 'sleaze' (see Table 5.1), problems which were almost exclusively the preserve of the Conservatives. Whilst allegations of extra-marital affairs revived memories of the Government's ill-fated 'Back to Basics' campaign, it was the corruption charges levelled against Tim Smith, Neil Hamilton and other MPs which did most to harm the Party's image. Smith's resignation as a candidate and Hamilton's determination not to only encouraged journalists to investigate further. Indeed, it was former BBC reporter Martin Bell who took the opportunity to stand as an anti-sleaze candidate in Hamilton's Tatton constituency, thereby guaranteeing continued media interest.

The decision by best-selling daily the *Sun* to support Blair was remarkable given the way the paper had mercilessly attacked Labour leader Neil Kinnock during the 1992 election.[11] Following the unexpected Conservative victory, the paper even claimed 'It's the *Sun* wot won it'. It was a view shared by former Conservative Party treasurer Lord McAlpine and Kinnock himself and one Blair appeared to endorse not long into his leadership when he made a trip to meet Rupert Murdoch, owner of the *Sun*. Murdoch was reportedly impressed by Blair and new Labour policies said to favour business interests in digital television. Table 5.2 shows the extent of continuity and change in the allegiance of newspapers.

Table 5.2 Newspapers' political allegiances and circulations (figures in millions)

Newspaper	*1997*		*1992*	
Dailies				
Sun	Labour	(3.84)	Conservative	(3.57)
Mirror/Record	Labour	(3.08)	Labour	(3.66)
Daily Star	Labour	(0.73)	Conservative	(0.81)
Daily Mail	Conservative	(2.15)	Conservative	(1.68)
Express	Conservative	(1.22)	Conservative	(1.53)
Daily Telegraph	Conservative	(1.13)	Conservative	(1.04)
Guardian	Labour	(0.40)	Labour	(0.43)
The Times	Euro-Sceptic	(0.72)	Conservative	(0.37)
Independent	Labour	(0.25)	None	(0.39)
Financial Times	Labour	(0.31)	Labour	(0.29)
Sundays				
News of the World	Labour	(4.37)	Conservative	(4.77)
Sunday Mirror	Labour	(2.24)	Labour	(2.77)
People	Labour	(1.98)	Labour	(2.17)
Mail on Sunday	Conservative	(2.11)	Conservative	(1.94)
Express on Sunday	Conservative	(1.16)	Conservative	(1.67)
Sunday Times	Conservative	(1.31)	Conservative	(1.17)
Sunday Telegraph	Conservative	(0.91)	Conservative	(0.56)
Observer	Labour	(0.45)	Labour	(0.54)
Ind. on Sunday	Labour	(0.28)	None	(0.40)

Source: Audit Bureau of Circulation.

The *Sun's* announcement 'We back Blair' the day after Major called the election was followed up with positive coverage of the Labour leader if not his Party. This culminated in unambiguous headlines like 'Who Blairs wins' and, emblazoned above Blair's picture, lottery slogan 'It must be you'. There was a clear expectation the leader would be a 'sleazebuster' and 'strongman' in Europe. Blair was interviewed and even given columns, one of which he used to state his commitment to the pound. On polling day even the page three model came out for Blair: in 1992 the paper had claimed Labour would ban the feature. John Major's response to the defection was blunt: 'I don't think that up and down the country, in the Dog and Duck or at No. 10 Acacia Avenue, they are going to say "Gosh, the *Sun's* backing Labour, and, therefore, I must change my mind."'[12] Predictably the paper sought to embarrass the Prime Minister with features on the said pubs and addresses complete with stories of recent Labour converts.

The largest-selling Sunday paper, *News of the World*, was initially less than favourable towards Labour in its limited coverage. One editorial questioned the 'sinister silence of the trade union barons' linked with the Party whilst columnist Woodrow Wyatt called Blair's campaign manager Peter Mandelson and press secretary Alastair Campbell 'satanic advisers'. Wyatt did, however, find himself relegated to the back of the paper and his space on the comment pages taken by pro-Labour journalist Richard Stott. If this suggested a bias, it was confirmed when the *News of the World* declared 'We back Blair' in its last edition before polling day.[13]

Like the *Sun*, populist former Conservative-supporting *Daily Star* gave Labour a better press than it had in 1992. The new approach was underlined by an editorial attack on Michael Howard following his questioning of Tony Blair's commitment to anti-terrorism measures. Despite a pro-Conservative political editor, the *Star* came out for Labour, declaring 'There's Tony one way to go'. The paper nevertheless warned against threats it perceived from 'scroungers', 'unions' and 'Europe'. The least political 'newspaper', the polling day edition of the *Sport*, allowed two men and a female model to state each party's case: perhaps an intended bias, the woman supported Labour.

Traditionally the most sympathetic title, the *Mirror* even incorporated the slogan 'Loyal to Labour, loyal to you' into its masthead, no doubt as a comment on its rivals' change of allegiance.[14] The *Sunday Mirror* and *People* were similarly enthusiastic. All ran articles highly critical of the Conservatives. Their approach distinguished the papers' coverage from that of Labour's newer tabloid supporters, which tended to concentrate on promoting Blair. It would have been hard to imagine the *Sun* publishing 'Ultimate nightmare', a *Mirror* supplement on the horrors that it believed would follow a Conservative victory. The paper also produced a tactical voting guide and urged readers to support Labour or Liberal Democrat candidates where they might beat a Conservative.

In spite of its acquisition by a company headed by Labour peer Lord Hollick, the *Express* continued to support the Conservatives. Editorials were reinforced by columnists like Peter Hitchens and former Downing Street press secretary Bernard Ingham. A prominent critic of Neil Kinnock during the last election, Hitchens fared less well this time and in his exasperation denounced the Labour leader as 'Big Brother Blair'. Like the *Express*, the *Daily Mail* attacked Labour policies and the 'Conspiracy of silence' it alleged surrounded the Party's trade union links. Reporting of sleaze emphasised individual moral failings rather than Conservative affiliations. Not all of the coverage was so sympathetic: columnist Richard Littlejohn declared he would not be voting whilst Simon Heffer was unenthusiastic about Major's leadership skills. Both cited disillusionment with Conservative policy on Europe, a sentiment expressed in 'Battle for Britain', an editorial which attacked 'the bipartisan omerta of the political elite' it believed supported further integration. More subversively the *Mail* also managed to lead on 'Scandal of our leaking water' and 'Water meters for everyone?', stories hardly supportive of the Government's privatisation programme.[15]

Unlike the tabloids, the self-styled qualities tend not to advertise political allegiance in such obvious ways. They are nevertheless partisan. Nor is the coverage similar: during the campaign 34 per cent of broadsheet news coverage was devoted to the election as opposed to 11 per cent in the tabloids; for lead stories on the campaign the figures were 90 per cent and 9 per cent respectively.[16]

An influential government critic, the *Guardian* predictably came out for Labour on polling day. Having vigorously fought Neil Hamilton in the courts over allegations it made about his financial dealings, the paper assiduously continued its anti-sleaze investigations throughout the campaign. Like its *Guardian* sibling, the *Observer* followed a pro-Labour line. In its final pre-election edition the title published results from constituency polls which indicated several leading Conservatives were vulnerable to tactical voting. The following week the paper claimed its analysis had helped unseat several Tories, including Michael Portillo, who was pictured under the headline 'It was the Obs wot won it'.

Priding themselves on their objectivity, the *Independent* and *Independent on Sunday* gave Labour a modest endorsement. This is not to suggest the titles' coverage was uncritical. If headlines like 'Whitehall wrecked by Tory years' were unsympathetic to the Conservatives, *Independent* editor Andrew Marr also expressed alarm about the Euro-sceptic tone of a *Sun* article written by Tony Blair.[17] Perhaps conscious of its popularity amongst Liberal Democrat supporters, the paper gave extensive coverage to Paddy Ashdown's warning that Labour was in danger of forgetting the disadvantaged in its bid to win over 70,000 people living in 'Middle England'.

In successive editorials, *The Times* expressed dissatisfaction with the leadership of John Major though it gave encouragement to Dame Angela Rumbold and other Conservative candidates opposed to a single European currency. On polling day *The Times* refused to support a party, preferring to endorse by name the several hundred potential MPs it claimed would strengthen the sceptical cause in Parliament. Whilst the overwhelming majority were Conservatives, *The Times* did find itself supporting erstwhilst opponents on the Labour left. Though sympathetic to its sister paper's stance, the *Sunday Times* grudgingly supported the Conservatives.

Both *Telegraph* newspapers publicised their anti-federalism with sympathetic coverage of prominent Conservative Euro-sceptics such as junior agriculture minister Angela Browning. The *Daily Telegraph* reserved its strongest comments, however, for a medium it accused of promoting sleaze to the detriment of other matters. Neil Hamilton was given space to publish documents he claimed exonerated him of any wrongdoing. Though supportive of the Conservatives, new title *Sunday Business* managed less sympathetic stories on dubious government arms sales. The unrelated *Financial Times* followed up its surprise 1992 endorsement of Labour with lukewarm support for the Party this time. A pro-European editorial explained that though Blair was inconsistent, the Conservatives had failed to represent British interests.

Addressing the question of whether press partisanship matters, Table 5.3 compares the voting intentions of readers in the 1992 and 1997 elections. The swing to Labour amongst these groups was, in most cases, above the 10.5 per cent national average. Care should be taken when seeking an explanation for this disparity: readerships are not static and change according to consumer taste and long-term factors like death.

Table 5.3: Partisanship of newspaper readers (%; 1992 equivalents in parenthesis)

Newspaper	*Con*	*Lab*	*Lib Dem*	*Swing (Con to Lab)*
Result	31 (43)	44 (35)	17 (18)	10.5
Sun	30 (45)	52 (36)	12 (14)	15.5
Mirror	14 (20)	72 (64)	11 (14)	7
Daily Star	17 (31)	66 (54)	12 (12)	13
Daily Mail	49 (65)	29 (15)	14 (18)	15
Express	49 (67)	29 (15)	16 (14)	16
Daily Telegraph	57 (72)	20 (11)	17 (16)	12
Guardian	8 (15)	67 (55)	22 (24)	9.5
Independent	16 (25)	47 (37)	30 (34)	9.5
The Times	42 (64)	28 (16)	25 (19)	17
Financial Times	48 (65)	29 (17)	19 (16)	14.5

Source: MORI.

New buyers attracted by *The Times*' high-profile marketing campaign may partly account for the large drop in readers' support for the Government. There is, however, a greater swing to Labour amongst readers of former Conservative titles. Though they suggest newspapers could have influenced the 1997 outcome, the figures may reveal more about the past. In particular, the disproportionately high swings amongst readers of four tabloids (*Sun*, *Star*, *Mail* and *Express*) which vilified Labour during the 1987 and 1992 elections could indicate these titles' more neutral/positive (*Sun* and *Star*) or less single-mindedly negative (*Mail* and *Express*) coverage of the party influenced a significant minority of readers to switch allegiance or abstain this time. If the pro-Labour papers (*Mirror* and *Guardian*) are considered, the less than average swing away from the Conservatives amongst their readers suggests these titles probably succeeded in mobilising support for Labour some time prior to the 1992 election.

Advertising

If management of 'free' media is the responsibility of so called 'spin doctors', 'image makers' promote the party through controlled use of broadcasts, advertisements and the Internet. Given that commercial-style political advertising is banned on the major radio and television networks, parties receive airtime in the form of five- or ten-minute party election broadcasts (PEBs). Though not purchased by recipients, PEBs nevertheless constitute a state subsidy and can be counted as a 'paid' media activity. Like other advertising formats, parties are wholly responsible for these broadcasts. PEBs provide an insight into what politicians, free of media filters, want the electorate to know about themselves and their policies.

PEB allocation is overseen by a committee of representatives from the main parties and broadcasters. Each broadcast is awarded on the basis of a formula which takes account of a party's previous vote and current number of parliamentary candidates.[19] In 1997 a record number received broadcasts; these were: Conservatives (five), Labour (five), Liberal Democrats (four) and one each for the minor parties. Regionally based parties in Scotland, Wales and Northern Ireland were allocated PEBs by their local networks. Parties also received radio airtime.

The highlight of the Conservatives' series, John Major's appeal to his Party for unity over Europe, marked a return to the unfashionable face-to-camera broadcast. Scheduled at short notice, the intervention necessitated the cancellation of a planned PEB. This and his appearance in two further broadcasts led one critic to denounce Major as 'egomaniacal'.[20] More stylistic PEBs featured actors playing voters lamenting a Blair victory and likened Labour policies to poorly rooted trees.

Labour PEBs were characteristically professional productions. Following in the tradition of Neil Kinnock in 1987 and John Major in 1992, the series' highlight was a feature on Tony Blair. Made by acclaimed producer Molly Dineen, the broadcast portrayed Blair as a visionary with a sense of humour. One PEB had business people like Anita Roddick endorsing the leader and 'Iron Chancellor' Gordon Brown. Another broadcast which moved away from traditional Labour themes featured a bulldog called Fitz and promoted Labour's patriotism by arguing the country, as depicted by the dog, was being held back by Conservative rule.

Patriotism also featured in a more negative broadcast contrasting the rhetorical indulgences of a Conservative conference with footage of crime and poverty. Set to the Tory anthem 'Land of Hope and Glory', the film ended with a sandcastle symbolising Britain being washed away. Made by director Stephen Frears and featuring film star Pete Postlethwaite, Labour's final broadcast showed a taxi picking up a father and daughter from hospital on election night. No usual driver, Postlethwaite turns out to be an angel intent on convincing his passenger of Conservative failures. Having agreed and pointed out that the polls have closed, the father is transported back in time to enable him to vote Labour.

A central feature of Liberal Democrat PEBs, the discussion group enabled Paddy Ashdown to appear natural. More revealing was the recognition of the presidential nature of campaigning that came in a biographical broadcast on Ashdown complete with endorsements from childhood and army acquaintances. Neither were the Liberal Democrats averse to attacking opponents, depicting Major and Blair as Punch and Judy in one film and the parties as two doddering footballers in another.

The legal attempt by Referendum leader Sir James Goldsmith to increase the Party's PEB allocation was more memorable than his sole broadcast. Featuring Goldsmith on the follies of European integration, the film was less interesting than an alarmist Party video hosted by former *That's Life* presenter Gavin Campbell sent to millions of households. Not to be outdone, the UK Independence Party used *Rumpole of the Bailey* actor Leo McKern to promote the case for withdrawal from the European Union. Aside from the controversy over allocations, the broadcasting authorities were drawn into a debate over censorship following their decision to ban part of an anti-abortion Pro-Life Alliance PEB showing a pregnancy termination. Whilst Channel 4 banned an anti-immigration broadcast by the far-right British National Party, other networks responded by censoring it so as to protect the identities of people featured.

The newly formed Socialist Labour Party commissioned director Ken Loach to make a broadcast which used the discussion group format favoured by the Liberal Democrats. Like the SLP, the Liberal Party attempted to win over those alienated by mainstream politics in a broadcast which owed more to the production values of the 1970s than the 1990s. Similarly radical, the Greens' relatively professional PEB concentrated on environmental issues. More surreal than rainbow party, Natural Law used its airtime to show how members' yogic flying could regenerate Merseyside. Perhaps the most bizarre and effective of all were commercial 'broadcasts' shown on behalf of the 'Old El Paso' party range of Mexican food and the thinly disguised ridicule of the three main parties' campaigns by soft drinks brand 'Tango'.

Turning to advertising, Labour's 'Enough is Enough' campaign was eventually abandoned in favour of promoting core policy pledges and the theme 'Britain Deserves Better'. The Party also experimented with other media. One was the pop charts with the re-release of D:Ream's 'Things Can Only Get Better', the song which became the campaign anthem. Advertising was targeted in women's magazines, pub and club toilets ('Now wash your hands of the Tories'), Asian cable channel Zee TV and Classic FM, Talk Radio and Virgin commercial stations.[21] Labour, like other parties and broadcasters, launched pages making this an 'Internet' election for the select group of voters who had Web access.

Conservative advertising was more negative than Labour's. One advert depicting Blair as a puppet of German leader Helmut Kohl earned a rebuke from former Premier Edward Heath who, before he heard it was Michael Heseltine, demanded the copywriter be sacked. Other material was similarly negative and included 'New Labour, Euro danger', 'Tony and Bill' (a reference to tax), and 'Britain is booming: don't let Labour blow it'. The Conservatives were also helped by two series of adverts paid for by Euro-sceptic businessman Paul Sykes and a group of sympathetic entrepreneurs. Labour, too, drew support from the knocking copy campaign of the Unison union and, with leader Sir James Goldsmith's personal fortune, the Referendum Party were also able to advertise. Whatever their relative merits, surveys reported high public recognition of both main parties' advertisements though there was considerable doubt over whether these were effective.[22]

Conclusion

Changes in the media coverage of the 1997 election were as dramatic as the result. Whilst broadcasters attempted to infuse programming with more voter questioning and critical examination of the parties' plans, it was the remarkable shift in newspaper allegiances which literally grabbed the headlines: the swing to Labour in the country was bettered by that in 'Fleet Street' (Table 5.4). Having been strained in recent years, the election signalled the end of the partnership forged between the Conservatives and the 'Tory press' over twenty years before. The relationship deteriorated for a number of reasons: Conservative Party divisions, 'New' Labour, marketing considerations and the need to 'back the winner', not to mention the contrast between party leaders whose presence once again dominated the media coverage. Michael Billig not unreasonably commented that, by comparison with the candidates, it was easier for editors to change their minds: 'The political leaders are continually exposed; the paper leaders trumpet freely.'[23]

Table 5.4 Daily circulation by partisanship (figures in millions)

	1997		*1992*	
Total circulation of all newspapers	13.83		14.3	
Supporting Conservative	4.5	(32.5%)	9.53	(66.7%)
Supporting Labour	8.63	(62.3%)	4.38	(30.6%)
Supporting Liberal Democrat	0		0	
Euro-sceptic	0.72	(5.2%)	0	
Non-aligned	0		0.39	(2.7%)

Source: Calculations based on figures in Table 5.2.[18]

Whilst there was a considerable *quantitative* change in newspaper allegiances, there was also a *qualitative* transformation in the way the press reported this election. Gone was the unapologetically anti-Labour lobby. In its place came recent converts keen to put the case for Tony Blair. Aside from the presumably positive effect newspaper partisanship had on Labour fortunes, there were other consequences. Arguably the press realignment had an effect on *elite* perceptions, reinforcing the dynamic image of Blair and his party at the expense of their opponents. This advantage was augmented by the *agenda-setting* function of media which focused on the very issues, European integration and sleaze, which ultimately did so much to expose Conservative divisions.

Notes

1 M. McLuhan, *The Medium is the Massage* (New York: Allen Lane, 1967), p. 26.
2 The limited media effects thesis was developed by P. Lazarfeld *et al.*, *The People's Choice* (New York: Columbia University Press, 1944). Recent work has challenged this, notably W. Miller, *Media and Voters* (Oxford: Clarendon, 1991) though others are sceptical; see J. Curtice and H. Semetko, 'Does it matter what the papers say?' in A. Heath *et al.* (eds), *Labour's Last Chance?* (Aldershot: Dartmouth, 1994).
3 See Miller, *Media and Voters*.
4 *Newsnight* specials featured discussion between partisan guests like comedienne Jo Brand and writer Frederick Forsyth.
5 The debate, which would have probably consolidated the media's influence, was abandoned following disagreements over whether an audience and Paddy Ashdown should be allowed to participate.
6 A. Frean, 'Viewers turn to the past in search of light relief', *The Times*, 10 April 1997.
7 Loughborough University Communication Research Centre analysed over 2,000 items from the newspapers listed in Table 5.1, *Today* (8–9 a.m.) on BBC Radio 4 and the five terrestrial television stations' main evening news bulletins. See P. Golding, D. Deacon and M. Billig, 'Dominant press backs "on message" winner', *Guardian*, 5 May 1997.

8 For background see C. Seymour-Ure, *The British Press and Broadcasting since 1945* (Oxford: Blackwell, 1996).
9 Broadcasters monitor newspapers for stories and, given their partisan interpretations, a consensus amongst part of the press can slant the news agenda.
10 For 1992 see Loughborough University figures in the *Guardian*, 11 April 1992.
11 M. Harrop and M. Scammell, 'A tabloid war', in D. Butler and D. Kavanagh, *The British General Election of 1992* (Basingstoke: Macmillan, 1992).
12 *Breakfast News*, BBC1, 18 March 1997.
13 There were reported disagreements within the editorial team over this decision (*Observer*, 23 March 1997). Similarly executives on the Scottish *Sun* were unhappy declaring for Blair given the paper backed the Conservatives in 1987 and SNP in 1992.
14 The *Mirror* group's Scottish papers, the *Daily Record* and *Sunday Mail*, strongly supported Labour.
15 Interestingly the *Mail*-owned London *Evening Standard* came out for Labour.
16 Golding, Deacon and Billig, 'Dominant press'.
17 A. Marr, 'Cry "God for Tony Blair, England and the Sun"', *Independent*, 23 April 1997.
18 These exclude small circulation titles like the Labour-inclined *Morning Star* and other, trivial newspapers such as the *Sport*. The figures for 1992 do, however, include the now defunct and then Conservative-supporting *Today* which regularly sold 533,000 copies. It should be remembered that readerships are two to three times the size of circulations.
19 M. Scammell and H. Semetko, 'Political advertising on television: the British experience', in L. L. Kaid and C. Holtz-Bacha (eds), *Political Advertising in Western Democracies* (London: Sage, 1995).
20 M. Lawson, 'Outpouring of poison', *Guardian*, 28 April 1997.
21 P. Barrett, 'Labour turns to off-beat media', *Marketing*, 17 April 1997.
22 'Poster watch', *Marketing*, 24 April and 22 May 1997.
23 M. Billig, 'Who exposes the exposers?', *Guardian*, 28 April 1997. It should be remembered that some proprietors effectively backed *both* parties. Newspapers belonging to the same group which supported different sides were the *Express* and *Daily Star*, *Sun*/*News of the World* and *The Times*/*Sunday Times*, and *Daily Mail*/*Mail on Sunday* and London *Evening Standard*.

Exeter

Most general elections have contests that test social attitudes and tolerance. In 1997 Exeter was one such seat. The Conservative candidate Dr Adrian Rogers inherited a majority of 3,064 secured by John Hannam at the 1992 general election. Exeter was very winnable for Labour, it was thirty-second on their list of key seats. Labour's candidate was a BBC journalist, Ben Bradshaw. Bradshaw, Dr Rogers stated, was a 'media man, a homosexual, he likes Europe, he studied German, he lived in Berlin, he lives in London and he rides a bike. He's everything about society which is wrong.' Before modern language students rush to hide their qualifications it should be noted that the crux of Rogers' campaign was a distaste for the open homosexuality of 'bent Ben', as he was known to some of his opponents.

'Race' rather than homosexuality has tended to be the issue most likely to arouse prejudice in British general elections. In the 1964 general election Peter Griffiths fought and won the Smethwick constituency for the Conservatives on a racist anti-immigration ticket with the slogan 'If you want a nigger neighbour, vote Labour'. At the 1992 general election John Taylor, the Conservative Party's first black candidate in a winnable seat, had been defeated in Cheltenham after racists in the local Conservative association refused to accept his candidacy. There have, of course, been gay MPs, but they have tended to conceal their sexuality or reveal it – either voluntarily or involuntarily – once elected.

Dr Rogers stood squarely on the morally authoritarian wing of the Conservative Party. He founded the Conservative Christian Fellowship and spread his ire wide. He called for an end to all primary immigration and said that he did not believe in a multicultural society of ethnic minorities. Controversially perhaps, he called for the firing of CS gas canisters into the tunnels containing protesters against the A30 road project. Bradshaw, too, was a man of God: a committed Christian and lay preacher in what was seen by some as Devon's holy war.

The election saw a decisive swing of 11.9 per cent in favour of Bradshaw, slightly above the average for the South West of England. Bradshaw secured a majority of 11,705 in an election that was seen as not just a win for Labour, but as a victory for tolerance over prejudice.

Result

Exeter			
Ben Bradshaw	Lab	29,398	
Dr Adrian Rogers	Con	17,693	
Dennis Brewer	Lib Dem	11,148	
	Others	3,625	
Total vote		61,864	Turnout 78.2%
Lab majority		11,705	
Lab gain from Con			
Swing Con to Lab 11.9%			

6

Europe: Major's nemesis?

Andrew Geddes

Introduction

In one of the most dramatic moments of the general election campaign, John Major made an appeal for support for his Government's policy on the European single currency. At a press conference on Wednesday 16 April 1997 he stated that: 'Whether you agree with me, disagree, like me or loathe me, don't bind my hands when I am negotiating on behalf of the British nation.' The startling thing was that this plea was not directed at the general public but at his own candidates, over 200 of whom disavowed the Government's 'negotiate and decide' (or 'wait and see') line. Even Government ministers opposed the Government's policy. For the first time at a British general election, European integration was propelled to the forefront of the campaign agenda.

The European issue had particularly divisive and corrosive effects on the Conservative Party. Some on the Party's Euro-sceptic wing argued that electoral benefits would accrue if 'clear blue water' was opened between the Conservatives and Labour. They were countered by a smaller, but influential, Euro-philic wing that included within its ranks the Deputy Prime Minister, Michael Heseltine, and Chancellor of the Exchequer, Kenneth Clarke. Years of in-fighting had exhausted the Party and alienated many of its supporters.

When the issue of Europe broke to the surface in the third week of the campaign it released a strong wave of Euro-scepticism within the Conservative Party. John Major chose to ride this wave and be perceived, he hoped, as the defender of 'national sovereignty'. However, even though evidence suggests that many British people are reluctant Europeans, the Conservative Party over-estimated the salience of the European issue. As the staunchly Euro-sceptical *Daily Express* observed: 'It's the issue that makes the parties swoon and the voters yawn'.[1] By playing the Euro-sceptic card the Conservatives actually drew attention to their own divisions and weakened still further the Party's electoral credibility.

The European issue

The reluctance of British governments to seek deeper economic and political integration within what was known as the European Community (EC), but which since 1993 has been the European Union (EU), is well documented.[2]

Britain did not join the Community until 1973, sixteen years after its creation. Successive British governments had disliked supranational integration because of its implications for national sovereignty. Looser free-trade arrangements based on intergovernmental co-operation were preferred. There was also a lingering supposition that integration would flounder when confronted by the stark reality of national interests although this has not yet proved to be the case.

European integration had played little part in British general elections prior to 1997. It was usually seen as a foreign policy issue divorced from the domestic concerns about tax, education, employment, health care and so on, that convulse campaigns. From the mid-1980s, a resurgence in European integration blurred still further the distinction between European and domestic politics. Responsibilities for policies which had been the preserve of national governments were ceded to the European level. For Euro-sceptics sovereignty had been 'lost' and the nation-state denuded as a direct result; for pro-Europeans it had been 'pooled' at European level where it could be used more effectively.

Dissent within the Conservative Party was impelled by the events of Wednesday 16 September 1992 when severe pressure from international financial markets wiped between $3 billion and $4 billion from Britain's currency reserves and forced sterling out of the EC's Exchange Rate Mechanism.[3] 'Black Wednesday' delivered a double blow to the Conservative Party: first, its reputation for economic competence was shattered; second, latent hostility to European integration within the Party bubbled to the surface.

The humiliating ejection from the ERM cast a shadow over the Treaty on European Union (TEU) – more commonly known as the Maastricht Treaty – and its plans for closer European integration. When John Major left the negotiating chamber at Maastricht in December 1991 he declared that the outcome was 'game, set and match for Britain'. The basis for this claim was the British opt-out from the extension of EU social policy contained within the TEU's Social Chapter. Britain also reserved the right to decide whether or not to opt in to the third stage of economic and monetary union (EMU) at which point a single currency was to be created, supposedly by 1999 at the latest. Major's Maastricht deal papered over the cracks in the Conservative Party and stymied dissent prior to the 1992 general election. None the less, for Conservative Euro-sceptics, Maastricht was 'a treaty too far'.[4]

A good deal of the unhappiness amongst Conservative MPs about European integration actually stemmed from the integrative consequences of the Single European Act (SEA), 1986, which most of them had keenly supported. The SEA laid plans for the creation of a single European market by the end of 1992 within which people, services, goods and capital could move freely.[5] Margaret Thatcher's Conservative governments were enthusiastic supporters of most aspects of the single market programme because it complemented domestic attempts at economic deregulation and liberalisation. The single market was, though, seen by the British Conservative Government as an end in itself and not as a means to an end, particularly if that end was a federal Europe.

For many other member states, and the European Commission – led between 1985 and 1995 by Jacques Delors – the single market programme was only the beginning of an ambitious plan for deeper political and economic integration. For instance, the advocates of integration argued that if there was a single market then it should have a single currency. The TEU laid out a three-stage plan for creation of an EMU based on economic convergence between the economies of participating countries. Convergence was to be measured by levels of government debt, interest rates, and inflation, and by participation in the ERM. In November 1990, Margaret Thatcher's vigorous rejection of a single currency provoked the resignation of Sir Geoffrey Howe which, in turn, instigated Michael Heseltine's challenge to her leadership. The perceived connection between Thatcher's hostility towards Europe and her party's very low opinion poll rating was a principal reason for her replacement by John Major who promised a more emollient style and pledged to put Britain 'at the heart of Europe'. In 1997, the ramifications of Thatcher's removal still hung over the Conservative Party. European integration became a defining issue which for some on the Party's right wing represented the betrayal of the Thatcherite inheritance.

EMU was not the only front on which the EU sought to advance. Plans for increased European-level social policy responsibilities provoked division between Britain and its European partners. European level social policy is not a recent innovation: there were social policy commitments in the Treaty of Rome (1957) which, in turn, had been extended by the SEA – both of which Britain signed. The late 1980s and early 1990s saw further expansion in the remit of European social policy which the British Conservative Government opposed because they saw it as running counter to the domestic emphasis on liberalisation and deregulation. The non-binding Social Charter of 1989 outlined a series of general principles, some of which were then given legal effect within the Social Chapter of the Treaty on European Union. The British Government refused to sign the Social Charter and opted out of the Social Chapter. Labour opposed the opt-out and said it would sign the Social Chapter if returned to government.

Labour's stance on European integration had been re-evaluated after the disastrous 1983 general election defeat when the Party was committed to withdrawal. This reassessment was linked to Party modernisation and to developments at European level which saw more focus placed on 'economic and social cohesion' alongside market-based purposes. By the 1997 general election, in terms of rhetoric at least, Labour had become the more pro-European of the two main parties. In terms of substantive European policies, Labour's stance was more ambivalent. The Social Chapter is a good example of equivocation: Labour pledged to sign the chapter, but made it clear that it would oppose new social legislation which hampered labour market flexibility.

The Liberal Democrats have been the most consistently pro-European of the British political parties. The Liberals had favoured accession to the EC's forerunner, the European Coal and Steel Community, in 1951. Since that time, they had remained determined advocates of European federation based on decentralisation and diversity. The nationalist parties in Scotland and Wales had also become more pro-European; 'independence in Europe' was seen as bolstering potential small states by providing them with an avenue to greater influence.

The intervention of Sir James Goldsmith's lavishly funded Referendum Party was another blow to the Conservative leadership. Goldsmith pledged to put to the people the question of Britain's future relations with Europe. The fear within the Conservative Party was that the Referendum Party would be a refuge for Euro-sceptic Tory voters alienated by the Conservative Party's 'soft' line on European integration. Even a relatively small number of votes cast for the Referendum Party could make a difference in key marginals if the election was close. The size of the Referendum Party's vote in the general election did exceed the majority of the winning candidate in nineteen seats where Conservatives were defeated. The Referendum Party was, though, a symptom not a cause of Tory disunity and eventual defeat. The Referendum Party also stole the thunder of the UK Independence Party, which was committed to withdrawal from the EU, which, they claimed, would save £19 billion.

Conservative Party intrigue

Plots and counter-plots within the Conservative Party added a Machiavellian twist to debates about Europe which enraptured keen observers of political life, but repelled most of the electorate, for whom the issues were remote. Compared with Margaret Thatcher, John Major faced the additional pressure of having only a small majority. Thatcher had been able to steamroller European legislation, such as the SEA, through the House of Commons. Major's 1992 majority of twenty-one – which soon dwindled – meant that he had to look anxiously over his shoulder to his Euro-sceptic backbenchers. Ultimately, only the introduction of a confidence motion secured TEU ratification. In November 1994, a hard core of eight intensely Euro-sceptic Conservative backbenchers had the whip withdrawn.

John Major was not able to rely on support for his European policy from across the floor of the House of Commons. Since British accession in 1973 there has been a cross-party pro-European majority in the Commons. British accession in 1973 had occurred as a result of sixty-nine Labour MPs defying a three-line whip and voting in favour of membership. The Labour Party, though, refused to support TEU ratification without inclusion of the Social Chapter and, of course, saw a golden opportunity to exploit Conservative disunity. The depth of Conservative divisions was illustrated on 22 July 1993 when twenty-three Conservative MPs voted for a Labour motion on the Social Chapter – a policy the Conservative Euro-rebels detested – with the intention of inflicting harm on their Government's European policy.

Eventual ratification of the TEU in August 1993 did not calm Conservative tensions. Major's attempts to draw lines in the sand were washed away by the rising watermark of proposals for closer integration. The strains of operating on two fronts within the 'two-level game' of international negotiations placed severe pressures on the Conservative leadership.[6] At European level a core group of member states pushed for more integration, whilst at national level there was growing opposition to the EU amongst Conservative backbenchers. In June 1995, Major resigned the Party leadership and invited a challenge from the Party's Euro-sceptic wing. The former Welsh Secretary, John Redwood, stood against him and was defeated, although Redwood did secure eighty-nine votes (a further twenty-two Conservative MPs abstained).

By the summer of 1996 there was a determination on the Conservative Party's Euro-sceptic wing not to be bound at the 1997 general election by a manifesto that did not rule out a single currency. At the 1992 general election most Conservatives had stood on a manifesto committing them to Maastricht ratification – a point about which the whips were eager to remind them during the ratification process itself. During the summer of 1996 members of the right-wing '92 Group' of Conservative backbenchers had been canvassing the adoption of a common line against the single currency in their personal manifestos.

Millionaire businessman Paul Sykes helped organise opposition to the single currency within the Conservative Party. Sykes had stood down as Conservative candidate for Barnsley because of his opposition to the single currency. In September 1996, the *Daily Telegraph* published a poll which showed that 186 Conservative candidates opposed the single currency. Sykes decided to offer donations to the campaigns of Conservative candidates who ruled out a single currency. By 30 April 1997, 237 Conservative candidates in previously Conservative-held seats had accepted campaign donations from Sykes of up to £3,000. Sykes also received advice from John Redwood's press spokesperson, Hywel Williams. Rumours around Redwood's preparations for a post-election leadership challenge compounded perceptions of disloyalty. Election night television pictures of his frequent mobile phone conversations gave the impression that a Redwood leadership campaign was being prepared before the dust had settled on the calamitous events of 1 May. This did little to help his leadership ambitions.

The manifestos

Despite the rumblings of dissent within the Conservative Party, the positions outlined by the Conservative and Labour Parties in their respective manifestos were strikingly similar. The Conservatives pledged that they would 'not allow Britain to be part of a federal European superstate'.[7] Labour's manifesto outlined a vision of Europe as 'an alliance of independent nations choosing to co-operate to achieve the goals they cannot achieve alone. We oppose a federal European superstate.'[8] Either form of words could have been used in either of the two manifestos. The similarities extended to other areas. The Conservatives prioritised three points: enlargement of the EU to bring in new members from Eastern Europe; completion of the single market; and reform of the Common Agricultural Policy (CAP). Us too, said Labour.

On the most salient of the Europe-related issues, the Conservative manifesto refused to countenance participation in a single currency without a 'yes' vote in a referendum, and made it clear that Britain was unlikely to participate in the first wave of members. The Major Government's line on a single currency had hardened in a cabinet statement made on 23 January 1997 which declared that: 'Upon the information available to us at present, we reached the conclusion that it was very unlikely, though not impossible, that countries' performance against the Maastricht criteria will be sufficiently clear and stable for a single currency to proceed on 1 January 1999. On that basis there is a strong argument for delay by the EU as a whole. If it did proceed without reliable convergence, we would not be part of it.'

Labour's draft manifesto saw EMU as 'a major step of integration which could bring benefits in terms of stability and lower interest rates'. The final version of the manifesto toughened the Party's line and dressed Labour's position more explicitly in the language of national self-interest. British participation in EMU under a Labour government would, it said, be based on 'a hard-headed assessment of Britain's economic interests'. It also saw 'formidable obstacles' to British participation in the first wave of members in 1999. In a televised debate on 9 April, Robin Cook appeared to rule out British participation in a single currency during the lifetime of Labour's first Parliament when he stated that: 'If you didn't join [the single currency] in 1999, it's very difficult to see a government that has taken the decision that Britain wasn't ready in 1999 coming to the decision that it would be ready the year after or the year after that.'[9]

Furthermore, Labour's manifesto pledged to uphold the national veto over taxation, defence and security, immigration, the budget and treaty changes, but did express willingness to countenance increased use of qualified majority voting in limited areas, such as environmental and regional policy. The principal difference between the two main parties was in their stance on the Social Chapter.

The Liberal Democrats had similar priorities to the Conservatives and Labour. They also saw the advantages of enlargement, single market completion, reform of the Common Agricultural and Fisheries Policies and a referendum on a single currency. They did, though, remain true to their federalist principles in a 'decentralised, democratic and diverse' EU and expressed support for the single currency because: 'Being part of a successful single currency will bring low inflation and low interest rates.'[10]

The European issue and the campaign

For the first two weeks of the campaign 'sleaze' dominated the election. The European issue broke to the surface when it became clear that the Government's line on the single currency was not holding. In March 1997 Major said he would allow some leeway for candidates who wanted to express opposition to the single currency in their personal election addresses, but also said: 'If ministers dissent in any respect, they should not expect to remain in office.'

When placed under pressure this policy buckled. Angela Browning, a junior agriculture minister, made a statement in her election address in which she said that EMU meant 'the end of sovereignty of the nation-state and, if that is what is offered, I have made it very clear that I will not support it'. Mrs Browning would not 'wait and see', but John Major refused to sack her because to do so would risk re-igniting the Conservatives' Euro-war.

Labour declared that it would not punish candidates who took what its foreign affairs spokesperson, Robin Cook, called an 'idiosyncratic' line on the single currency. Cook did, though, make it clear that the leeway extended to candidates was not open to frontbenchers, or anyone who aspired to such a position. Labour had its Euro-sceptics, but Party discipline was maintained throughout the campaign. For most Labour MPs and candidates internal divisions and anti-Europeanism were associated with electoral disaster. Many Conservatives had not yet learnt this lesson.

The first test of the parties' stances on Europe came when the EU Commission proposed reductions of 30 per cent in fish catch quotas. The cuts aimed to preserve fish stocks in the long term, but would have adverse effects on the UK fishing industry. Many in the industry were already angered by the selling off of parts of the UK quota to fishermen from other EU member states. This 'quota-hopping' was lawful, but fostered resentment. Major threatened to block progress at the Amsterdam summit meeting of EU heads of government to be held in June 1997 unless quota-hopping was ended. As soon as the Conservatives threatened to block progress at the Amsterdam summit, Mr Blair did the same and, thereby, displayed Labour's eagerness to neutralise the European issue.

The Conservatives' 'wait and see' line on the single currency soon suffered another setback when Angela Rumbold, the Conservative candidate for Mitcham and Morden in Surrey and a party vice-chairman, made it clear in her election address that she did not want any more powers transferred to Brussels, that she opposed a single currency and thought there should be a referendum before any further steps were taken on European integration.

The simmering discontent within Conservative ranks was capitalised upon by the Tory press. Newspapers that had been staunch supporters of the Conservative cause were no friends of John Major during the difficult years of his premiership. Right-wing newspapers such as *The Times*, *Daily Telegraph*, *Sunday Telegraph* and *Daily Mail* were hostile to Major personally – whom they saw as a weak leader – and to the EU – which they saw as a threat to the integrity of the nation-state. These Euro-sceptic newspapers also adopted a rather different stance on the issue of Europe from the one they had taken when sleaze dominated the election agenda. Writing on the subject of sleaze in the *Daily Telegraph*, Stephen Glover argued that: 'It is not the proper role for journalists to set the agenda for this election. We are not, after all, elected representatives. To determine what the election should be about is an abuse of power.'[11] Paul Johnson demanded to know who governs Britain: elected politicians or unelected journalists?[12]

The same newspapers were, though, keen to fan the flames of Euro-scepticism. On 15 April the *Daily Mail* stated that the 'battle for Britain' had begun. In a front-page editorial it declared that 'There is a deafening silence at the heart of the campaign and its name is Europe.' On the same day, two more junior Conservative ministers, John Horam and James Paice, breached the wait-and-see line. The next day the *Daily Mail* proclaimed that 'the great revolt' had begun. The *Daily Express*, which had remained loyal to Major, urged that it was 'time to come clean on Europe'. Even though the *Sun* had announced its support for Tony Blair at the start of the campaign, it still maintained a Euro-sceptic stance. Blair felt moved – or at least his press spokesperson did – to write an article for the *Sun* which reassured its readers that he 'loved the £'.

Coverage of the European issue was a major part of the media agenda. Research for the *Guardian* by Loughborough University academics showed that between 31 March and 25 April, 16 per cent of media coverage was devoted to Europe. This was more than double the amount of coverage of issues such as education and tax, which actually had a far greater impact on how people cast their vote.[13]

By the fourth week of the campaign, John Major was backed into a corner by his own candidates. At the Conservative Party's press conference on Wednesday 16 April he made an impassioned statement to them via the assembled press. He urged them to support his wait-and-see stance. Flanked by his pro-European Chancellor of the Exchequer, Kenneth Clarke, Major outlined the possible costs and benefits of EMU participation and said that he had been 'scarred' by the ERM calamity.

That evening Major scrapped the planned Conservative Party election broadcast and instead chose to speak directly to the nation in a manner reminiscent of a war-time broadcast. Major stood aside from his Party and made a personal appeal for support. In a telling review of the broadcast, the *Daily Telegraph* reflected on the broadcast's sub-text: 'My Party may look a bit of a shower, but don't be alarmed about that. I, John Major, am in charge.'[14] Unfortunately for the Conservatives, the European issue was centre-stage on the same day that unemployment, as measured by the number of benefit claimants, fell by 41,000 to 1.7 million – the lowest level in over six years. By pursuing the European issue, Major went 'off-message' and drew attention to Conservative divisions. As one Labour campaign adviser tellingly remarked: 'It may sound a terribly simple point to make, but they did not give anyone a reason to back the Tories.'[15]

The European issue rumbled on at the next day's press conference when Major declared that he would offer a free vote on the single currency to his backbenchers. Even though it had been discussed with ministerial colleagues, Major made this policy change without consulting senior colleagues. The Chancellor of the Exchequer was campaigning in the West Country and knew nothing of the policy shift. Major defended his stance by stating that he was only answering the question he had been asked and that he could not be expected to say: 'I'm frightfully sorry, that's a very interesting question, but I'd better go and ask Ken Clarke or Joe Bloggs or someone else before I give you an answer.' The next day the *Guardian* printed a picture of Kenneth Clarke with the headline 'Meet Joe Bloggs: Major's Chancellor'.

Despite the evidence of serious internal divisions, the Conservatives thought that they could wrong-foot Labour by contrasting the experience of Major with the inexperience of Blair and the Labour Party. The Conservatives claimed that Labour would surrender Britain's interests in Europe and import the allegedly ruinous 'European social model'. A campaign poster devised by Michael Heseltine showed a tiny Tony Blair perched on Chancellor Kohl's knee with the slogan 'Labour's position on Europe' and the warning 'Don't send a boy to do a man's job'. Blair responded by remarking that he did not feel the need to take lessons in the art of negotiation from a Prime Minister and Government that had lurched from disaster to disaster in their European policy and, in particular, had shown themselves incapable of resolving the BSE crisis and the export ban on British beef.

The Euro-sceptic tone of the British general election campaign was viewed with dismay in other EU member states. In a speech in Amsterdam the EU Commission president, Jacques Santer, attacked Euro-sceptic 'doom merchants' for offering no positive alternative to the EU. 'We have only one option,' he said, 'to move on.'[16] Santer's intervention provoked further bouts of Euro-scepticism. The Foreign Secretary, Malcolm Rifkind, used Santer's speech to raise fears of a federalist agenda for the Amsterdam summit to which, he contended, Labour would surrender. Robin Cook gave Santer's remarks an equally frosty response. Santer's intervention was viewed as unhelpful and likely to do little to offset the Euro-scepticism about which he expressed concern.

Major used intercessions such as Santer's to play the Euro-sceptic card. In response to Santer's speech, he said that he would 'keep his feet on the brakes' whereas Tony Blair would 'put his foot on the accelerator to a federal Europe'.[17] In an interview with the *Sunday Telegraph* on 20 April, Major dismissed as 'a silly piece of Euro-babble' the commitment at the heart of the Treaty of Rome to forge an 'ever closer union between the peoples of Europe'. Meanwhile the divisions within the cabinet were becoming increasingly evident. Home Secretary Michael Howard confirmed his Euro-sceptic credentials by claiming that the meeting of the EU heads of government in Amsterdam in June 1997 had such far-reaching implications that it put the survival of Britain as a nation-state in question. Kenneth Clarke described as paranoid nonsense the idea that the EU was a threat and stated that he did not think that the survival of Britain as a nation-state was at issue.

The impact of Europe

It could be construed as rather eccentric that the Conservative Party seemed so keen to discuss the European issue when they were palpably divided upon it. The stance could be viewed as a rationalisation of disunity. By portraying themselves as defenders of the nation-state and national sovereignty – or at least their perceptions of these notions – the Conservatives hoped to wrong-foot Labour and turn a weakness into a strength and defence into attack. For Major, European integration was closely linked with domestic constitutional reforms, which he also opposed. Major believed that his anti-devolution stance and 'defence of the Union' had contributed to the Conservatives' 1992 general election victory.

When taken at face value, opinion poll evidence suggests the British public could be amenable to a Euro-sceptic message. Table 6.1 shows that 47 per cent of British respondents in autumn 1996 thought the UK had not benefited from EU membership, 10 per cent more than the EU average. Table 6.2 shows that 60 per cent opposed the creation of a single European currency to replace sterling.

Why, then, were the Conservatives unable to exploit Euro-scepticism to their electoral advantage? To answer this question the impact of the European issue on voting intentions needs to be analysed.[18] Neither issue awareness nor evidence of people's opinions on an issue is sufficient for a judgement on that issue's impact on voting to be formed. It is also important to assess how strongly people feel about the issue and whether or not one of the political parties represents such views.

Despite the furore in certain newspapers, opinion poll evidence suggests that Europe was not a highly prioritised concern. A Gallup poll in the *Daily Telegraph* on 13 April showed that only 22 per cent of voters saw Europe as one of the two most urgent problems facing the country, and most of these were Conservative voters anyway. The same poll also showed that when asked which party could best handle the issue, 31 per cent of respondents said the Conservatives, but 35 per cent said Labour. This marked a turnaround from

Table 6.1 The benefits of EU membership (%)

Q: Everything considered, in your opinion has the UK benefited or not from its membership of the EU?		
	UK	*EU 15*
Benefited	34	42
Not benefited	47	37
Don't know	19	21

Source: *Eurobarometer* 46, autumn 1996.

Table 6.2 Support for the single currency (%)

Q: What is your opinion on the following proposal: there should be a European Monetary Union with one single currency replacing the pound and all other national currencies of the member states of the EU?		
	UK	*EU 15*
For	29	51
Against	60	37
Don't know	11	12

Source: *Eurobarometer* 46, autumn 1996.

the situation in 1992 when Gallup put the Conservatives a massive twenty-seven points ahead on Europe. Despite Conservative efforts to portray Blair as weak and inexperienced, a Gallup poll printed in the *Sunday Telegraph* on 20 April showed that 45 per cent thought Blair was the best negotiator on Britain's behalf, compared with 42 per cent who thought Major was. Even towards the end of the campaign, when the profile of the European issue was raised, Labour's lead held, as Table 6.3 shows.

Table 6.3 Perceptions of party stances on Europe (%)

Q: Which of the main parties – Conservative or Labour – most closely reflects your views on Europe?	
Labour closer	40
Conservatives closer	37
Neither/other	9
Don't know	9

Source: Gallup/*Daily Telegraph*, 24 April 1997.

In terms of substantive policy commitments there were few differences between the two main parties. Labour was keen to neutralise Euro-scepticism, as shown by its adoption of a tougher line on the single currency and fish quotas. More important, the Conservatives were divided on Europe. These divisions had a significant negative effect on their electoral appeal. An NOP poll for the *Sunday Times* on 20 April showed 27 per cent of respondents to be less likely to vote Conservative because of the Party's divisions on Europe and only 8 per cent to be more likely (62 per cent said it made no difference). A Gallup poll for the *Daily Telegraph* on 24 April showed 80 per cent of respondents viewed the Conservatives as a divided party. The Conservative Party's attempt to rationalise its disunity and portray itself as the defender of the national interest failed.

Conclusion

On polling day there was little discernible variation in swing between Euro-sceptics and Euro-philes. On the Party's pro-European wing, Hugh Dykes lost his Harrow East seat and Edwina Currie was defeated in Derbyshire South. On the anti-European wing, Nicholas Budgen lost in Wolverhampton South West, Tony Marlow in Northampton North and Norman Lamont in Harrogate.

The general election was, though, not won or lost in the six-week campaign. For nearly five years prior to the 1992 general election the Conservative Party was bitterly divided. The fissures ran too deep to be concealed and broke to the surface in the campaign's third week. The TEU's plans for deeper economic and political integration in Europe were to be Major's undoing. The calamitous exit from the ERM in September 1992 emboldened the Euro-sceptics and swelled their numbers. The Euro-sceptics were then able to exploit the Party's small majority to propound their anti-EU cause.

In opposition, the Conservatives remain skewed towards Euro-scepticism, although there is a Euro-philic tendency and, therefore, the potential for further division. Analysis of Conservative MPs elected in 1997 suggests that 21 per cent of the Conservative Party are on the pro-European integration left wing of the Party and 30 per cent on the Euro-sceptic right wing; Party loyalists constitute the remainder, although 34 per cent of the faithful have Euro-sceptic leanings.[19] During his successful leadership campaign, William Hague ruled out Conservative support for a single currency for – what seems a rather arbitrary – ten years. Out of government the strains of the European issue are unlikely to be so acute; although a principal reason why the Conservatives are out of government is the European issue.

During the campaign, Labour, as it had done throughout the Conservatives' Euro-war, sat back and enjoyed the spectacle of the Conservative Party turning on itself. Labour's quest for electoral victory meant that it was quick to adjust its position when the Conservatives played the Euro-sceptic card. In government, Labour's vast majority and stern party discipline seem likely to reduce the effect of troublesome rebellions. Blair's government has also made it clear that Britain is highly unlikely to participate in the first wave of countries to join a single currency in 1999.

Blair's Government, like Major's before it, has stated its intention to take a leading role in the EU. In his first meeting with fellow EU heads of government, Blair spoke of modernising the EU in the same way that Labour had been modernised. However, like the Conservatives before it, the Labour Government will have to respond to the ambitions of a core group of EU member states to push for 'ever closer union'. For over fifty years successive British governments of whatever political hue have consistently under-estimated – or preferred to ignore in the hope that it would go away – the drive for economic and political integration. If Britain is to lead, it must engage in constructive dialogue, but doing so means that difficult issues that impinge on understandings of national sovereignty have to be faced. If they are not, then the idea of Britain at the heart of Europe will remain a pipe dream.

Notes

1 *Daily Express*, 16 April 1997.
2 See, for example, S. George, *An Awkward Partner: Britain in the European Community* (Oxford: Oxford University Press, 1994); A. Geddes, *Britain in the European Community* (Manchester: Baseline, 1993).
3 P. Stephens, *Politics and the Pound: The Conservatives' Struggle with Sterling* (London: Macmillan, 1996).
4 M. Spicer, *A Treaty Too Far: A New Policy for Europe* (London: Guardian Books, 1992).
5 D. Dinan, *Ever Closer Union? An Introduction to the European Community* (London: Macmillan, 1994), Ch. 5.
6 R. Putnam, 'Diplomacy and domestic politics', *International Organization*, 42 (1988): 427–60.
7 Conservative Party, *You Can Only Be Sure with the Conservatives: The Conservative Manifesto 1997* (London: Conservative Central Office, 1997), p. 46.
8 Labour Party, *New Labour: Because Britain Deserves Better* (London, 1997), p. 37.
9 *Guardian*, 10 April 1997.
10 Liberal Democrat Party, *Make the Difference: The Liberal Democrat Manifesto 1997* (London, 1997), p. 57.
11 *Daily Telegraph*, 4 April 1997.
12 *Daily Telegraph*, 8 April 1997.
13 *Guardian*, 28 April 1997.
14 *Daily Telegraph*, 17 April 1997.
15 *Sunday Telegraph*, 20 April 1997.
16 *Daily Telegraph*, 22 April 1997.
17 *Daily Telegraph*, 22 April 1997.
18 D. Butler and D. Stokes, *Political Change in Britain* (London: Macmillan, second edition, 1974).
19 I am grateful to Professor Philip Norton, University of Hull, for permission to use these data.

Putney

The south-west London constituency saw the battle of the plutocrats. The seat was defended by former cabinet minister David Mellor, who was appointed in 1992 as the inaugural 'Minister of Fun' at the Department of National Heritage. Revelations about Mellor's seemingly fun-filled personal life had forced him out of ministerial office in 1993. Without the pressure of red boxes he had turned his attention to making his fortune from, amongst other things, numerous business consultancies and football phone-in shows on Radio 5 Live. Millionaire businessman Tony Colman fought the seat for Labour. Putney was eighty-ninth on Labour's key seats list; a swing of 8 per cent would unseat Mellor.

It was not just the contest between Labour and the Conservatives that attracted attention. There was also the intervention of billionaire financier and French MEP, Sir James Goldsmith, who founded and funded the Referendum Party. Goldsmith's fortune dwarfed that of the other candidates; he was able to spend £20 million of his own money to create the Referendum Party as a vehicle for his views on Europe. He was, of course, restricted to the normal candidates' expenses in the Putney contest, although many local residents along with millions of other Britons received a free copy of a short video from the Referendum Party outlining the apparent evils of the EU. The Liberal Democrats' candidate, Russell Pyne, felt rather outgunned and pointed out that he was the only non-millionaire amongst the main candidates.

The Putney contest had a by-election feel to it. Six other candidates also exercised their right to stand at the risk of their £500 deposit. These included the UK Independence Party, which despite some good by-election performances had been crowded out of the Euro-phobic market by Goldsmith's Referendum Party; and the so-called Sportsman's Alliance, which defended 'shooters' rights' (Mellor had been vocal in the campaign for a total ban on hand guns).

The outcome in Putney was no great surprise: Mellor was defeated by an 11.2 per cent swing from the Conservatives to Labour. Equally unsurprisingly, Goldsmith lost his deposit, as did all the other minor party candidates. What were extraordinary were the scenes at the count. As Mellor made his loser's speech he was heckled and jeered by other candidates. Goldsmith and the Sportsman's Alliance candidate led the cry of 'Out, out, out' as Mellor tried to address the audience. Mellor responded in kind by referring to Goldsmith's Mexican home and the rather unlikely basis of his claim to be a champion of British national interests: 'Up your hacienda, Jimmy' was Mellor's defiant rejoinder. Goldsmith's 1,518 votes added to a grand total of 810,778 in 547 seats, which, when the £20 million campaign is taken into account, works out at £24.67 for each vote.

Result

Putney			
Antony Colman	Lab	20,084	
David Mellor	Con	17,108	
Russell Pyne	Lib Dem	4,739	
Sir James Goldsmith	Ref	1,518	
	Others	546	
Total vote		43,995	Turnout 73.1%
Lab majority		2,976	
Lab gain from Con			
Swing Con to Lab 11.2%			

How the Conservatives lost the economic argument

Mark Wickham-Jones

Introduction

Economic issues played a central role in Labour's 1992 election defeat. In the months before the campaign, a series of private polls indicated to the Party's leadership that they trailed the Conservatives badly over the question of economic competence. Moreover, the gap between the parties was widening. A key consideration for voters was Labour's proposed taxation increases. Although their overall impact was moderate, over half the electorate thought their own taxes would rise. Furthermore, a majority of voters were opposed to such measures. Difficulties over tax were characteristic of the Party's more general failure to project an image of economic proficiency. Throughout the twelve months before the 1992 election, the Conservatives led Labour by at least 12 per cent on this subject. Many commentators concluded that, as at previous elections since 1979, this lead played an important part in the outcome.[1]

The economy was no less important in the outcome of the 1997 election than it had been five years earlier. Economic issues remained amongst the most salient with voters. There was, however, a significant difference. In 1992 the Conservatives won a twenty-one-seat majority in spite of a prolonged and deep recession. By contrast, five years later Labour led strongly on economic policy (by 14 per cent) and won a landslide at a time of relative economic success. In recent work analysing elections, political scientists have distinguished between 'sociotropic' and 'egocentric' voting.[2] Under sociotropic motivations, individuals are concerned by the general economic outlook. Under egocentric reasoning, they are influenced by their own personal well-being. Both approaches might have been expected to result in a Conservative victory in 1997. Indeed, of the four elections since 1983, in many ways 1997 should have been the easiest at which to secure re-election. Inflation and interest rates (influences upon egocentric voting) were lower than at any previous election in the sequence of Conservative victories. Determinants of sociotropic voting were equally impressive. Unemployment was lower than at any national poll since 1979. Growth was higher than at all but one (1987). Only the growth of wages was slightly disappointing in comparison with other elections (see Table 7.1). Moreover, the UK economy had recovered dramatically from the recession of 1990–92 and had for the past few years outperformed most of its European rivals. That the Conservatives lost so heavily at a time of relative economic success has led some commentators to question the importance of economic matters in determining election outcomes. A leader in the *Spectator* concluded, 'Whatever else it was, the election result was a defeat for economic determinism.'[3] Likewise, at the start of the campaign, Anatole Kaletsky commented in *The Times*, 'If the Tories lose, the theory of "economic determinism" which has dominated British politics for decades will have to be junked once and for all.'[4]

Table 7.1 Economic data from British general elections 1983–1997

Economic issue	*1983*	*1987*	*1992*	*1997*
Growth (% of GDP)	2.0	3.6	−1.7	3.0
Unemployment (% of workforce)	12.7	10.9	9.4	6.1
Inflation (%)	3.7	4.2	4.3	2.7
Growth of earnings (%)	7.5	7.5	7.3	5.0
Interest rates (%)	10.0	9.5	10.5	6.0

Source: The *Economist*, 4 June 1983, 6 June 1987, 4 April 1992 and 3 May 1997; and David Butler and Dennis Kavanagh, *The British General Election of 1992* (London: Macmillan, 1992).

The failure of the Conservatives to benefit in electoral terms from a sustained economic recovery highlights a noteworthy paradox about the 1997 election. In addressing this failure much has been made of Britain's ejection from the European Exchange Rate Mechanism in September 1992. The exit had an adverse effect on Conservative political fortunes and on popular perceptions of the Government's economic competence. Yet it was a fortunate event, paving the way as it did for a new economic package which laid the foundations of the subsequent economic upturn. Voters chose not to re-elect the Government despite its economic achievements between September 1992 and April 1997.

The paradox of the Conservatives' inability to benefit from the economic revival is greater because Labour adopted a similar stance on British membership of the ERM. Labour endorsed entry and affirmed its support for stable exchange rates in the summer of 1992. Yet it benefited in political terms from the exchange rate crisis and established a strong lead over the Conservatives on the question of handling the economy without offering a distinct alternative policy. At the election itself, voters appeared to be remarkably indifferent as to whether they endorsed either Labour's commitment to sustain existing personal tax rates or the Liberal Democrats' pledge to increase income tax by a penny. This chapter examines the paradoxical failure of the Major Government to benefit from Britain's improved economic performance. The development of the Conservative Government's economic policy and the evolution of Labour's strategy are assessed before consideration of the central themes: how did the Conservatives lose the economic argument and what do voters' attitudes towards economic issues tell us about the election result?

Conservative economic policy: from rules to discretion

In terms of its economic strategy, John Major's second administration got off to a disastrous start.[5] It had fought the 1992 campaign mainly on two issues. The Party was committed to low inflation through UK membership of the ERM and to successive tax cuts through strict control of public spending. Within twelve months the Government had been forced to abandon each commitment.

Britain joined the ERM in October 1990. The arrangement meant that the value of sterling became fixed within a 6 per cent band to the exchange rates of other participating European countries. Most notably the level of the pound was established at DM2.95. Advocates of the system maintained that it gave much-needed stability to trade with Europe and that, by linking UK interest rates with German interest rates, it acted as an anti-inflationary anchor for the economy. In the summer of 1992, however, the ERM was coming under immense strain. The costs of German reunification (and the accompanying high German interest rates) meant that UK interest rates were high at a time when the British economy was struggling to recover from recession. Some observers concluded that the UK had entered the ERM at too high a rate and that British exports were being priced out of foreign markets. More concluded that there was simply a structural tension within the system, a fault line as John Major would later claim, which demanded resolution.

Political difficulties added to the pressures on the pound's membership of the ERM. On 2 June 1992 the Danish electorate voted in a referendum against the Maastricht Treaty, thus throwing the process of European integration into considerable uncertainty. It was also evident that splits within the Conservative Party over Maastricht ran much deeper and were broader than had previously been anticipated.

The mechanism by which the tension within the ERM could be resolved was by no means obvious. The German Bundesbank was under no obligation to cut interest rates simply to ease the strain on the British economy. The Major Government was equally unwilling to raise them in order to alleviate the pressure on the pound, given that the effect of such an increase would be to damage economic confidence and so prolong the recession. In July and August, the Conservatives attempted to resolve the dilemma by continually reaffirming their commitment to the ERM. In one theatrical statement, Norman Lamont, the Chancellor of the Exchequer, announced, 'We are absolutely committed to the ERM. That is our policy. It is at the centre of our policy ... I hope there is no room for any doubt about that at all.'[6] A *Financial Times* leader noted, 'Words are cheap. Deeds may yet be required.'[7] A year later, in his resignation speech, Lamont observed, apparently without irony, 'Credibility and confidence depend not on words, but on objective conditions.'[8] In August 1992 the pound fell close to its bottom band within the ERM but the Treasury did not step in and raise interest rates. The Government's nerve appeared to have failed.

The effect of a devaluation by Italy on 13 September 1992 was to increase market concerns about the value of sterling. The pound's position was not helped by the publication of off-the-record comments from the Bundesbank president concluding that the realignment involving Italy should have been more widespread. His message was straightforward: Major's Government should have devalued with the Italians. On 16 September sterling came under huge pressure. The pound opened at the bottom of its band within the ERM: it was plain that the Government's reserves would soon be expended. Lamont announced that interest rates would go up from 10 to 12 per cent. The decision had no impact on markets as selling continued. The Chancellor quickly concluded that UK membership of the ERM could no longer be sustained. After some discussion, another interest rate increase (to 15 per cent) was announced, largely in the hope that it might ease the pressure on sterling. There was no expectation that it would allow the UK to remain a member of the ERM. It was rescinded later that day and, with the foreign exchange reserves nearly exhausted, the suspension of the UK's membership was announced.

The UK's ejection from the ERM represented a catastrophic reversal of the Government's economic policy. Philip Stephens estimates that in two days nearly $38 billion of reserves had been used up at a cost of between $3 billion and $4 billion.[9] The overall figure was higher still, probably around $5 billion. Arguably, it was the greatest defeat suffered by a post-war administration in terms of its management of the economy. The humiliation suffered by Norman Lamont and John Major was all the greater because of the promises they had made over the preceding months. In seeking to assure markets they had repeatedly defended the ERM and attacked devaluation. The alternatives to the ERM, Lamont had argued, 'are all illusory or destined to fail'.[10] Likewise, John Major told the Confederation of British Industry (CBI) in Glasgow just before the sterling crisis, 'There is going to be no devaluation, no realignment. The soft option, the devaluer's option, the inflationary option would be a betrayal of our future and it is not the government's policy.'[11]

In the aftermath of the débâcle, the Government blamed the Bundesbank and the trajectory of German economic policy as well as the political uncertainty. Mistakes by the Government in its management of the economy had played a significant part as the crisis had unfolded. The administration had failed to demonstrate its commitment to sterling through the use of interest rates. In giving ambiguous signals to currency markets, it had raised doubts about the credibility of its support for the ERM. Other countries had intervened well before their currencies fell as low as sterling had within its given band. Furthermore, the Treasury was isolated within Europe and had few allies.

More than that, however, the Government had locked itself into a trajectory from which it was unwilling to extricate itself at the appropriate time. A better course would have been to compromise and voluntarily accept a realignment involving devaluation, even though it would have meant a reversal of the Government's policy. Worst of all was 'the elevation of the exchange rate parity into a badge of pride'.[12] The Conservatives had persisted in an extremely dogmatic fashion with a strategy regardless of the cost to the economy and ultimately to the Government's own credibility.

'Black Wednesday' left the Government without an economic strategy. Over the next few months a new set of measures, based around an inflation target, gradually emerged. Taken together, they marked an important change in direction for the Government in terms of both the means and the objectives of policy. In effect, it abandoned its enthusiasm for a rules-based system in favour of an approach based upon discretion and pragmatism. The ERM was a rules-based framework for the conduct of policy. At the heart of its economic strategy, the Government had locked the exchange rate into a formal setting. If the Government's policies were to be credible, there could be no deviation from that commitment: any measures necessary to defend sterling had to be taken. Under the new policies, post-September 1992, the Conservative Government was much more flexible. Policies were adapted as necessary to secure the administration's objectives. They were justified by the results they secured and not by fulfilling any overarching theoretical criteria. In a further contrast to the nature of policy during UK membership of the ERM, Lamont now talked of 'British' monetary policy.[13] Previously, he had been scathing about the potential of nationally based economic policies.

The consequence of the UK's ejection from the ERM and the adoption of these measures was that interest rates came down rapidly: by January 1993 they were at 6 per cent as the pound fell further. Interestingly, there was an ambiguity about the Government's commitment to price stability. In October 1992, both Lamont and Major stated that growth had to be a priority alongside inflation. It was a reflection in part of the poor state of the economy and the prolonged recession as well as a recognition of the isolated political position of both Chancellor and Prime Minister. The Government would attempt to juggle low inflation and growth through an *ad hoc* and accommodating policy mix.

Britain's membership of the ERM was not the only aspect of the Conservatives' economic strategy to run into trouble during 1992–93. The level of Government borrowing was much higher than had previously been anticipated (up from £32 billion to £51 billion for 1993–94). This outcome reflected the legacy of the general election (and a neglect of public borrowing during the run-up to it) as well as the prolonged recession in which tax revenues had fallen. In his March 1993 budget, Lamont introduced huge tax increases including higher national insurance contributions (from 1994) and lower personal allowances. Most controversially, he announced that VAT would be added to domestic fuel in two stages in 1994 and 1995. The reason for this strategy was a desire to indicate to markets that action was being taken to deal with the precarious state of public finances whilst not derailing the fragile recovery through any damage to confidence.

The political impact of Lamont's measures was devastating. Whilst many economists endorsed the tax increases, opinion polls indicated that it was the most unpopular budget since records began in 1949 (see Table 7.2). After disastrous local election results and the loss of the Newbury by-election in May 1993, something was needed to induce a revival in Conservative fortunes and Lamont was manifestly vulnerable in any cabinet reshuffle. He enjoyed little credibility with either financial markets or voters. Major offered him the Department of Environment. Lamont refused it and returned to the back benches, feeling he had been unfairly scapegoated after bravely taking unpopular but economically necessary decisions. In his resignation speech he launched a vitriolic attack on the Prime Minister in which he suggested Major had overruled the Treasury on occasion and made interest rate decisions on the basis of political, rather than economic, criteria. 'We give the impression,' he concluded, 'of being in office, but not in power.'[14]

Table 7.2 The popularity of budgets and Chancellors 1992–1996 (%)

Q: Is the budget fair?			
Date	*Yes*	*No*	*Don't know*
Mar 92	45	44	11
Mar 93	19	75	6
Nov 93	35	56	9
Nov 94	23	65	13
Nov 95	31	57	12
Nov 96	30	57	13

Source: *Gallup Political and Economic Index* (December 1996).

Q: Is the Chancellor doing a good or a bad job?			
Date	*Good*	*Bad*	*Don't know*
Mar 92	43	43	14
Mar 93	18	70	13
Nov 93	36	40	24
Nov 94	24	59	17
Nov 95	33	49	18
Nov 96	38	46	16

Source: *Gallup Political and Economic Index* (December 1996).

Kenneth Clarke, the new Chancellor, endorsed Lamont's discretionary framework for economic policy and repeated the ambiguous commitment to both price stability and growth. Over the next three years he proved to be extremely flexible in his conduct of monetary policy, trusting his own judgement over that of the Treasury and the Bank of England. On several occasions his conclusions proved correct and he skilfully avoided interest rate increases. Like his predecessor, Clarke was not afraid to take tough decisions over fiscal policy. In his first budget in November 1993 he increased taxation and cut public spending. Together, the two budgets in 1993 had seen the largest peacetime increases in taxation ever introduced in the UK. A year later, Clarke reduced mortgage tax relief and was forced to introduce further levies on petrol, alcohol and cigarettes when the second stage of VAT on fuel was defeated in the House of Commons. By 1995, he felt able to cut a penny off income tax, a measure which was repeated a year later. Such reductions had little impact on popular perceptions of the Government's policy. The two tax-cutting budgets of 1995 and 1996 were regarded as being less fair than the revenue-raising one of 1993. Polls suggested that the tax cuts were seen as attempts to bribe the electorate, efforts which might well be reversed after the election.

In the summer of 1992, Norman Lamont had asserted that 'devaluation just does not work for Britain'.[15] The Conservatives' management of the economy over the next four and a half years demonstrated otherwise. By 1993 inflation was down to a thirty-year low and unemployment had peaked. In 1994 GDP rose by 4 per cent, unemployment fell by 280,000, prices rose by only 2.4 per cent and the balance of payments deficit came down from £11 billion to £2 billion.[16] The recovery faltered slightly in 1995 but the general trajectory of key economic indicators was impressive. The outcome of a lower pound, reduced interest rates and tight fiscal policy was a sustained and, in the eyes of many, sustainable economic recovery. The Government continued to juggle its objectives of low price stability and growth through the mix of monetary and fiscal policy. Inflation came down, unemployment fell and GDP rose. The discretionary framework, established in the aftermath of Black Wednesday and adeptly operated by Kenneth Clarke since 1993, had been successful. In electoral terms, however, it failed.

The evolution of Labour's 'new economics': from discretion to rules

After the Labour Party's 1992 election defeat, Gordon Brown was given the job, as the new Shadow Chancellor, of redesigning Labour's economic strategy. It was a difficult task. Although the Party's policies were taken by many to be a significant cause of the defeat, Labour had campaigned on a limited set of proposals. It was unclear as to what changes Brown could make which would further moderate the Party's image whilst leaving it with a distinctive and attractive package of measures with which to secure electoral support. He was further restrained by the Party's existing commitment to the ERM.

In the spring of 1993, over a year before Tony Blair became leader of the

Party and adopted the slogan of 'New Labour', Brown laid out his proposals in a series of speeches entitled 'the new economics'. Many of his themes had been Party policy before the 1992 election. Members of the Parliamentary Labour Party expressed concern, usually in private, about the Shadow Chancellor's unambitious objectives: some backbenchers (and a few others) pressed him publicly without success to adopt expansionist measures.[17] On occasion, John Smith, the Party's leader between 1992 and 1994, laid out aspirations towards more radical goals: he endorsed full employment in robust terms to the Trades Union Congress (TUC) in September 1993. He was equally concerned, however, to ensure the Party's image of moderation was understood by both the electorate and business. In 1993 he became the first Labour leader to address the conference of the Confederation of British Industry (CBI) (though many attributed that achievement to his successor two years later). Overall, Brown found the first two years of his Shadow Chancellorship tough going. His performance may even have cost him the leadership in July 1994.

Tony Blair's accession to the leadership gave impetus to Gordon Brown's search for a new economics. The new leader quickly demonstrated his determination to reform the Party's economic policy. Some of his reforms were symbolic and rhetorical whilst others simply confirmed changes that had been made under previous leaders long before his accession. Nevertheless the overall impression was of far-reaching and permanent change. One of Blair's first initiatives on economic matters was to persuade the Party to abandon its historical and largely token commitment to common ownership through the reform of Clause Four of its constitution. In the new clause, the Party endorsed the mixed economy and the profit-making activities of the private sector. It was a dramatic reformulation which had been regarded as impossible by many commentators and members of the Party.

In May 1995, in the Mais lecture, Blair pledged his Party to the goal of low inflation above all economic targets and painted a bleak picture of the options available to a reformist government. His argument was blunt: the environment in which Labour took office would set tight parameters on the decisions it took. Economic circumstances confined the options available to any administration and sustaining business confidence was vital in such conditions. Blair concluded that markets 'can swiftly move against policies which fail to win investors' confidence'. He went on to suggest 'to that extent the room for manoeuvre of any government in Britain is already heavily circumscribed'.[18] If firms were concerned about either the inflationary intentions or the other policies of a Labour government, they would cut investment and so damage growth and prosperity. Accordingly, a central theme of the Party's economic strategy between 1994 and 1997 was the need to reassure business and to convince markets of its moderation once in office: there must be no fears about the election of a Labour government. Blair and Brown adopted a series of extremely modest measures.

In January 1996 in a speech in Singapore, Blair argued that the foundations of long-term economic prosperity in the UK would be found through the introduction of a 'stakeholder economy': 'We need to build a relationship of trust not just within a firm but within society ... It is a stakeholder economy, in which opportunity is available to all, advancement is through merit and from which no group or class is set apart or excluded.'[19] Stakeholding was an ambiguous concept. It could be applied specifically to firms or more generally to society as a whole. In 1995, Will Hutton had published *The State We're In*, a surprise bestseller, in which he outlined a radical programme of stakeholding, including far-reaching reforms of corporate governance.[20] Blair's conception, drawn in part from the work of John Kay, was much less ambitious, being based largely on the observation that ethically-minded companies were more successful economically than others. It was therefore rational, even in a narrowly self-interested fashion, for firms to take decisions in a socially responsible manner. But he was quick to assure business that it would not be legislatively enforced: 'The whole concept of stakeholding as developed by many people in business is saying, "Look, we get better value for our shareholders if we behave this way." But it is not something I envisage a government being able to come through and enforce.'[21] Any changes to corporate practice would be voluntary: at most Labour might introduce a code of conduct. The Party did not explain how a wider responsibility would be fostered amongst British business. At the societal level, Blair offered stakeholding as a rather bland ethic of social inclusion: it served as a unifying theme upon which to hang already existing policies.

The adoption of stakeholding did not, therefore, involve new initiatives in terms of the policies put forward by Labour. Indeed the Party's 1994 document, *Winning for Britain*, produced by Robin Cook, had proposed reforms to corporate governance, explicitly as part of a stakeholding initiative. Blair backed away from these measures as he replaced one kind of stakeholding with another more moderate version. The place of even this weak form within Labour's programme was uncertain. Given the possibility of radical interpretations, some of Blair's advisers had doubts about such measures and opinion polls suggested that the concept was not an asset to the Party's electoral prospects. Question marks existed over the feasibility of stakeholding (how could it be introduced?) and its desirability (would it produce the benefits claimed for it?). Critics argued that the extreme *laissez-faire* nature of the UK's economy was especially unsuited to any stakeholding-type reforms. The phrase appeared occasionally in policy documents, but little use was made of it during the election campaign. Although stakeholding attracted considerable publicity when first floated, the idea had little impact on Labour's economic strategy between 1994 and 1997.

Further modifications were made to Labour's electoral proposals in the long run-up to the election. For a long time the Party prevaricated over any changes in taxation – the issue that had apparently done so much damage in 1992. In January 1997 Brown stated that there would be no increase at all in personal taxation rates during the first term of a Labour administration. The top rate of tax would stay at 40 per cent. Press reports indicated that Blair had taken the lead over the decision, which was against Brown's own judgement. It was described as a 'conclusive break' with Labour's past and an end to the 'politics of envy'.[22] The pledge reflected an acceptance of the difficulties that the Party had encountered in convincing the electorate that it had broken with tax-and-spend. The Shadow Chancellor also announced that, during its first two years, the new Labour government would accept the levels of public spending planned by the Conservatives. Commentators doubted the realism of this pledge, given the implausibility of Clarke's existing plans. Most felt it made political sense.

The measures adopted by Blair and Brown marked the abandonment of Labour's discretionary approach to economic policy. In 1992 Labour had endorsed the rules-based ERM. But alongside exchange rate stability, the Party proposed a flexible taxation policy designed both to promote equality and to raise revenue for state spending. Labour also laid out a detailed and wide-ranging set of industrial policies including proposals for training, research and development and increased investment. The Party's economic approach was essentially discretionary and pragmatic in the means by which it would secure its goals. By 1997, the Party had largely relinquished that discretion in favour of a series of rules. These rules governed monetary and fiscal policy as well as taxation. Their advantage was that they gave private agents a clear indication of the moderate trajectory upon which a Labour government would embark. There would be no surprises once elected to office, given the resources and political capital which had been sunk into the Party's plans. The disadvantage of such rules was that they limited the flexibility a Blair administration would enjoy, especially in the face of the kind of stochastic shock to which economies are liable. Fiscal and monetary policy was not the only area of economic policy to be guided by rules under Labour's proposals: regulation was a predominant feature of the Party's economic and industrial strategy. The financial sector and the privatised utilities would both be subject to new frameworks in which detailed rules and tight regulation would a play a prominent part. Given this change in the nature of Labour's economic strategy, Brown's quick decision, once elected to office, to give the Bank of England operational responsibility for setting interest rates is unsurprising. Such a move demonstrated the anti-inflationary intent of the new Government and indicated the support within it for the rules-based approach.

Much changed in Labour's economic strategy between 1992 and 1997, but most reforms were evolutionary. It is also the case that many of them were neither as dramatic nor as original as has been claimed. The most radical features of Labour's economic strategy by the time of the election were the

Party's promise of a minimum wage and its pledge to sign the EU's Social Chapter. Other policies, those for reducing unemployment for example, remained potentially far-reaching but also extremely unspecific. The main taxation proposal of the Party was for a windfall tax on the excess profits of privatised utilities to generate funds for reducing unemployment.

For all the emphasis placed by Brown on the Party's break with the past, a substantial minority of the electorate remained unconvinced by his moderation on taxation and spending. According to polls, they persisted in thinking that they would pay more tax under a Labour government. In January 1992 57 per cent of voters thought taxation would increase. By March 1994 it had fallen to 40 per cent and, by the time Blair was elected leader in the July of that year, it was 34 per cent. But it fell no further and, during the next three years the figure was often higher (up to 42 per cent). In the same period between just 9 and 20 per cent thought they would pay less tax under a Blair administration. Only three months before the election, 60 per cent were worried that taxation would rise under Labour. In March 1997, 75 per cent expected increases. Whatever reason voters had for choosing the Party, it was not because they believed the fine detail of Brown's promises on tax-and-spend. Perhaps it was sufficient that the electorate no longer perceived the Conservatives as a party of low taxation: in polls, respondents felt that tax was as likely to go up under the Tories as with Labour (73 to 75 per cent).[23]

How the Conservatives lost the economic argument

Contrary to John Major's hopes, the economy played little part in the election campaign. He opted for a long campaign partly because the publication of good economic statistics would take place in successive months. Yet little attention was paid to further falls in unemployment and good results were reported for GDP and the balance of payments. The Government looked likely to overshoot its inflation target, but only by a small margin. The figures for public debt showed it to be lower than had been forecast.

The party manifestos contained little that was unexpected for those who had noted the trajectory of the parties' economic proposals over the previous five years. Many of the arguments were equally stale. Campaigning on the slogan 'Britain is booming. Don't let Labour ruin it', the Conservatives criticised the opposition's vague spending plans and argued that tax would have to rise. Unlike 1992, the claim appeared to have little impact. Labour attacked what amounted, the Party asserted, to twenty-two tax increases under Lamont and Clarke. The changes were equivalent to a seven pence increase on the basic rate of tax. The Party further alleged that official figures disguised the true extent of joblessness and claimed that in international terms Britain's relative economic position had declined.

As part of its determination to win over business, Labour published a separate manifesto aimed at employers. It repeated earlier promises of economic stability and emphasised the Private Finance Initiative as part of a new partnership with industry and finance. There was a slight wobble over plans to give workers rights of union recognition but the issue never really caught fire. In 1992 markets had been nervous about the election of a Labour government: sterling had fallen within its ERM bands and the FTSE share index had declined by about 10 per cent. Such nerves were absent in 1997. Indeed, it was ironic that during the campaign the pound recovered for the first time to the level at which it had left the ERM on Black Wednesday in September 1992.

A mild surprise occurred when Blair expressed support for privatisation, albeit in a roundabout way. In fact his pragmatic stance on the issue had been established for some time. It was reported that Labour was prepared to consider the privatisation of air traffic control, largely in order to sustain public revenues as planned by the Conservatives. That the issue caused so little furore within the Party was a reflection of Labour's transformation under Blair's leadership and the extent of his dominance of policy-making. There were hints of differences between Blair and Brown over the extent of the windfall tax on the utilities and the Party's policy on the overall burden of personal taxation. These disagreements none the less came to nothing. Overall, the economy was nothing like as visible an issue as such matters as sleaze and the Conservative split on Europe.

Traditionally, the economy has been viewed as one of the Conservatives' strongest cards. Yet in 1997, during a prolonged upturn, they suffered a massive defeat. When asked which party was best able to handle Britain's economic difficulties, the Conservatives trailed Labour from September 1992 until the election (see Table 7.3). At no time from the ERM crisis onwards was the Government able to recover its previous position of strength on economic matters. After Blair's election as leader, Labour's economic rating peaked at a lead of 32 per cent in December 1994. It declined in the latter half of 1996, but much of this fall is attributable to a change in technique by Gallup from face-to-face interviews to telephone polling. The results suggest either that earlier polls had exaggerated Labour's lead or that subsequently they underestimated the Government's weakness on the economy. Even under the new method, Labour was ahead by an average of 10 per cent in 1996. It was a marked contrast to April 1992 when they had trailed by 21 per cent.

Why did the Conservative Government not profit from the recovery? There are four potential economic causes. First, it may be that the recovery was not as strong as commentators asserted it to be. Second, voters may have been concerned by other issues affecting their welfare. Third, it may be that, whatever the 'objective' state of the economy, 'subjectively' voters still perceived it to be in a weak condition: perhaps the so-called 'feel-good factor' did not re-emerge as the recovery developed. Fourth, it is possible that voters were more optimistic by the time of the 1997 election than they had been during the preceding years but that they decided, for whatever reason, not to vote

Table 7.3 Party competence ratings on economic issues 1991–1997 (%)

Q: With Britain in economic difficulties which party do you think could handle the problem best – the Conservatives under Mr Major or Labour under Mr Blair?

Date	*Conservative (%)*	*Labour (%)*	*Labour lead*	*High point*		*Low point*	
1991–92	44	30	–14	Feb	–12	Apr	–21
1992 pre-ERM	45	34	–11	Aug	–5	Apr	–18
1992 Sept–Dec	31	43	12	Sept	1	Dec	21
1993	27	41	14	Jun	18	Jan	8
1994	22	46	24	Dec	32	Jan/Feb	18
1995	22	48	26	May/Jun	30	Sept	20
1996 Jan–Jun	24	46	22	Mar/Apr	24	Jun	20
1996 Jul–Dec [a]	26	43	17	Oct/Dec	18	Jul–Sept	16
1996 Jul–Dec [b]	30	40	10	Oct/Dec	12	Aug	9
1997	36	47	11	Mar	14	Jan/Feb	9

Note: Conservative and Labour figures given as annual percentages based on monthly surveys by Gallup. 'Don't know' and 'neither' respondents are excluded.

Sources: Data refer to the Gallup 9000 series with the exception of April–December 1992 figures. 1991–92 figures (Gallup 9000) taken from David Sanders, 'Why the Conservatives won – again', in A. King (ed.), *Britain at the Polls 1992* (Chatham, New Jersey: Chatham House, 1992), p. 202. 1992 figures taken from *Gallup Political and Economic Index* (September 1992), p. 12 and from *Gallup Political and Economic Index* (January 1993), p. 14. [a] 1996 Jul–Dec refers to figures using old polling techniques; [b] Jul–Dec refers to figures using new techniques.

Conservative. These explanations are not mutually exclusive: indeed, it is likely that all four contributed to the scale of the Government's defeat. (Incidentally, an additional cause may be found in the indirect effect that economic crisis had in further demoralising the membership of the Conservative Party as the Government became increasingly unpopular.)[24]

The first possible factor concerns the extent and permanence of economic improvement. Between September 1992 and April 1997, gross domestic product (GDP) grew by about 11 per cent. Despite this performance, fears persisted over the nature of the recovery and certain indicators. At times economists were worried about the sustainability of the trajectory established by the Government, fearing that it would give way to some sort of inflationary boom. Interest rates were increased several times in the autumn of 1994–95. By 1997, some commentators were apprehensive about price rises and potential over-heating in the economy. They decided that interest rates would have to rise in order to rein in inflation. Other economists noted the uncertainties of public finances, arguing that tax increases would be necessary. The impact of these uncertainties on the electorate is hard to gauge: most observers concluded that the economy was in fundamentally good shape. In a discussion of the economic conditions that foster electoral success for an incumbent,

David Sanders gives five criteria: falling interest rates; falling rates of unemployment; falling taxation; rapidly growing GDP and personal disposable income; and positive press coverage.[25] The Major administration met most of these: unemployment was coming down; there had been cuts in direct tax; GDP and incomes were growing (perhaps a little slowly); interest rates were low (though likely to go up); and press coverage was mixed. Of all the five explanations, this cause, on its own, is probably the least significant.

The second possible cause relates to the effect that other economic issues may have had on voting. Although unemployment fell from 1993 onwards, there was widespread concern about the future of work. That many of the new jobs were part-time, flexible and temporary added to the fears of the workforce. Labour promised to tackle job insecurity and, at its 1995 conference, Blair offered a vision of 'one-nation socialism' in which anxieties about work would be resolved. The housing market was a further cause for concern. In some regions it had picked up by 1997, but in others it continued to be sluggish. The number of repossessions remained considerably above the levels of the 1980s, and about one in twenty borrowers was trapped by negative equity (owning a house worth less than the mortgage taken to finance its purchase). Moreover, private disposable income was growing in the spring of 1997 by less than at previous elections.

The third cause notes the importance of the 'feel-good factor', defined as that proportion of households who think their financial situation will improve over the coming year against those who think it will deteriorate. If the number of optimists outweighs the pessimists then the feel-good factor is positive. If there are more pessimists, it is negative. At the time of the April 1992 election, according to one set of results, the feel-good factor was +15 per cent.[26] It declined during the summer and was negative before the exchange rate crisis of that September. Thereafter, according to the Gallup 9000 series of figures, it was negative until September 1996. It was especially low following the proclamations of tax increases in 1993, as well as after the introduction of VAT on fuel in the spring of 1994 and the budget of that November. When it did recover, the improvement was slight (see Table 7.4).

Despite the economic upturn, any feel-good factor proved to be exceptionally elusive. Between September 1992 and March 1997 the feel-good factor was negative for fifty months out of fifty-four. It was positive for the first time at the start of the campaign. Persistent negative scores during the recovery reflected the depth of the recession and the impact of Conservative tax increases. In a moment of candour in March 1995, Kenneth Clarke admitted that the Government's measures might result in a negative feel-good factor for up to two years. The weakness of economic expectations also followed from the nature of the recovery engineered by the Government following devaluation in 1992. Though the economy grew, for a time, at any rate, real incomes fell. This fall reflected the tight fiscal measures to improve the state of public finances and

Table 7.4 The 'feel-good factor' 1991–1997

Q: How do you think the financial situation of your household will change over the next twelve months?

Date	Get better (%)	Get worse (%)	Feel-good factor	High point		Low point	
1991–92	24	26	−2	Sept	4	Jun–Jul	−5
1992 pre-ERM	22	28	−6	May	5	Aug	−15
1992 post-ERM	15	39	−24	Dec	−22	Oct 92	−24
1993	18	38	−20	Jan	−10	Dec	−36
1994	16	42	−26	Aug/Oct	−16	Dec	−34
1995	18	32	−14	Aug	−10	Feb/Mar	−20
1996 Jan–Jun	21	26	−5	Jun	−2	Feb/Mar	−9
1996 Jul–Dec [a]	21	24	−3	Oct	1	Dec	−11
1996 Jul–Dec [b]	21	24	−3	Sept/Oct	0	Dec	−10
1997	24	23	1	Mar	5	Feb	−2

Note: 'Get better' and 'get worse' figures given as annual percentages based on averages of monthly surveys by Gallup. 'Don't know' and 'stay the same' respondents are excluded.

Sources: Data refer to the Gallup 9000 series. September 1992 omitted as polling occurred before and after ERM crisis. [a] 1996 Jul–Dec refers to figures using old polling techniques; [b] Jul–Dec refers to figures using new techniques.

to ensure that the lower pound did not result in a flood of imports. The economic upturn was in part possible precisely because of the squeeze on consumer spending: in 1993 GDP grew by 5.3 per cent (in constant price terms) whilst personal disposable incomes rose by just 1.2 per cent.[27] Exports performed especially strongly during the recovery whilst the proportion of national income taken by wages fell and that taken by profits rose. The result was that consumer confidence remained low. Only once the tax increases were out of the way did low interest rates start to have an impact on consumer confidence.

Given the alteration in polling technique, it is hard to compare the feel-good data between 1992 and 1997. However, by the spring of 1997, economic expectations appeared no better than at the time of the April 1992 election. On Gallup's 1974 series (discontinued in January 1997) they were worse in the preceding months. In the 1990–92 recession, voters had been at least as optimistic about their future well-being as they were in the subsequent recovery. In March 1997 barely a quarter of respondents expected their own situation to improve financially; nearly 70 per cent thought it would either stay the same or get worse. Such figures suggest an electorate prepared to vote out the incumbent administration on economic grounds. The economic recovery did not foster positive subjective perceptions of individual well-being and the weak feel-good factor explains why individuals would be motivated to vote egocentrically for change. Sociotropic perceptions were slightly more favourable towards the Conservative Government. From September 1992 onwards, for all but thirteen months, those who expected the general economic situation to deteriorate outnumbered those who anticipated improvement. In the four months before the election, however, the average was +16 per cent.[28] (In the run-up to 1992 the monthly mean was +8 per cent.) Egocentric voting appears to have been more prevalent than sociotropic.

The last interpretation to be addressed is the possibility that voters decided to vote against the Conservatives in spite of their economic record in the last few years. The modest improvement in expectations during 1996 led only to an even more modest erosion of Labour's lead on economic competence (see Table 7.5). Some of this decline is, as noted above, due to a changed polling technique. When asked about which party could best handle the economy and whether they would be better off under a Blair administration, a plurality of respondents favoured Labour over the Conservatives. Both series remained positive in 1996–97. Moreover, the Party continued to perform strongly in terms of individuals' voting intentions. In the past economic expectations had provided a good indication of political allegiances. The erratic and slight improvement of the feel-good factor had relatively little impact on Labour's standing in the polls during 1996–97 because, whatever their doubts about the Party's taxation policies, voters perceived that they would be better off under a Blair administration. Even during the months in which the feel good factor was neutral or positive during 1996–97, it was outweighed by the number of respondents who positively wanted a change of government for material reasons.

This explanation emphasises the damage done to the Government's political fortunes during the economic crisis of 1992–93. In effect voters punished the Government for its failures over the ERM and the state of public finances, rather than rewarded it for its subsequent success. The slight upturn of the feel-good factor, accordingly, did not have a consequential impact on voting intentions. Most members of the electorate had already made up their minds because of the results of the first year of the administration and the costs they perceived its mistakes to have imposed on them. Black Wednesday alone did not have quite the cataclysmic and immediate impact on the Government's standing that some commentators have attributed to it. In the short term the exchange rate crisis gave Labour the most marginal of advantages on economic competence (35–6 per cent).[29] Moreover, the Government was able to pass some of the blame for the crisis on to others. More voters attributed responsibility to the world recession (45 per cent) than to the Major Government (28 per cent).[30] Almost as many (22 per cent) felt that the Bundesbank was as responsible as the Treasury. A similar poll in November 1992 indicated that voters felt that liability for the recession lay with the preceding Thatcher administration (37 per cent) and not that of John Major (9 per cent). The issue of blame is germane: in April 1992 those who blamed world-wide influences for the recession were likely to vote Conservative whilst those who blamed

Table 7.5 The 'feel-good factor' and Labour's lead 1996–1997

Date	*Feel-good factor*	*Lab lead on economy (%)*	*Better off under Lab (%)*	*Lab poll lead (%)*
Jan 96	–5	22	21	33
Feb 96	–9	21	11	30
Mar 96	–9	24	17	33
Apr 96	–7	24	11	33
May 96	–3	21	14	31
Jun 96	–2	20	12	29
Jul 96	–2 (–2)	11 (16)	15	20 (27)
Aug 96	–2 (–2)	9 (16)	14	18 (26)
Sept 96	0 (–2)	10 (16)	10	19 (27)
Oct 96	0 (1)	12 (18)	13	21 (29)
Nov 96	–3 (–4)	11 (17)	9	21 (30)
Dec 96	–10 (–11)	12 (18)	15	21 (30)
Jan 97	0	9	3	18
Feb 97	–2	9	3	18
Mar 97	5	14	5	24

Notes: 'Feel-good factor' defined as pessimists removed from optimists. 'Labour lead on economy' defined as Labour lead in answer to question: with Britain in economic difficulties which party do you think could handle the problem best? 'Better off under Labour' defined as percentage lead of those who think they will be better off under a Labour government against those who think they will be worse off. 'Labour poll lead' gives Labour's lead in terms of voting intentions.

Sources: Gallup 9000 series for feel-good factor, handling of economic difficulties and voting intentions. Gallup state of the economy series for better off under a Labour government data. July 1996–March 1997 figures collected with new polling techniques. Figures in parentheses give old data.

successive administrations were likely to vote Labour.[31] By October 1994, on a differently worded question, 69 per cent attributed responsibility to Major's administration.

Conclusion

What explains the collapse of Conservative Party support after September 1992? The exchange rate crisis was manifestly significant and, as the magnitude of the crisis sunk in, so Conservative popularity plummeted. The Government's approval rating fell steadily to record depths (16 per cent in October, 13 per cent in November and 12 per cent in May 1993).[32] Two other economic events were notable. The first was the Government's attempt to close thirty-one remaining coal pits in October 1992 which generated a public outcry. The second was Norman Lamont's tax-increasing budget of March 1993. It was the combination of these three events which explains the steep decline of support for the Conservative Government. Positive support for Labour's specific proposals about taxation and spending was limited. Nevertheless Blair and Brown successfully projected an image of Labour as a moderate party under which people would be better off. Two significant causes of the strong lead it enjoyed over the Conservatives were the failure of the economic recovery to spark a strong feel-good factor amongst the electorate and the failure of voters to respond positively to economic success by approving the Government's trajectory. The Conservatives' economic competence rating continued to decline in 1994 and 1995. The feel-good factor fell further in 1994 (Table 7.5). This pattern was a reflection of the Government's strategic decision to stagger the tax increases between April 1993 and April 1995. It may have made economic sense: in political terms it was a disaster.

Three conclusions can be noted from the above discussion. It would be a mistake to regard the election result as the end of economic voting in some way. Economic issues remain salient. There is an economic explanation as to why, despite the recovery, voters abandoned the Conservatives. Second, it is evident that the electorate's perceptions of parties' economic competence is an important indicator of their political allegiance. In 1997 subjective perceptions were more important than objective economic conditions. Third, in certain ways, voters appear to be backward-looking. Economic theorists have argued that agents make decisions on the basis of forward-looking rational expectations. The election results indicate that backward-looking adaptive expectations may be as important in motivating decisions within the polling booths. Economists have often treated the electorate as a myopic collection of individuals who have no memory of the ills that have befallen them. The experience of 1992–97 indicates that voters may not be as short-sighted as some commentators have asserted. Their memories of those events and the associated costs played a pivotal part in the election outcome. In March 1997, John Major accepted that the manner of the UK's ejection from the ERM had been a mistake: two months later he was made to realise just how big a blunder his Government's management of the exchange rate and public finances had comprised. Politics can be a brutal business. Whether history will be more forgiving of Kenneth Clarke, Norman Lamont and John Major remains to be seen.

Notes

1 D. Butler and D. Kavanagh, *The British General Election of 1992* (London: Macmillan, 1992).
2 D. Sanders, 'Why the Conservatives won – again', in A. King (ed.), *Britain at the Polls* (Oxford: Oxford University Press, 1992), p. 179.
3 *The Spectator*, 10 May 1997.
4 *The Times*, 18 March 1997.

5 This section draws heavily upon Treasury and Civil Service Committee, *The 1992 Autumn Statement and the Conduct of Economic Policy* (London: HMSO, 1992) and the excellent account of Phillip Stephens, *Politics and the Pound* (London: Macmillan, 1996), pp. 193–296. See also P. Jay, 'The economy 1990–94' in A. Seldon and D. Kavanagh (eds), *The Major Effect* (London: Macmillan, 1994) and P. Sinclair, 'Financial sector' in Seldon and Kavanagh, *The Major Effect*.
6 *Financial Times*, 27 August 1992.
7 Ibid.
8 *Hansard*, 9 June 1993, col. 283.
9 Stephens, *Politics and the Pound*, pp. 254–5.
10 *Financial Times*, 11 July 1992.
11 *Financial Times*, 11 September 1992.
12 Stephens, *Politics and the Pound*, p. 259.
13 *Hansard*, 24 September 1992, col. 106.
14 *Hansard*, 9 June 1993, cols 281–5.
15 *Financial Times*, 11 July 1992.
16 L. Elliott, 'Treasury: economic policy' in M. Linton (ed.), *The Election* (London: Fourth Estate, 1997), p. 156.
17 See, for example, R. Berry and P. Hain, *Labour and the Economy* (London: Tribune, 1994).
18 T. Blair, *The Mais Lecture*, May 1995.
19 T. Blair, *New Britain* (London: Fourth Estate, 1996), p. 292.
20 W. Hutton, *The State We're In* (London: Jonathan Cape, 1995), pp. 298–318.
21 *Financial Times*, 16 January 1997.
22 *Financial Times*, 24 January 1997.
23 *Gallup Political and Economic Index* (March 1997), p. 11.
24 P. Whiteley, P. Seyd and J. Richardson, *True Blues: The Politics of Conservative Party Membership* (Oxford: Clarendon, 1994), p. 235.
25 D. Sanders, 'New Labour, new Machiavelli: a cynic's guide to economic policy', *Political Quarterly*, 67:4 (1996): 290–302, at p. 294.
26 *Gallup Political and Economic Index* (July 1992), p. 20.
27 D. McKie (ed.), *The Guardian Political Almanac 1994/95* (London: Fourth Estate, 1994), p. 32.
28 *Gallup Political and Economic Index* (April 1997), p. 11.
29 *Gallup Political and Economic Index* (November 1992), p. 18.
30 *Gallup Political and Economic Index* (September 1992), p. 20.
31 Sanders, 'Why the Conservatives won – again', pp. 200–1.
32 *Gallup Political and Economic Index* (January 1993), p. 6; (June 1993), p. 9.

Southport

A prosperous seaside town, Southport ought to represent a reasonably safe Conservative seat. However, even during the national Conservative triumphs of the 1980s, the seat changed hands, captured by the Liberal–SDP Alliance in 1987. To the surprise of many, the seat reverted to the Conservatives in 1992. Now the veteran Liberal Democrat candidate, Ronnie Fearn, attempted to join the select band of 'retread' MPs, returning to Parliament after temporarily being ousted.

Southport was significant for the Liberal Democrats as it represented a seat that would help demonstrate their ability to capture target seats outside their West Country heartland. With representation in northern industrial towns threatened by the Labour revival, Liberal Democrats looked for alternative seats in more prosperous areas. Southport lay eleventh on their list of targets.

As early as 10 April, Paddy Ashdown staged a public rally in the town. The arrival of national Liberal Democrats consolidated years of effort by local supporters, reflected in their dominance of Southport wards on Sefton Council. The local card was also played by Fearn, a councillor who had lived all his life in the town and was acknowledged as a hard worker, points made regularly to the local newspaper, the *Southport Visitor*.

In the event, the main national feature, the collapse of the Conservative vote, was decisive in allowing the Liberal Democrats a success much more comfortable than envisaged. Local Conservatives hoped that a hostile swing might be mitigated by persistent strength amongst Southport's very large elderly population, but the Party's share of the vote fell to a new low. Tactical voting was evident. The increase in Labour's vote was tiny, as electors saw the contest as a two-way fight. Even the stalwart Labour *Daily Mirror* (1 May) had identified Southport amongst its constituencies where people should vote tactically to oust the sitting Conservative. The result was that the Conservative to Liberal Democrat swing more than trebled the 2.76 per cent swing required.

Result

	Southport		
Ronnie Fearn	Lib Dem	24,346	
Matthew Banks	Con	18,186	
Sarah Norman	Lab	6,125	
Frank Buckle	Ref	1,368	
	Others	571	
Total vote		50,596	Turnout 72.08%
Lib Dem majority		6,160	
Lib Dem gain from Con			
Swing Con to Lib Dem 8.85%			

8

The provision of services: trouble in store for Labour?

Ian Holliday

Introduction

The British state provides its citizens with so many services – in sectors as diverse as defence, law and order, trade and industry, transport, the environment, and the many parts of the welfare state – that the first task of this chapter is simply to identify the public services on which it will focus. The choice is fairly straightforward. Of £274 billion spent on public services in 1996–97, fully £190 billion – or nearly 70 per cent – went on the five classic elements of the welfare state: social security, health care, education, personal social services and housing (Table 8.1). Although there were other important areas of public service provision in 1996–97 – notably defence (£21.2 billion) and law and order (£16.5 billion) – this chapter will therefore deal with welfare services. Furthermore, in keeping with the substantially diminished importance of public housing since the last Labour Government left office in 1979 and ushered in eighteen years of Conservative Government under Margaret Thatcher and John Major, the chapter will also restrict its analysis to what are now the four big areas of welfare provision: social security, health care, education and personal social services. The chapter focuses on the campaigns run by the three big parties – Conservative, Labour and Liberal Democrat – which made most of the political running in this sphere.

At the outset two general contextual points need to be made about the 1997 campaign. The first is that this campaign paid less attention to welfare provision than had its immediate predecessors. Although voters remained as concerned as ever about the future of the social security system, the fate of the National Health Service (NHS), the state of the education system and the condition of personal social services, leading politicians preferred to focus on Europe, the economy and sleaze as central campaign issues. The media also preferred to concentrate on Europe and sleaze. Researchers at Loughborough University found that media coverage of Europe (16 per cent of total) and sleaze (11 per cent) was much higher than coverage of education (7 per cent) or health (2 per cent).[1] The second is that the future of Britain's social security, health, education and personal social services systems did not come together to form a single campaign theme. There was no unified debate on welfare,

Table 8.1 Real public expenditure on welfare services 1978–1979 and 1996–1997

	1996–97		*1978–79*		
Service	*£bn*[a]	*%GDP*	*£bn*[b]	*%GDP*	*Real £ growth (%)*
Social security	97.5	13.1	52.0	9.9	88
Health care	41.2	5.5	24.1	4.6	71
Education	36.9	4.9	28.0	5.4	32
Personal social services	10.0	1.4	4.2	0.8	138
Housing	4.0	0.5	13.8	2.6	–72
Total expend. on services	274.2	36.8	200.6	38.3	37

Notes: [a] Estimated.
[b] In 1996–97 prices.

Source: Calculated from H.M. Treasury, *Public Expenditure: Statistical Analyses 1997–98*, Cm 3601 (London: HMSO, 1997), pp. 26–8.

and given the diversity of the sectors that constitute the welfare state it is hard to see how there could have been one. Instead, debate broke down by sector and even sub-sector. It is therefore analysed by sector here.

Social security

Social security is by far the biggest expenditure area in the entire British public sector. It had a mixed experience under the Conservatives. The real amount of money spent on social security came close to doubling in the Thatcher–Major years and now stands at around £100 billion, most of which goes on pensions, family, disability and unemployment benefits. However, the social security system was also restructured as Conservative Governments sought to make it more efficient, target it more effectively, and reduce the burden it placed on taxpayers. Key changes were made to the biggest spending item, the state earnings-related pension scheme (Serps), which was created by the Social Security Pensions Act 1975 and introduced in 1977 (as the latest in a line of state pensions first implemented in 1908). The Social Security Act 1980 linked pension payments with prices instead of earnings. The Social Security Act 1986 created a right to opt out of Serps into personal pension schemes. The Pensions Act 1995 equalised the state pension age at sixty-five for men and women. Each of these measures did something to reduce the weight of claims on Serps. The wider social security system was restructured chiefly by means of the Social Security Act 1986, which amongst other things simplified and extended means-testing of benefits and created the income support and family credit systems.[2] In the 1997 campaign the two aspects of the social security system which received most attention were pension reform and 'welfare to work' schemes.

The initiative in debating pension reform was taken by the Conservatives.

On 5 March 1997, less than two weeks before the formal opening of the campaign, the Secretary of State for Social Security, Peter Lilley, announced that in the course of a generation the Conservative Government would abolish Serps and replace it with compulsory private pension contributions. New entrants to the workforce would be given a rebate on their national insurance contributions of around £9 per week, which would have to be invested in an approved pension fund and would in due course take the place of Serps as their basic pension entitlement (though there would continue to be a state safety net for those who fell outside this scheme for one reason or another). This initiative, which subsequently featured amongst the Conservatives' twenty-five pledges for the nation,[3] was both radical and surprising. It was radical because it comprised nothing less than the eventual privatisation of the state pension. It was surprising because it was thus likely to strike terror into the hearts of many voters. The initiative was nevertheless taken by the Conservatives for two main reasons. One was that only radical reform will prevent the state pension from becoming overwhelmed by the claims made on it some time towards the middle of the twenty-first century, by which time the British population will have aged considerably and the proportion of individuals in employment will have shrunk substantially. The other was that it showed that an allegedly tired and washed-out Government had not entirely run out of radical ideas or steam.

The problem for the Conservatives was that this initiative also opened them up to clear risks, which were duly exploited by Labour in particular. Despite the fact that Tony Blair himself was on record (in 1996) as promising to 'think the unthinkable' about welfare, and despite the equally important fact that Frank Field, the most creative thinker about welfare issues in Labour Party ranks, had in the mid-1990s devised a scheme for stakeholder pensions that was rather similar to Lilley's proposal in key respects,[4] Labour chose to play pension reform as a scare story, and did so to good effect. On the penultimate weekend of the campaign – 19–20 April – Blair made the claim that the Conservative Party was planning to privatise the basic state pension (which was true) and to 'destroy the foundation of security in retirement' (which was not).[5] Harriet Harman, Shadow (subsequently actual) Social Security Secretary, said that Lilley's plans were a 'chilling prospect'.[6] The Conservatives responded in kind, with Michael Heseltine claiming that Labour had 'cynically played with the fears of the elderly and the frail' and that Blair 'was not fit to be Prime Minister of Britain'.[7] Lilley was also brought back to London from a campaign visit to Taunton to rebut the claim in detail. However, the pensions scare story proved to be a critical part of Labour's campaign strategy. In contrast to 1992, when Labour had suffered badly from the tax-and-spend 'double whammy' and lost control of the campaign agenda in its final stages, in 1997 it was able to use the pensions issue as part of its management of the news agenda against the Conservatives.

Neither Labour nor the Liberal Democrats had substantial reformist plans of their own. Labour favoured multi-employer and industry-wide occupational alternatives to Serps, the Liberal Democrats a compulsory occupational second-tier pension. Neither, therefore, was prepared to offer the British people a credible solution to the pensions crisis which will confront the British state some time in the middle of the next century unless something is done to avert it.

In a different realm of social security Labour launched one of its central campaign themes by holding that under a Blair Government a 'windfall levy' on privatised utilities' profits could be used to take 250,000 under-twenty-five-year-olds off benefit and into compulsory work or education. Using the American understanding of welfare, this was known as the 'welfare to work' scheme. It was not far removed from the equally American notion of 'workfare'. The Conservatives strongly objected to the notion of a windfall tax on privatised utilities, but were themselves proponents of variants of workfare, with which they had already experimented in office. They thus proposed to extend their 'contract for work' scheme to help (or require) people on benefit to seek work and their 'parent plus' scheme to help single parents into work. The Conservatives also proposed to set up a Benefit Fraud Inspectorate.

The Liberal Democrats floated a series of ideas intended to break the poverty trap. One was a general raising of tax thresholds to take half a million people out of the income tax system altogether, to be paid for by a fifty pence top tax rate on taxable incomes of over £100,000 per year. Another was a 'self-financing' 'Benefit Transfer Programme' designed to turn unemployment benefit into employer incentives to take people on. The other ideas were less precise or substantial.[8]

Health care

Health care – essentially the NHS – was a persistent source of controversy in the Thatcher–Major years. Although the NHS experienced real annual funding increases totalling 71 per cent during eighteen years of Conservative Government, it was almost universally thought to be underfunded. Similarly, although Conservative reforms made no more than marginal changes to the public–private frontier in health care, they were widely held to embody implicit or explicit privatisation. In fact, the major reforms contained in the National Health Service and Community Care Act 1990 involved separating 'purchasers' from 'providers' in the NHS, and obliging them to trade with each other in an 'internal market' for health care. These reforms thereby forced the NHS to quicken a transition to business practices and market principles which was already under way in the 1980s, but they did not make radical changes to its underlying ethos of universal health care offered free of charge at the point of delivery.[9]

The sound and fury which enveloped the NHS in the 1980s and early 1990s usually fed into the heart of general election campaigns. This was certainly the case in 1992, when the 'Jennifer's ear' saga developed from a Labour Party political broadcast about the NHS, and exploded into a row not only about the NHS but also about campaign tactics and ethics more generally.[10] In 1997, by contrast, health care was comparatively marginal to debate. Although all parties made noises about the NHS, none of them set it at the centre of its electoral strategy.

The charge away from health-care controversy was led by Labour. Fifth in its ten-point contract was a commitment to 'rebuild the NHS, reducing spending on administration and increasing spending on patient care'. Third in its list of five election pledges was a promise to 'cut NHS waiting lists by treating an extra 100,000 patients as a first step by releasing £100 million saved from NHS red tape'.[11] However, although the Labour manifesto also headlined a commitment to 'End the Tory internal market', in reality the Party offered little more than a revision of this critical aspect of the Conservatives' NHS reform programme. Purchaser and provider functions – the key aspects of the internal market – would not be abolished (as Labour had once promised they would be). Instead, each would be revised to a limited extent. Labour in 1997 was very keen not to get embroiled in rows about the NHS, and pursued a softly, softly strategy in this sphere. The Liberal Democrats made similar pledges to Labour's, but sought to demonstrate the seriousness of their commitment by identifying sources of funding for health-care improvement. Their manifesto stated that 'at least an extra £540 million every year' would be invested in the NHS 'by closing the loophole that allows employers to avoid paying National Insurance contributions on certain benefits in kind and by putting five pence on the price of a packet of twenty cigarettes'.[12] The Conservatives were content to trumpet the success of their reforms and to pledge their extension, being, as they put it, 'proud of the part we are playing in improving the NHS still further'. Moreover, against the claim that 'Labour created the NHS fifty years ago',[13] the Conservatives sought to remind people that they too had played a part in this 'British success story': 'We have been the guardians of the NHS for most of its life, improving its services and securing its funding.'[14] An 'NHS funding pledge' – to continue to increase real NHS resources – and a commitment to extend the shift towards family doctors (and away from hospitals) featured amongst the Conservatives' twenty-five key pledges.[15]

Behind this essentially pseudo-debate about health care lay the critical issue of NHS funding. Though certain to become vexed before too long, the resource issue was glossed over by both the Conservatives and Labour. The Conservative Party was committed to a real resource increase of 0.3 per cent between 1996 and 1999. Labour promised to respect all Conservative spending commitments for at least its first two years in office. It is very hard to conceive of circumstances in which these plans could ever approach viability. Even the real annual rise of 3 per cent in NHS resources witnessed in the period 1979–97 was held to be woefully inadequate by the bulk of the British people.

Education

Education did not fare particularly well under the Conservatives. Its budget grew by only 32 per cent in the entire Thatcher–Major years, or about 1 per cent annually. As a proportion of GDP, state spending on education actually fell between 1979 and 1997. At the same time, education (like all other aspects of the welfare state) was restructured by the Conservatives. Their key initiative was the Education Reform Act 1987, which was consolidated and extended by the Education Act 1993. Central to the Conservative reforms were institutional reshaping, chiefly through the creation of grant-maintained schools, and monitoring of standards, chiefly through the introduction of testing at many stages of school life.[16] At the very start of the Conservative years a fairly small 'assisted places scheme' was created to extend access to private-sector schools. At the very end of those years vouchers for nursery education for four-year-olds were introduced.

The main opposition parties concurred in making education an important campaign theme in 1997. The Liberal Democrats placed it at the centre of their campaign, backing their pledge to 'make education the next Government's top priority' with a commitment to 'invest an additional £2 billion per year in education funded by an extra penny in the pound on the basic rate of income tax'.[17] Labour matched the pledge, but not the commitment of resources. At the top of its ten-point contract was the statement 'Education will be our number one priority'. Equally, the first of the Party's five election pledges was to 'cut class sizes to thirty or under for five-, six- and seven-year-olds by using money from the assisted places scheme'.[18] The Conservatives were content simply to hold that the future of Britain and of its citizens 'depends on the quality of their education'.[19] Their twenty-five key pledges contained commitments on school standards – which they claimed central intervention would be able to 'guarantee' – and school choice through specialisation and selection.[20] As the campaign developed, so a series of educational themes was played out.

Labour struck a careful balance between rejection and acceptance of eighteen years of educational reform by promising to abolish the assisted places scheme, scrap nursery vouchers, reshape grant-maintained schools and cut class sizes whilst at the same time maintaining a commitment to testing, allowing grammar schools to stay unless rejected in a ballot of parents and making no radical suggestions for overhaul of the British educational system. One new idea was the creation of 'education action zones'. Others were study support centres at Premier League football grounds, linkage of schools to the information superhighway (in a deal struck with British Telecom prior to the election campaign), creation of a National Grid for Learning to place schools on the Internet and a University for Industry. The idea of 'zero tolerance of underperformance' suggested that a Labour Education Secretary would be just as interventionist as his or her Conservative predecessors.[21]

The Conservatives committed themselves to the notions of standards and choice which have long been their watchwords in this sphere. They placed most of their eggs in the basket of selection, pursuing Major's dream of a grammar school in every town (which became one of the key campaign slogans) and, more generally, an increase in selection in all secondary schools. In opposition to Labour's determination to abolish the assisted places scheme, the Conservatives declared that they would double it. Like Labour, the Conservatives suggested that central intervention would certainly be employed to ensure standards were met.[22]

The Liberal Democrats were content to ridicule their opponents' 'unfunded' promises and to make the probably valid claim that they alone had a serious commitment to educational improvement through the three Rs of 'resources, resources, resources'. Their £2 billion a year educational pledge was, however, curiously limited in its reformist ambition. According to the Liberal Democrats' manifesto they would buy more books and equipment, reduce primary school class sizes, increase building repair and maintenance and improve the chances of those returning to education in adult life.[23]

However, although education was an important campaign theme in 1997, eliciting a chorus of approval and a wealth of commitment, it never became central. Chiefly this was because Labour was placed on the defensive by the Liberal Democrats' open commitment to raising taxes for educational gain. The Conservatives were placed on the defensive by doubts about the plausibility of Major's vision of a grammar school in every town, and the Liberal Democrats were never able to control the election agenda and insist that their chosen territory of education become decisive.

Personal social services

Personal social services are often the responsibility of local authority social services departments, and divide into residential care, day care, domiciliary services and fieldwork. In the Conservative years services for children were reformed chiefly by means of the Children Act 1989, which sought to enhance the role of the family in the assessment of children's needs and to keep families together whenever possible. Services for adults were reformed chiefly by means of the National Health Service and Community Care Act 1990, which created purchasers and providers in personal social services much as it did in the NHS.[24] Personal social services were an important growth area in the Conservative years, with real expenditure more than doubling to £10 billion.

Personal social services were also one of the rising electoral stars in 1997. From a position of substantial marginalisation in previous campaigns, 'caring' moved not to centre-stage in 1997 but at least to an important walk-on part. Mainly responsible for this were the Conservatives, who took two key initiatives. One was the 'Respite Care Programme' which, the Conservative manifesto stated, would 'enable family members with heavy responsibilities caring for a relative to take a much needed break'.[25] In the course of the campaign, this initiative was clarified. Each year £53 million would be allocated to fund a one-week break for carers with major responsibilities, local social services departments stepping in to undertake their duties for free.[26] The Conservatives also made it clear that the programme would be cash-limited, meaning that breaks for carers would have to be fitted into £53 million rather than money being made available to fund one week off for all legitimate claimants. This was still a key initiative which went a long way to meeting one of the main demands made by the lobbying organisation Carers National Association. The Conservatives' second major initiative was part of a broader attempt to 'boost family life', and was one of the few new policies launched in the course of the campaign. It was trailed as a commitment to allow men and women not in employment to transfer their £3,765 tax allowance to their working spouse, but it seemed likely to benefit carers too. It would have been worth up to £17.50 a week.[27]

Beyond this, the Conservatives launched further initiatives, such as a 'partnership scheme' for long-term care intended to balance costs between the individual and the state, and a more general promotion of private-sector involvement in personal social services. Labour and the Liberal Democrats made little more than vague declarations of intent. Labour stated that it would 'establish a Royal Commission to work out a fair system of funding long-term care for the elderly' and that it would introduce something called a 'long-term care charter'.[28] The Liberal Democrats floated the idea of a new 'Carers' Benefit'.[29]

The impact of the campaign on policy development

The 1997 general election was eventually won by the party which said the least about welfare services, took the fewest initiatives, and made the smallest number of promises. Despite claiming that 'We will be the party of welfare reform',[30] Labour was actually very quiet about the welfare state in 1997, and allowed much of the political running to be made by the Liberal Democrats (which was largely to be expected) and the Conservatives (which was in many ways rather surprising). Broadly, the Conservatives took the initiative in shaping discussion of the social security and personal social services systems, the Liberal Democrats made most of the running in the education debate, and the NHS was rather strangely neglected by all the main parties, none of which came up with a decent reform initiative. After spending the bulk of the Thatcher–Major years prioritising welfare issues and losing general elections, Labour in 1997 toned down its 'social' message and won its first election in five attempts. Sobriety, moderation and a certain 'toughness', when allied with conspicuous inadequacies on the part of Major's Conservative Government, paid handsome dividends for Labour. The question which arises from this is whether, in the end, the campaign mattered to the future of welfare. This question has short- and long-term dimensions.

The short-term dimension is whether the campaign on public service provision made a difference to the election result. Although during the campaign welfare issues were not prioritised by politicians or the media, they remained salient for voters. A MORI poll conducted on 8 April found that the issues voters considered most important were health (68 per cent), education (61 per cent), law and order (51 per cent), unemployment (49 per cent) and pensions (39 per cent). Welfare thus dominated the issue agenda from the electorate's point of view. Managing the economy (30 per cent) and Europe (22 per cent) were comparatively unimportant. On welfare issues MORI also found that Labour had a substantial lead over all other parties. For policies on health, 47 per cent of voters supported Labour, 15 per cent the Conservatives and 9 per cent the Liberal Democrats. On education, the figures were 40 per cent, 21 per cent and 15 per cent. On pensions, they were 37 per cent, 17 per cent and 5 per cent.[31] Although welfare issues were marginal to a campaign which was played defensively by Labour in particular, and are unlikely to have been established as a vote winner for Labour in the campaign itself, they would therefore seem to have contributed to the Labour landslide.

The long-term dimension is whether a party which said little about welfare in the campaign is likely to be constrained in making welfare policy in government. The answer is that it will be, because the campaign established clear parameters for policy development which will affect the shape of welfare reform for at least the first few years of the Blair Government. In some respects it did this with more than usual force, because the Labour programme was centred on the ten-point contract and five election pledges on which Labour has said it wants to be judged when it next faces the people in a general election. This is certain to generate a real desire on the part of Labour to deliver on its promises. In other respects, that force is not especially great, for Labour was very careful to ensure that it did not constrain itself too closely in writing its contract and its pledges. The parameters which resulted from this exercise have both negative and positive dimensions.

Negatively, the most important theme of the Labour campaign was its commitment to respect declared Conservative expenditure plans for at least its first two years in government. In many welfare sectors those plans are almost unmanageably tight, the case of the NHS (which has already been mentioned) being the best example of this. The result is that supply is likely to continue to lag a long way behind demand in the health-care sector, and that no prospect of real change is in sight this side of the millennium. This is true of many other sectors too. The Labour campaign imposed further constraints on the Blair Government. In pension reform, the Government could be constrained by its cynical (and predictable) response to the Lilley initiative, and could find it difficult to 'think the unthinkable' when it has reacted so negatively to a privatisation initiative. In education, Labour could find it hard to introduce real changes when it has signed up to so much of what was again a controversial Conservative agenda and has also rejected the Liberal Democrats' proposal of tax increases for educational gain. In personal social services, spending constraints could equally prevent the Government from embarking on reform. In general, then, the main negative parameter which Labour in the campaign imposed on Labour in government was the commitment to austerity budgets, competitiveness in the international arena and limitation of the social wage. All of this was most succinctly expressed in the second point of Labour's ten-point contract with the British people: 'There will be no increase in the basic or top rates of income tax.'[32]

However, not everything that Labour said about social issues in the 1997 campaign was negative. Some elements were in fact positive. Chief amongst these was a refusal to denounce changes made by the Thatcher–Major Governments as wholly evil and misguided. Instead, Labour undertook to respect not only Conservative spending plans but also the central drive of much welfare reform as part of its 'pragmatism, not dogmatism' political stance. In general terms, this means that there is very little that Labour is actually committed to abolishing or reforming in government, and therefore a great deal that it can now judge on its merits. Not much beyond the assisted places scheme and nursery vouchers must go. The rest – including the NHS internal market, grant-maintained schools and testing at all stages of school life – can be retained in one form or another. The value of this positive sphere of political manoeuvre is likely to be substantial, and British politics should finally be delivered from the ideological and pendulum-swing policy-making which has characterised too many aspects of it for too long. The Blair Government is constrained in important ways, but has also been careful to protect its freedom of manoeuvre in other ways.

The future

The result of Labour's refusal to take the lead in shaping many aspects of welfare debate in 1997 is that the future is likely to exhibit important continuities with the past. Crucially, the key policy dynamic of the Thatcher–Major years is unlikely to be revised in anything other than marginal ways by the Blair Government. That dynamic had a number of sub-elements, but at its core was a marketisation drive designed to undermine the focus on strategic planning which experienced its heyday in the 1960s and 1970s, the dominance of professional (as opposed to business) modes of working which has been a feature of the British welfare state since it was first invented, and the year-on-year real cash increases which have also been a permanent aspect of the British welfare state. None of this is likely to be challenged by the Blair Government, and for this reason the welfare state will move further down the road which has seen political priorities increasingly replaced by the dictates of the market. The movement away from strategic planning is the clearest manifestation of this. One important consequence is that change will be driven more than ever by extra-political factors. Chief amongst these will be economic and social change, though in some spheres (such as health care) technological change could also play an important role. Reform in specific sectors will range from limited to substantial.

Least likely to be affected by reform are the headline welfare sectors of education and health. Elements of personal social services also fall into this category. Indeed, despite the 'number one priority' status accorded to education by Labour, and the genuine concern about the NHS which is always felt and expressed by Labour politicians, neither of these sectors is likely to experience radical change as a result of the election of a Labour government. Labour has said that education can only secure real funding increases as public spending on unemployment falls, though radicalism is possible in the higher education sector, where the Dearing Report (commissioned by the Major Government) has recommended the introduction of student fee payments, to be met incrementally by those who earn above a certain level of income. The overall result could be no more than marginal change in school education in the next few years. Structurally, little change is in prospect. Labour may be nice to teachers – which would make a welcome change – but beyond that it could be difficult to spot the difference from the Conservatives. The health-care sector is, if anything, more strapped for cash, and despite the loud Labour protests of recent years will see no more than marginal structural changes: community representatives on NHS Trust boards, moves to counter the excessive fragmentation that GP fundholding represents on the purchaser side of the internal market, and other cosmetic reforms. Here, too, Labour may build a reasonable relationship with health service workers, but could otherwise look pretty much like more of what the British became used to under the Conservatives. Similar points can be made about community care.

The area in which policy change will surely be greatest is, in fact, that in which Labour was expressly most resistant to change in the general election campaign: pensions. Here campaign statements could prove to be a highly unreliable guide to government action, for something like the Lilley initiative that was so derided by Blair and Harman in the campaign will almost certainly be launched by Labour in the course of this Parliament. One reason for this is that the British pension system, though better placed than most others in the developed world, is facing a deep crisis unless radical reform is introduced soon. A second reason is that Blair's most imaginative appointment to his first government was Frank Field's fairly open brief to examine welfare reform as minister of state in Harriet Harman's Department of Social Security. Like Lilley, Field is committed to deconstructing the present state-run system. Also like Lilley, he is therefore certain to move in the direction of privatisation.

Conclusion

In its first weeks in office the Blair Government demonstrated that it had no intention of being confined by its campaign promises. Neither operational independence for the Bank of England nor statutory regulation of the financial services sector by an enlarged Securities and Investments Board featured in the Labour manifesto, yet within three weeks of taking office both had been announced by Chancellor of the Exchequer Gordon Brown. Radical moves can therefore be expected from a Party elite which was terrified of alienating voters when campaigning for office but which is determined to make an impact having attained it. In the sphere of public service provision, however, campaign statements do appear to have been mainly reliable, except in the area of pension reform. Labour should be able to deliver on its promises, but may still find that it upsets voters who now, as under successive Conservative Governments, expect a first-rate welfare state but are highly resistant to parting with the resources necessary to fund it.

Notes

1 *Guardian*, 28 April 1997.
2 M. Hill, *Understanding Social Policy*, 5th edn (Oxford: Blackwell, 1997), ch. 5.
3 Conservative Party, *You Can Only Be Sure with the Conservatives. The Conservative Manifesto 1997* (London: Conservative Central Office, 1997), p. 54.
4 F. Field and M. Owen, *Private Pensions for All: Squaring the Circle* (London: Fabian Society, 1993); F. Field, *Making Welfare Work: Reconstructing Welfare for the Millennium* (London: Institute of Community Studies, 1995); F. Field, *Stakeholder Welfare* (London: Institute of Economic Affairs, 1996).
5 *Financial Times*, 22 April 1997.
6 *Economist*, 10 May 1997.
7 *Daily Telegraph*, 26 April 1997.
8 Liberal Democrats, *Make the Difference: The Liberal Democrat Manifesto 1997* (London, 1997), p. 49.
9 I. Holliday, *The NHS Transformed: A Guide to the Health Reforms*, 2nd edn (Manchester: Baseline, 1995).
10 D. Butler and D. Kavanagh, *The British General Election of 1992* (Basingstoke: Macmillan, 1992), pp. 122–3.
11 Labour Party, *New Labour* (London, 1997) pp. 5, 40.
12 Liberal Democrats, *Make the Difference*, p. 37.
13 Labour Party, *New Labour*, p. 20.
14 Conservative Party, *You Can Only Be Sure*, pp. 27–8.
15 Ibid., p. 55.
16 C. Chitty, *The Education System Transformed: A Guide to the School Reforms* (Manchester: Baseline, 1992).
17 Liberal Democrats, *Make the Difference*, p. 10.
18 Labour Party, *New Labour*, pp. 5, 40.
19 Conservative Central Office, *You Can Only Be Sure*, p. 21.

20 Ibid., p. 54.
21 Labour Party, *New Labour*, pp. 6–9.
22 Conservative Party, *You Can Only Be Sure*, pp. 21–4.
23 Liberal Democrats, *Make the Difference*, p. 11.
24 Hill, *Understanding Social Policy*, ch. 7.
25 Conservative Party, *You Can Only Be Sure*, p. 17.
26 *Financial Times*, 3 April 1997.
27 Conservative Party, *You Can Only Be Sure*, p. 20.
28 Labour Party, *New Labour*, p. 27.
29 Liberal Democrats, *Make the Difference*, p. 39.
30 Labour Party, *New Labour*, p. 4.
31 *The Times*, 10 April 1997.
32 Ibid.

Bury North

Bury North is a classic barometer seat. Captured by the Conservatives in 1983, it remained a marginal which Labour knew they had to capture if they were to form a government. At fifty-fourth position on Labour's list of fifty-seven marginals needing capture for an overall majority, few seats were regarded as more significant. Labour required a swing of 4.1 per cent. John Major and Tony Blair visited Bury, along with hordes of other prominent figures. Granada screened a national television debate there.

Labour believed they faced an awkward task. The incumbent MP, Social Security Minister Alistair Burt, was respected as a good constituency MP even by opponents. His political career was untainted even by its association with the controversial Child Support Agency. In 1992 the swing to Labour, despite vigorous local campaigning, had been a desultory 2 per cent. This flop was echoed in Bury South, yet more marginal. In 1997, there was even a local feel-good factor, with a second successive promotion for the town's football club; Burt is a fervent supporter. It appeared that Bury North was an increasingly prosperous northern industrial constituency with a high (79 per cent) level of owner occupation which belied simplistic talk of a North–South divide.

Despite these negatives for Labour, they enjoyed a very comfortable success, dispelling the fiction that an MP's personal vote is highly significant. Burt was swept aside by the Labour tide, as the swing against the Conservatives slightly exceeded the national average and was typical of marginal seats in the region. As Burt commented to the *Bury Times* (6 May) there was 'nothing locally we could do'. Labour nullified Conservative campaigning on local issues. Questioned, for example, about the impact of abolition of the assisted places scheme upon those attending Bury Grammar School (attended by both main candidates) Tony Blair stressed to the *Bury Times* (25 April) that all those currently on the scheme would be protected.

Victorious Labour candidate David Chaytor found his majority enlarged by Conservative absentees, defections to the Referendum Party and lack of support for the Liberal Democrats in what is always a two-party contest. However, it was the Conservative to Labour swing that proved decisive. At the count and in the local press (*Bury Times*, 9 May) Chaytor paid tribute to his defeated rival. The winner had been described by the *Sunday Times* (23 March) as 'old Labour'. The *Manchester Evening News* (18 April) marked him as an 'unswerving Blairite'. It made not the slightest difference to the result which view was correct.

Result

Bury North			
David Chaytor	Lab	28,253	
Alistair Burt	Con	20,657	
Neville Kenyon	Lib Dem	4,536	
Richard Hallewell	Ref	1,337	
Total vote		55,053	Turnout 78.07%
Lab majority		7,866	
Lab gain from Con			
Swing Con to Lab 11.19%			

9

The battle for Britain? Constitutional reform and the election

James Mitchell

Introduction

A constitution is, quite simply, the set of rules which govern the political process. It is the 'law behind the law – the legal source of legitimate authority'.[1] Those who lose out under the rules of the game, including political parties, tend to support change. Those who benefit tend to support the *status quo*. 'Constitutionalism' refers to a system in which accepted rules and procedures govern the process of politics. Those in power have no more power over these procedures than those in opposition and changes in the procedures must be agreed by more than those holding power. The United Kingdom is unusual in that the rules of the game are so malleable as to raise questions as to whether it could properly be described as exhibiting constitutional government. There are fragments of a system of constitutional government, most notably in the shape of constitutional conventions. However, as Marshall remarked, constitutional conventions are 'somewhat vague and slippery – resembling the procreation of eels'.[2] The British constitution is unwritten in the sense that there is no entrenched set of rules and procedures. This was an important background to the campaign.

There were significant differences between the parties on constitutional issues in the 1997 election. This does not mean that such differences were a key aspect of the campaign. There have been few occasions this century when the constitution has been at the heart of an election campaign. Ireland, the empire, the European Community/Union, electoral reform and the position of the Lords have been issues in elections, but rarely have any of these been at the forefront of the campaigns of either of the two main parties throughout Britain and never have all of these issues played a part as a package. In an overview of elections since 1945, the foremost chronicler of events had little to say about constitutional politics.[3] When these issues have arisen, they have been isolated, episodic and of concern either in only one part of the United Kingdom or for a small proportion of the electorate. It would be wrong to suggest that the constitution dominated the 1997 election. Yet constitutional politics played a more significant part in the election, across the UK as a whole and including a wider variety of issues, than at any previous election in modern times. Most significantly, constitutional politics was symbolically important for each of the parties in presenting themselves and their opponents in the election even if the substance of constitutional politics may not have had a great impact.

For the most part, the components of constitutional politics excited little enthusiasm amongst the electorate. Support for constitutional change, where it existed, was broadly based but shallow. What made it electorally important was the manner in which the constitution was tied into the contrasting images Labour sought for itself and for the Conservatives. Labour's task was made much easier following the emergence of 'sleaze' as an issue. The notion that Conservative MPs were receiving 'cash for questions' added to the feeling that something was rotten at the core of British politics. Labour's proposals for new rules governing the financing of political parties and support for inquiries into the conduct of MPs could be presented as part of a critique of British government.

One issue which fuelled the debate on the constitution was Scotland's constitutional status. In Scotland itself, home rule had been a secondary issue at elections from the 1920s and had come to the fore in 1974 only to recede again in 1979 before rising again in the 1980s largely as a result of the electoral weakness of the Conservatives in Scotland. The belief that the Tories were anti-Scottish, an English party foisting its policies on Scotland, had been acknowledged as a problem after the 1987 election in a private internal document leaked to the press.[4] Following that election a constitutional convention was established consisting of Labour, the Liberal Democrats, local authorities, trade unions and churches which drew up a scheme of home rule. These proposals became a focal point in 1992 and again in 1997.

In large measure, the debate on the constitution was about how each of the parties saw Britain. Central to this was the role of Parliament. Should parliamentary sovereignty be compromised by further European integration, devolution or a Bill of Rights? How should its members conduct themselves?

New Labour, new Britain

Emphasis was placed on 'new' and 'modern' in Labour rhetoric. This was as much a feature of its discussion of the constitution as anything else. At Labour's 1995 conference, Blair had spoken of his desire to make Britain a 'young country again'.[5] The thrust of the Party's strategy was to alter its image and stress that it was not the old Labour Party associated with trade unions, state intervention and high taxes. Detail was less important, indeed would be resisted for fear that it might distract attention from the general image Labour wanted to project. Labour's approach to the constitution, therefore, involved projecting an image which was in keeping with its electoral strategy. Devised as an electoral strategy rather than a blueprint for a new constitutional order, there were many loose ends in Labour's proposals. Labour wanted to imply that it was sympathetic to constitutional change without supporting anything too radical.

There were a number of reasons why constitutional politics was important for Labour in 1997. The convergence of Labour and the Conservatives on economic and social policy meant that the constitution was one of the few areas where real differences existed. The perceived need inside the Labour Party to avoid appearing willing to 'tax and spend' made the constitution a useful means of distinguishing it from the Conservatives. In its widest sense, constitutional politics also offered Labour an opening for attacking the Conservative record. Labour wanted to highlight what they perceived as the partisan and unconstitutional nature of Conservative rule: that the British constitution had become, more than ever, what the government of the day deemed it to be. Labour's critique of the years of Conservative government noted that local authorities had lost power or been abolished and power had become increasingly centralised, the civil service had lost its independence, the Government had increased its power at the expense of Parliament which had grown corrupt and individual liberties had been compromised. This emphasis on how politics was conducted rather than on policies allowed Labour to side-step the awkward matter of the converging policy agendas of the two parties.

Labour had reluctantly come to support devolution in 1974 as a result of the threat posed by the SNP. The problem back then for Labour was that many members opposed the policy whilst others supported it for reasons of Party loyalty and not conviction. Labour members still had a view of Britain as a unitary state, with 'one unambiguous political centre which enjoys economic dominance and pursues a more or less undeviating policy of administrative standardization'.[6] This was difficult to reconcile with support for devolution. By the mid-1980s, the SNP threat was greater. Though the SNP's peak of 30 per cent in a general election was achieved in October 1974, its profile increasingly resembled that of the Labour Party both in terms of the nature of its support and the policies and image it projected.[7] The ease with which Labour supporters could shift to the SNP presented the main electoral challenge in Scotland, but there were other reasons. Devolution had become associated with a progressive political agenda and it was accepted in Scottish Labour circles that a Scottish Assembly, even one as weak as that which had been proposed by the Labour Government, would have been able to protect services which had been undermined by the Conservative-controlled Scottish Office. In the early 1980s, Scottish devolution became part of the Bennite alternative strategy. It was to be one of the very few policies from that period which was to withstand the modernisation of the Labour Party after 1983.

Labour's devolution policy evolved in the 1980s but in most respects the substance remained the same as that proposed in the late 1970s.[8] In other respects, it changed dramatically. Labour no longer talked of establishing a devolved Parliament but instead talked about a Scottish Parliament. It was to be given tax-raising powers (though in fact these were fiscally rather feeble) and its range of responsibilities was to be increased. These changes all occurred in the early 1980s before the modernisation of the Party. Labour entered the constitutional convention with the Liberal Democrats in 1989 and agreed a scheme which included an alternative voting system for the proposed Scottish Parliament.

Most significantly, Scottish Labour members rejected the notion that Britain was a unitary state. Though this was not the language they adopted, their thinking was informed by a wholly new notion of Britain. Britain came to be seen as a union state, where integration was 'less than perfect. Whilst administrative standardization prevails over most of the territory, the consequences of personal union entail the survival in some areas of pre-union rights and institutional infrastructures which reserve some degree of regional autonomy and serve as agencies of indigenous elite recruitment.'[9] This perception of Britain was more compatible with support for devolution. Scottish Labour had undergone a sea-change in outlook involving a dramatic paradigm shift. Parliament was at the heart of the unitary state view of Britain whereas Parliament's position was less central to the union state view.

Labour could use its devolution policy to present its Scottish credentials to the electorate. Yet just as Labour had portrayed the Tories in Scotland as anti-Scottish, there was a danger that the Tories might portray Labour as a party of the Celtic peripheries with little sympathy for the English heartlands. During John Smith's brief leadership there was much comment on the 'tartanisation' of the Labour Party with senior positions held by Scots. The possibility of a Conservative onslaught focusing on this was not beyond possibility. However, Labour under Tony Blair was more difficult to portray as Scoto-centric. Blair was quintessentially a British politician. Given the highly personalised style of Labour's electoral strategy, the issue of the leader's background and image proved crucial. He had been born in Edinburgh, attended fee-paying schools in Durham and Edinburgh, studied at Oxford, joined the English bar, lived in Islington and represented a North of England constituency. Blair could be presented as a British politician in a way that John Smith or John Major could not. The notion of 'creating a young country', of understanding the component parts of Britain and offering a fresh start, could be achieved more easily through Blair than any previous Labour leader.

Playing up its Scottishness in Scotland had been the strategy in the past but in 1997 this would present problems. The Party could not afford to appear too Scottish for fear of offending voters in England but needed to highlight devolution to the Scottish electorate. Devolution may have been a vote winner in Scotland, but it was potentially a vote loser in England; even though successive polls had suggested that a majority of people in England supported Scottish devolution, there was a possibility that the Conservatives would play the 'English card' against Labour. The problem remained that devolution might be an issue for the Scottish public, but it had implications for England and could become a British issue. The so-called 'West Lothian question', relating to the rights of Scottish MPs at Westminster after devolution, had not been addressed by devolutionists. By 1997, devolution had become a British issue and anything said by Labour in Scotland would, if possible, be used against them in England. Labour had to find a balance between maintaining its support in Scotland with the ever-present SNP threat in mind whilst reaching out to new supporters in the South of England.

Prior to the launch of Scottish Labour's manifesto, Blair was asked whether his Sedgefield constituents might think it unfair that Scotland should have its own Parliament responsible for a range of matters whilst Scottish MPs at Westminster would still be able to vote on comparable English affairs. 'I will say to them we have devolved these matters to the Scottish parliament but as far as we are concerned sovereignty rests with me as an English MP and that's the way it will stay.'[10] This contradicted the Scottish Labour position, as agreed in the Constitutional Convention, that sovereignty resided with the Scottish public. The Scottish media interpreted it as a gaffe. The fact that Blair had said it in an interview with a Scottish newspaper suggests that it was deliberate. The underlying thinking was that Labour needed to prevent the Conservatives from successfully playing the English card more than it needed to fear the SNP. Labour needed to demonstrate its British patriotism especially with Conservative taunts that its devolution policy would rip the country apart and its European policy would destroy British sovereignty.

Fitz, a British bulldog, put in an appearance in a Labour Party political broadcast in the middle of the campaign. Fitz was, as the Party claimed, a 'metaphor for Britain'. The problem was that the connotation behind the metaphor for ethnic minorities was racist and xenophobic. The Conservatives countered by pointing out that Labour supported a Council of Europe convention on the protection of pets which, they claimed, would threaten the future of British dog breeds, including bulldogs.[11] Labour insisted that it only supported the convention in principle and wanted some elements clarified. There was no desire to be painted as a party which was in thrall to Johnny Foreigner. Metaphors and symbols could be double-edged weapons and Labour abandoned the bulldog after complaints from minorities who associated it with the British National Party. The Union Jack, however, appeared as the backdrop to press conferences and at party meetings. An SNP news release noted Labour's use of symbols: 'Blair has now completed his love-in with the Tories. First he took their policies, now he has taken the symbols.'[12] Labour were determined to prevent any notion developing that their devolution policy and attitude towards the European Union meant that they were unpatriotic.

House of Lords reform was also high on Labour's agenda. In particular,

Labour wanted immediate legislation to remove the right of hereditary peers to sit and vote in the House of Lords. The Lords never became a major issue in the election but were raised by Labour politicians when Conservatives threatened to use the Lords to disrupt the progress of Labour's devolution proposals. Lord Fraser, for the Tories, maintained that the Lords would have every right to amend the devolution legislation if, as Labour intended, the details would be considered in the Commons by a standing committee rather than a committee of the whole House. The Tories noted that almost all major constitutional bills in the twentieth century had been debated in committee by the Commons as a whole. Labour pointed out that only the first clause of the bill abolishing the Greater London Council in 1985 had been debated in that way. Whilst, constitutionally, the Conservatives were on quite strong ground, Labour's reference to a Peers versus the People battle probably had more resonance, if the issue was picked up by the pubic at all.

On some difficult issues, Labour made use of the pledge to hold a referendum or the promise of an inquiry. These were New Labour's equivalents of a Royal Commission which Harold Wilson had once described as an institution which 'spent years taking minutes'. John Smith had committed Labour to holding a referendum on electoral reform in May 1993. In an article on the constitution published in the *Economist* in September 1996, Blair agreed to this but stated that he was 'unpersuaded that proportional representation would be beneficial for the Commons'.[13] This commitment got round the issue which had caused Labour difficulties in the closing stages of the 1992 election when Neil Kinnock had failed to clarify his position on electoral reform.

Similarly, Labour agreed to a referendum on a single European currency and regional government in England. Open-mindedness was suggested without being committed either way. The image of indecisiveness never hung over the Party despite this because of the firm leadership which Blair had shown during his period as leader in reforming his Party. Labour also promised to incorporate the rights and duties enshrined in the European Convention on Human Rights into law, establish a Human Rights Commission, pass freedom of information legislation, alter the procedures in Parliament for questioning the Prime Minister, overhaul the scrutiny of European legislation and pass legislation to ensure the political neutrality of public officials. Whilst each in turn was significant, and taken together these proposals would potentially fundamentally alter the British constitution, there was remarkably little public debate or much made of them in Labour's national campaign. The central message of a 'New Britain', however, encapsulated the reform programme even if the electorate could have been excused for not appreciating all that was being proposed.

Labour was on the offensive in the election. The Conservative record was under detailed scrutiny, not Labour's proposals. Constitutional issues as such were not electorally salient and were often quite technical. Symbolically, however, they were important. The image projected on this as on other matters was of a party offering something new and fresh but cautious.

Conservatives, unionism and British nationalism

A myth developed in Conservative circles after the 1992 election. It was believed that the Tories had been pulled back from the brink of defeat because John Major made the constitution a central issue. Late in the campaign, the Prime Minister had made his most impassioned speech of the campaign on the subject of devolution. He had declared, 'If I could summon up all the authority of this office, I would put it into this single warning – the United Kingdom is in danger. Wake up, my fellow countrymen! Wake up now before it is too late!' [14] The belief that this had been a powerful rallying cry for the Conservatives was to influence campaigning in the next Parliament and election.

The Conservatives had once supported Scottish devolution and in opposition in the late 1970s had toyed with other constitutional reforms. Under Margaret Thatcher, however, the Conservative position on devolution, Europe and other constitutional reforms hardened. The old Tory view of Britain as a country consisting of distinct national communities was replaced with a view of Britain as an almost uniform entity. As Labour's understanding of Britain shifted from a unitary to a union state, the Conservatives moved in the opposite direction.[15] Indeed, an assimilationist strand of thinking developed within the Party as some Conservatives questioned whether Scotland should be treated as a special case. In her memoirs, Thatcher made clear her contempt for the Scottish Office.[16] For the Thatcherites, parliamentary sovereignty – which in practice meant Prime Ministerial power under Thatcher – was supreme.

Under Major, the Conservatives attempted to soften their image. This was reflected in debates on Europe and Scotland's constitutional status. The Prime Minister had offered to 'take stock' of Scotland's constitutional status after the 1992 election. In the event, the stock-taking exercise, undertaken by Ian Lang, Major loyalist and Scottish Secretary, proved a missed opportunity. After a number of postponements *Scotland in the Union – a Partnership for Good* was produced (Scottish Office, 1993). The build-up to its publication had given an impression that the Conservatives might have something imaginative to offer, but in the event the document proposed only minor reforms in parliamentary procedures plus a few other minor changes and even had a number of basic factual errors on the history of Scottish government. Lang proved one of the weakest and most unimaginative Scottish Secretaries in a long line of uninspiring holders of the office. His successor, Michael Forsyth, was one of the most impressive holders of the office.

Forsyth's appointment in June 1995 gave a new lease of life to the moribund Scottish Conservatives. For the first time in almost twenty years, the Conservatives went on the offensive in Scotland on the constitution. The new Scottish Secretary focused on the proposed tax-raising powers in Labour's proposals and dubbed them the 'tartan tax'. This caused Labour a great deal of discomfort and George Robertson, the shadow Scottish Secretary, struggled to find a response. For the first time in many years, Labour was under attack on the constitution from the Conservatives rather than the Nationalists. Labour's problem was that it was determined to avoid being labelled a high-tax party but the tax-raising power was a long-standing commitment which would be defended vigorously by Party members and it had been part of the scheme agreed in the Constitutional Convention with others. Whilst the Party leadership may have preferred to have abandoned this commitment, the political costs in terms of Party unity in Scotland and for its public image would have been considerable.

In a bold U-turn in June 1996, the Labour leadership in London decided to support a referendum in which two questions would be put to the Scottish people: whether they wanted devolution and whether they wanted a Parliament with tax-raising powers. In February, Robertson had ruled out the need for a referendum but was forced to accept the policy. His own position was gravely weakened and it was no surprise that Donald Dewar was appointed Scottish Secretary after Labour's victory and Robertson was given Defence. John McAllion, Labour's Scottish constitutional spokesperson, had not been consulted and resigned, as did Lord Ewing, who had been a Scottish Office minister when Labour were last in power, as joint chair of the Constitutional Convention. The Scottish Labour executive met in August when a proposal to have just one all-embracing question was defeated by twenty-one votes to eighteen before a proposal was accepted which would have required the two-question pre-legislative referendum plus a further referendum before the Scottish Parliament could activate the tax. This was accepted by twenty-six votes to sixteen. This position held for six days before Blair announced that there would be no need for a second referendum. *The Conservative Campaign Guide 1997* described the events with relish. During the election, the Conservatives attacked Labour for exactly what they had been accused of over the previous seventeen years: 'Labour's three U-turns showed the total impotence of Mr Robertson and the Scottish Labour Party. They have had to accept fundamental changes of policy dictated to them by Mr Blair and his advisers in London who have no interest in their views.'[17]

Forsyth forced Labour on to the defensive but also attempted to 'put a kilt' on the Scottish Tories. In his brief and controversial period as chairperson of the Scottish Tories in 1989–90, he had shown little appreciation of the Scottish dimension, but as Scottish Secretary he attempted to rekindle the Scottish dimension of Conservatism. The Conservatives were rediscovering the union state, but it would prove too little, too late. Forsyth literally put a kilt on when he turned up for the première of *Braveheart*, the Hollywood version of the story of William Wallace, the Scottish patriot hanged for his leadership of Scotland's fight for independence centuries before. On St Andrew's Day 1995, Forsyth gave a public lecture outlining proposals for reform in the government of Scotland. These amounted to little more than what had been proposed by Lang after the 'taking stock' exercise. The difference was in presentation. The Constitutional Convention – consisting of Labour, Liberal Democrats and others who had been meeting since 1989 to devise a scheme of home rule – were to publish their final report that day and the SNP were planning a major press conference on 'Scotland in Europe' from Brussels. Forsyth hijacked the day and dominated the news.

Forsyth's most audacious idea was the return of the Stone of Destiny to Scotland. The stone was the subject of nationalist folklore. It had been in London from the end of the thirteenth century, but had been retrieved by a group of nationalist students in 1950 and returned after much hilarity in Scotland and outrage on the part of the London establishment. Forsyth's decision to return the stone was an act of symbolism again designed to emphasise the Scottishness of the Tories. The stone was returned amidst considerable media hype.

A criticism levelled against Forsyth from within the Party in the run-up to and during the election campaign was that the timing of his anti-devolution campaigning had been wrong. Throughout the campaign proper, Forsyth and the Conservatives attacked the 'tartan tax' and devolution but the arguments and slogans were no longer new. He had forced Labour to change its policy almost a year before but failed to make an impact when the election came. His other problem was that reversing the English image the Party had in Scotland required more than symbolic gestures. Putting a kilt on – both literally and metaphorically – would no longer suffice.

Conservative disunity and weak leadership were also evident when it came to 'sleaze'. In essence, one aspect of sleaze was about the conduct of politics and the working of the political system. By the time of the election proper, the focus of attention was on Neil Hamilton, MP for Tatton and former junior minister. Hamilton had dropped a libel action against the *Guardian* after it had claimed that he had received thousands of pounds and a free trip to the Paris Ritz for tabling parliamentary questions on behalf of Mohammed Al Fayed, the owner of Harrods. The evidence against Hamilton was mounting and an official inquiry had failed to clear his name and, after the election, found him guilty. Hamilton's determination to stand again as Conservative candidate and the withdrawal of Labour and Liberal Democrat candidates in favour of Martin Bell, BBC reporter and Independent candidate, was given prominent media coverage much to the dismay of the Conservative leadership. The issue was a gift for Labour. Instead of being faced with the charge that the Party was inexperienced, having been out of office for so long, the Conservatives were having to face the charge that their long tenure in power had led to 'sleaze'. Had this been an isolated case, it might not have had the same impact. The opposition parties promised reforms in the funding of parties and in parliamentary procedures. Sleaze was, in this sense, a constitutional issue but, once more, was more important in that it was tied up with the imagery of the parties.

Liberal Democrats and Nationalists: the constitutional radicals

Constitutional reform has been at the heart of Liberal Democrat politics for generations. In part, the desire to change the rules of the game follow from the Party's distance from power but also reflects its liberalism and support for individual rights. Electoral reform has been at the forefront of its reform package. In addition, the Party supported Scottish home rule and federalism throughout the UK, a Freedom of Information Act, a Bill of Rights including the incorporation of the European Convention on Human Rights into UK law and establishing a Human Rights Commission, decentralisation, reform of Parliament and European integration which amounted to the most radical reform package on offer from the main parties.

As ever, the Liberal Democrats hoped to be pivotal in the next Parliament and bring about constitutional change, particularly electoral reform. A number of contacts had been made between the Liberal Democrats and the Labour Party on the constitution. Both parties had worked together in the Scottish Constitutional Convention and the Liberal Democrats maintained that they were the guardians of the constitutional reform movement. The Party had dropped a demand that Blair should personally endorse a change in the electoral system in February.[18] Relaxation of this demand made a deal on constitutional change possible between the parties. Though little was made of this during the campaign, there was substantial common ground between the two parties which may have made tactical voting more likely than at any previous election.

The Liberal Democrats started the campaign on the defensive when Malcolm Bruce, its Treasury spokesperson, and Ray Michie, Scottish affairs spokesperson, issued a paper on constitutional reform entitled 'Towards a Federal United Kingdom'. It advocated federalism but media attention focused almost exclusively on the proposal for a new national flag. The abolition of the Union Jack was rejected by Paddy Ashdown and played down by its proponents whilst Conservatives locally made much of it in an attempt to embarrass Bruce and Michie. This encapsulated the Liberal Democrat approach to the constitution in 1997. Its proposals may have been constitutionally coherent and logical but they lacked the coherent packaging and imagery so evident in Labour's campaign.

The Scottish National Party and Plaid Cymru attempted to attract votes for independence and urge voters to support them to maintain pressure on Labour. Facing the prospect of Labour coming to power and, more significantly, the public anticipating this, the nationalists could not use their familiar charge that voting Labour in Scotland and Wales was a lost cause. Shortly before the election, the parties shifted their position and argued that Labour would win in England and therefore across Britain as a whole. A Labour vote in these circumstances was pointless. The nationalists focused less on Labour's constitutional politics than on 'social justice', charging Labour with having adopted a Conservative agenda. The SNP avoided the issue of devolution, arguing that any referendum should offer the Scots three options: independence within the EU, devolution and the *status quo*. The SNP made much of Treasury statistics published just before the start of the campaign proper which showed that Scotland had made a net contribution of £27 billion to the Treasury over the previous eighteen years. The arguments over this were highly technical and whilst the SNP went into much detail, their opponents largely preferred a broad-brush approach, responding with ridicule for the most part. Absent from the SNP's 1997 campaign were Jim Sillars and his fiery oratory. In his place were SNP economists. Accounting and statistics shored up the SNP vote across Scotland, but failed to ignite its campaign. A much more targeted approach allied with the collapse of the Conservative Party gave the SNP an additional three seats, including the Perth seat won in a by-election. In Scotland and Wales, the nationalists' best hope was the return of a Labour government which implemented home rule. The 1997 general election proved a very British affair in which the nationalists were squeezed.

Conclusion

The constitution in 1997 was more important than in previous elections and the new Parliament was set to be one of the most constitutionally radical of the twentieth century. A new image of Britain had gained ground within the Labour Party which was both conservative – with its emphasis on symbols such as the Union Jack and the patriotism of Tony Blair – and radical – with the rhetorical emphasis on the new and creating a 'young country'. Proposals for substantial change in the shape of devolution or the possibility of change, including the commitments to referendums suggested cautious support for change which matched the public mood. Most important, unlike the Conservative Party, which remained much more conservative both in its imagery and policies, Labour appeared united and coherent. Labour's Achilles heel would have been in the details of constitutional reform had these existed or had there been a greater effort to focus on them by the media. Labour's emphasis on the big picture and symbols allied with the troubles inside the Conservative Party left it in a strong position.

The growing dissatisfaction with the conduct of politics had focused on 'sleaze'. This and disunity over Europe seriously damaged the Conservatives. As the constitutional party, and having been in power for so long, the Conservatives were on the defensive. It was much more difficult to play the patriotic card as Major had in 1992 with such deep divisions in the Party and the general sense that something was rotten in how politics in Britain was conducted.

There was less reason to feel proud of the British constitution in 1997, at least under the Conservatives, and this removed a weapon from the Conservative armoury which had proved so powerful in the past. The nearest the Conservatives came to emulating Labour was Michael Forsyth's onslaught against devolution and his attempt to put a kilt on the Scottish Tories, but this proved insufficient and badly timed.

The other parties were marginalised in the process and despite, or perhaps because of, the central importance of the constitution to the Liberal Democrats, SNP and Plaid Cymru they were unable to have much impact. The gains for the third parties were part of the fall-out from the Conservative collapse. The paradox of the 1997 election in which the constitution was more important than in previous elections but parties which placed it at the heart of their agendas gained only in the wake of others is explained by the manner in which constitutional politics were articulated and understood. Symbols and imagery were more important than substance and in these New Labour proved masterly.

Notes

1 S. de Smith and R. Brazier, *Constitutional and Administrative Law*, 7th edn (London: Penguin, 1994), p. 5.
2 G. Marshall, *Constitutional Convention* (Oxford: Clarendon, 1984).
3 D. Butler, *British General Elections since 1945* (Oxford: Blackwell, 1989).
4 J. Mitchell, *Conservatives and the Union* (Edinburgh: Edinburgh University Press, 1990).
5 T. Blair, 'Speech to the Labour Party Conference', Brighton, 3 October 1995.
6 D. Rokkan and S. Urwin, *The Politics of Territorial Idenitity* (London: Sage, 1982), p. 11.
7 J. Brand, J. Mitchell and P. Surridge, 'Social constituency and ideological profile: Scottish Nationalism in the 1990s', *Political Studies*, 42 (1994): 616–29.
8 J. Mitchell, 'Conceptual lenses and territorial government in Britain' in U. Jordan and W. Kaiser (eds), *Political Reform in Britain, 1886–1996; Themes, Ideas, Policies* (Bochum: Universitätsverlag Dr. Brochmeyer, 1997).
9 Rokkan and Urwin, *The Politics of Territorial Identity*, p. 11.
10 *Scotsman*, 4 April 1997.
11 *Daily Telegraph*, 16 April 1997.
12 SNP News Release, 11 April 1997.
13 *Economist*, 14 September 1996.
14 D. Butler and D. Kavanagh, *The British General Election of 1992* (Basingstoke: Macmillan, 1992), p. 130.
15 J. Mitchell 'Conservatives and the changing meaning of union', *Regional and Federal Studies*, 6:1 (1996): 30–44.
16 M. Thatcher, *The Downing Street Years* (London: Harper Collins, 1993), p. 67.
17 Conservative Party, *Conservative Campaign Guide* (London: Conservative Central Office, 1997).
18 *Financial Times*, 1 February 1997.

Stirling

Defending the sixth most vulnerable Conservative seat, the chances of Michael Forsyth, Secretary of State for Scotland, remaining as MP for Stirling always appeared remote. Labour needed a mere 0.3 per cent swing to capture the seat, one of the more prosperous areas in Scotland's urban central belt.

Forsyth's hopes depended upon a repetition of the 1992 result, when, against expectations, there was no swing against the Conservatives. Now, 12 per cent changes worked marginally in Labour's favour. Another factor against the Conservatives was the relatively small previous SNP vote, reducing the chances of a divided opposition allowing a Conservative success by default.

The constituency had undergone the trauma of the massacre at Dunblane. Its aftermath saw a concerted effort, led by the Snowdrop Campaign, for a total ban on hand guns. Forsyth, whilst not unsympathetic to this cause, was bound by his responsibilities in government to support the compromise offered: a partial prohibition.

Regarded as an effective political campaigner, Forsyth had led a strong Conservative campaign against Labour's proposals for a devolved Scottish Parliament. His criticism of the 'tartan tax' which he claimed such an institution was bound to impose added to the controversy over such proposals. Appointed Scottish Secretary in July 1995, Forsyth appeared to have moderated slightly his Thatcherite zeal, whilst concurrently promoting himself as Scotland's champion. His campaigning skills and the four-cornered nature of the contest, even allowing for the lack of strength of the SNP and Liberal Democrats, reduced the swing against the Conservatives, but the seat was a comfortable Labour gain, forming part of the obliteration of the Conservatives in Scotland.

Result

Stirling			
Anne McGuire	Lab	20,382	
Michael Forsyth	Con	13,971	
Ewan Dow	SNP	5,752	
Alistair Tough	Lib Dem	2,675	
	Others	178	
Total vote		42,958	Turnout 81.84%
Lab majority		6,411	
Lab gain from Con			
Swing Con to Lab 7.74%			

10

The dog that didn't bark? Immigration, race and the general election

Shamit Saggar

Introduction

In the long run-up to May 1997, most informed commentators had suggested that race and immigration concerns were *unlikely* to play a prominent part in the approaching general election. Racial politics, it was assumed, was the stuff of inner-city ethnic minority-dominated districts, and thus held limited saliency on the broader electoral map. It was accepted that racial and ethnic loyalties were capable of throwing up volatile results in a handful of constituencies, but had virtually no impact beyond. Additionally, the older, heated arguments over immigration, that had become a familiar feature of the 1960s and 1970s, appeared to have fallen off the agenda of electoral competition as far back as the 1983 election. By the late 1990s, then, the immigration theme, far from causing a deep fault line across the political landscape, was an issue of limited and predictable passions.

This chapter examines the experience of the 1997 election against this minimalist backdrop. On the one hand, there were a number of forces at play that dampened interest in race and immigration issues. These forces described a broader pattern at work which portrayed race as electorally dead in modern British politics. However, on the other hand, the election campaign itself revealed fresh interest in several distinct racial themes. The most visible of these was, arguably, the renewed Conservative campaign to attract ethnic-minority support. The return of additional black and Asian faces to the Commons also stood out, in contrast to the Conservatives' anti-immigration rhetoric, which, significantly, did not. In this respect, race appeared far from dead and, in fact, appeared to play an important role in (i) party strategy, (ii) political communications, and (iii) assessments of representation.

This chapter will focus on three inter-related themes in order to evaluate the 'electoral death' thesis. First, the electoral engagement of the ethnic minorities[1] will be surveyed; second, the question of party strategy in relation to ethnic minorities and towards anti-minority sentiment will be analysed; and third, the problems over ethnic minority representatives and representation will be discussed. Finally, some concluding remarks based on these areas of evidence will argue that the 'electoral death' thesis has been overstated in several important senses.

Electoral engagement and leverage

Prior to 1997 most general elections had followed a predictable pattern in which a range of minority politicians, press barons and assorted public figures would suggest that considerable electoral influence could be exerted by black and Asian voters. The 1997 contest was no exception, though it was startling to witness the seriousness with which the claim was made. Moreover, whereas in earlier elections this argument was usually met with only moderate interest by the major parties, in 1997 it was given a considerable push by the pre-emptive Conservative attempt to woo minority voters.

Geography and ethnicity: ethnic marginals

To be certain, there was nothing especially new in these electoral muscle claims. Such claims have historically been closely linked to boasts about so-called 'ethnic marginals', that is, seats where local minority groups outnumber the scale of existing MPs' majorities. Ethnic marginal calculations, sadly, have often been exaggerated in number, owing, principally, to the failure to allow for the younger age structure of blacks and Asians and differential registration and turnout rates, as compared with white voters. Moreover, the secret ballot in itself serves to make judgements about differential inter-ethnic swings extremely unreliable.

However, despite these notes of caution, the 1997 contest witnessed a re-run of the bluster over ethnic marginals. An Asian satellite television company, Zee TV, published a list of forty-five Asian marginals, whilst a comparable list of forty-nine black marginals emerged from Operation Black Vote (OBV), a pressure group set up in 1996 by Charter 88 campaigning for greater black electoral involvement. A more sober assessment would suggest around fifty-four seats in all were subject to potential influence (see Table 10.1). However, the strong national swing enjoyed by Labour, coupled with the small number of close results in this fifty-four-seat list, meant that minority influence mattered in perhaps as few as fifteen to twenty of these constituencies. Even this figure may be an overstatement since the polling evidence of differential swing amongst minorities remains very sketchy.[2]

Weighing up potential

Such debates over minority electoral muscle are ultimately contingent upon three background factors. First, there is the question of the demography of minority populations. Electoral leverage, in a single-member-constituency system, is heavily dependent on basic numbers.[3] In Britain, the numbers of blacks and Asians remain far from substantial when measured in macro terms. However, these are heavily clustered populations giving rise to concentrated

Table 10.1 Estimated 'ethnic marginals' 1997 (%)

All seats in which majority of sitting MP is equalled or exceeded by size [a] of local ethnic minority electorate [b]

Seat	*1992 notional majority*	*Ethnic minority electorate (notional estimate)*
Con-held seats		
Vale of Glamorgan	0.0	0.5
Hayes & Harlington	0.1	11.7
Halesowen & Rowley Regis	0.2	2.2
Croydon North	0.3	16.8
Portsmouth South	0.5	1.4
Luton South	1.0	12.7
Oldham East & Sadd'worth	1.0	3.2
Edmonton	1.2	10.5
Bury South	1.3	1.3
Batley & Spen	1.7	6.6
Brentford & Isleworth	2.8	11.3
Mitcham & Morden	3.4	9.8
Crawley	3.7	4.2
Ilford South	4.8	19.7
Coventry South	5.1	5.3
Battersea	9.1	11.6
Wolverhampton South West	9.4	13.1
Total Con: 17		
Lab-held seats		
Rossendale & Darwen	0.1	0.8
Slough	0.1	17.1
B'ham Yardley	0.4	4.3
Ipswich	0.6	5.2
Halifax	0.8	4.7
Cambridge	1.1	2.1
Dudley North	1.8	4.1
S'hampton Itchen	1.8	2.1
Feltham & Heston	2.6	15.1
Lewisham East	2.6	7.8
Dulwich & Norwood	3.5	12.8
B'ham Selly Oak	3.7	6.4
Pendle	4.0	6.5
Lewisham West	4.2	10.3
Hampstead & Highgate	5.4	5.5

Nottingham South	5.9	6.6
Walsall South	6.3	12.7
Ealing, Acton & S/Bush	7.0	11.6
Walthamstow	7.1	16.1
Dewsbury	7.2	8.4
Regents Pk & Ken. North	7.3	10.9
Derby South	7.4	10.9
Tooting	8.0	13.8
Leicester West	8.2	8.9
Ealing Southall	9.0	27.6
Hornsey & Wood Green	9.3	9.7
Blackburn	11.0	12.3
Streatham	11.0	15.6
B'ham Perry Barr	14.6	23.2
Leyton & Wanstead	14.9	18.1
Brent East	16.3	19.4
Leicester South	17.7	19.3
Bradford West	19.4	22.6
East Ham	22.0	28.2
Leicester East	22.7	23.6
Brent South	26.5	31.6
Total Lab: 36		
Lib Dem-held seats		
Rochdale	0.2	9.2
Total Lib Dem: 1		
Grand total: 54 seats		

Notes:

[a] Resident population of Asian and black origin, adjusted downwards for younger age profile of ethnic minority population (controlling for estimated proportions below sixteen years of age).

[b] Ethnic minority defined as those who declared themselves to be of Indian, Pakistani, Bangladeshi or black origin (1991 General Census).

Source: Author's calculations, derived from P. Norris, *UK Election Results (New Constituency Boundaries)* (Cambridge, Mass.: Harvard University Press, 1996).

strength in a small number of constituencies. In 1997 there were no less than twenty-six Labour-held seats in which blacks and Asians comprised more than a fifth of the population. There were just four such Conservative seats and none defended by the Liberal Democrats.[4] The 1991 General Census had shown just under 1.5 million Asians resident in Britain, plus a further 900,000 or so black people of various African and Caribbean origins. The ethnic Chinese, another tightly clustered group, numbered 157,000. One estimate just prior to the election suggested that Britain's ethnic minorities may have grown by a further 12 per cent between the last census (1991) and 1996.[5]

Second, electoral muscle necessarily involves a large degree of political participation within the democratic process. On this point there has been clear disagreement between commentators over the years. Some data have tended to paint a picture of low levels of minority electoral registration and turnout.[6] Meanwhile, there has been plenty of evidence to suggest high levels of engagement, especially amongst the Asian electorate,[7] and also in local studies going back many years of Asian activism, for example in Bradford.[8] The scenario in 1997 provided some support for both these contending views. As Table 10.2 shows, planned turnout amongst Asians and the (mainly white) general public was extraordinarily similar. That of blacks meanwhile lagged behind somewhat, though arguably not by as much as many sceptics believed. To be sure, a great deal was made by OBV and others in the campaign about the risk of as many as four in five blacks abstaining from the democratic process, when in fact these alarming ratios related to those who at the time of the survey (June 1996) were 'not absolutely certain' they would vote.[9]

Table 10.2 Voting turnout; black, Asian and general public 1996–1997 (%)

Voting intention	*Black*	*Asian*	*General public*
Certain not to vote	13	10	8
Not very likely to vote	11	7	7
Quite likely to vote	14	11	11
Very likely to vote	17	13	15
Certain to vote	40	58	57
Don't know	5	1	2

Sources: MORI, 'Asian voting: preliminary results', unpublished briefing notes, February 1997; MORI, 'Black Britain', *British Public Opinion*, July 1996; data on general public from nationwide survey by MORI on behalf of *The Times*, January 1997.

What was clear was that, beyond these disputes over participation, the black and Asian electorates were the subject of unprecedented efforts to mobilise their electoral force. In 1997 this objective was singled out by OBV, and to a lesser degree by an initiative known as 'Race for the Vote' (a loose cross-group campaign body). The combined impact of both was such that the threat of supposed black non-participation featured as a central and continuing element in any media coverage of racial affairs. The dilemma for OBV and others was that in highlighting black abstention, they unintentionally raised the possibility that black electoral muscle was, in truth, rather less than had been claimed.

Third, it remains broadly true, though perhaps unfashionable to remind ourselves, that discrete social groups that aspire to electoral brawn will be frustrated in their efforts if their party allegiances are heavily skewed in one direction. This, bluntly, has been the single greatest impediment facing minorities in Britain to date. As Table 10.3 notes, the historical track record has been one of overwhelming devotion to the Labour Party. A crude rearrangement of limited polling data from 1996–97 (right-hand column) indicates that combined minority loyalties in May 1997 were broadly in line with earlier elections. *Plus ça change.*

Table 10.3 Levels of Labour and Conservative support amongst ethnic minorities 1974–1997 (%)

Party	*1974*[a]	*1979*	*1983*[b]	*1987*	*1992*[b]	*1997*[b]
Lab	81	86	83	72	81	78
Con	9	8	7	18	10	17

Notes:
[a] October 1974 general election.
[b] Recalculated average of Asian and Afro-Caribbean support levels.

Sources: Adapted from: Community Relations Commission, *Participation of Ethnic Minorities in the General Election of October 1974* (London: CRC, 1975); Commission for Racial Equality, *Votes and Policies* (London, CRE, 1980); Commission for Racial Equality, *Ethnic Minorities and the 1983 General Election* (London: CRE, 1984); Harris Research Centre, 'Political attitudes amongst ethnic minorities', unpublished data set JN98746 (London: Harris, 1987); A. Ali and G. Percival, *Race and Representation: Ethnic Minorities and the 1992 Elections* (London: CRE, 1993); MORI, 'Asian voting: preliminary results', unpublished briefing notes, February 1997; MORI, 'Black Britain', *British Public Opinion*, July 1996.

Voter loyalty or voter drift?

There are, inevitably, a number of ways to read these figures. To begin with, there is no doubting the persistence of the 'ethnic gap', if the differential minority–white split can be dubbed as such. Four in every five backed Labour, repeating a long-running pattern. However, it would appear that the sizeable increase in vote share that New Labour enjoyed in the country as a whole was not reflected amongst minority voters. Previously, the blip that had occurred in 1987 had proven to be nothing more than a temporary surge in Conservative fortunes. That increase for the right had of course taken place in the context of Conservative electoral hegemony and a second successive landslide.

No such context existed in 1997. The ability of the Conservatives to substantially improve their minority vote share, despite a humiliating débâcle amongst voters more generally, must be one of the remarkable features of the election. Closer examination of the MORI polling data in fact reveals that two contrasting trends were at work concurrently. Amongst Asians, the MORI evidence points to a Conservative surge of 25 per cent of all respondents naming a preferred party choice; in sharp contrast Conservative fortunes amongst blacks intending to vote slumped to just 8 per cent. Therefore, for one group amongst the minority electorate, 1997 amounted to a small yet significant breakthrough.

Party strategy and 'race politics'

How might this picture be interpreted amongst the major political parties? Any party that held such a commanding share of the votes of a discrete social group – as Labour still does – would naturally have minimal cause for anxiety. Labour's position after 1997 therefore remains enviable, though lurking worries stemming from the spillover effects of rows about candidate selection mean that complacency remains a lurking possibility. The success in retaining its minority supporters in 1997 is largely down to two factors. First, the force of the Party's massive polling lead and commanding ballot box victory clearly raised the chances of its minority supporters remaining loyal. It is possible to speculate that a more slender win over the Conservatives could have allowed some real erosion in its minority support.

Second, the success in holding on to minority voters was a testimony to Labour's determination to offer only limited policy pledges targeting minority voters. Indeed, the bulk of Labour's appeal towards minorities was couched in non-race-specific terms. A few exceptions could be found in the Party's programme, manifesto and campaign pledges, notably on scrapping the 1983 'primary purpose' immigration rules (of principal concern to Asians). Beyond that, programmes to tackle long-term unemployment, educational under-achievement and suchlike were all presented as mainstream policies, but from which minorities might be disproportionate beneficiaries. This approach had the virtue of avoiding any close association between the Party and (electorally unpopular) minority vested interests.

On the debit side, Labour strategists would have noted that short-term successes were unlikely to halt, fully or permanently, the long-term erosion in the Party's lead. The Conservatives have long recognised such a potential; to be sure, over the past twenty years there have been a series of Conservative breakthrough predictions.

The Conservative campaign for minority voters in 1997 continued this trend and homed in on two core themes. First, Conservative politicians re-turned to the familiar cultural arguments that putatively linked the Party with middle-class Asians. Common bourgeois values, so these arguments ran, underpinned the British Asian experience and were reflected *inter alia* in aspects of family life, attitudes towards education, emphasis upon thrift, moral conservatism, and so on. The Conservatives, it was claimed, uniquely offered such values in their approach to politics and public policy, thus rendering Labour as unelectable on quasi-deterministic grounds. The cultural thesis arguably ran into severe difficulties in 1997 since it was increasingly apparent that much of the ideological soil upon which the argument was rooted was now shared between the Conservatives and their Labour opponents. This made it extremely hard, almost impossible, for Conservative strategists to dwell on the uniqueness of the Asian–Conservative cultural bond.

Second, the Conservatives' appeal also tended to emphasise economic confidence as an especially relevant factor to promote their cause amongst Asian voters. To begin with, bullishness about the Conservatives' economic record plainly drove the Party's campaign strategy, and arguably would have featured even more in the absence of unwelcome party disunity on Europe. Building on this, strategists seemed to calculate (i) that the pocket book factor mattered rather more to Asians than their white counterparts, and/or (ii) that Asians took a somewhat more supportive view of the Tory record than their white counterparts. It is hard to know for certain which way the lines of causation were perceived in the minds of strategists, many of whom were merely in search of plausible arguments of any kind. Table 10.4 cites evidence from a MORI survey indicating that the strategy might have been on the right lines for a section amongst the Asian electorate. The difficulty, however, lay in projecting and capitalising on the slim advantage amongst Asian voters shown in these figures, not least of all in an election in which precious few dividends based on the so-called 'feel-good factor' accrued to the Conservatives.

Table 10.4 Asian and general public economic expectations 1997 (%)

Q: Do you think that the general economic condition of the country will improve, stay the same, or get worse over the next twelve months?

Opinion	*Asians*	*General public*
Improve	32	25
Stay the same	30	39
Get worse	24	25
Don't know	14	10

Source: MORI, 'Asian voting: preliminary results', unpublished briefing notes, February 1997.

One might speculate, thus, that economic competence served as a useful metaphor for traditional class-based appeals by the Conservatives. In fact, the Conservatives' failure to make greater headway in attracting middle-class support from black, Asian and other minority groups has been the subject of extended academic interest in the past.[10] Significantly, however, very little of the content of the 1997 Conservative 'ethnic campaign' in fact involved class-based appeals. The attraction of the 'Your values are our values, and our values are your values' slogan served to eclipse any substantive class-based message the Conservatives may have hoped to deploy.

Two further obstacles existed in 1997. The first was that the Conservatives' great cross-class coalitions of the 1980s were finally coming apart. Despite heroic efforts, it was clear that the Party had surrendered valuable ground amongst its traditional middle-class constituency as well as in the eyes of many aspirant working-class supporters. The upshot was unmistakable confusion and hesitancy in the Party's campaign efforts to attract class-based support. This missing ingredient in the wider strategy seemed to spill over into the Party's targeted efforts towards minorities, where, it might be argued, so much class-related territory still had to be gained. Additionally, the Conservatives' stand-alone, cultural rhetoric directed towards minority voters had the deficiency of not obviously complementing the wider Conservative campaign, much of which was driven by simple, and less colourful, claims about economic management. There is revealing evidence within the two MORI pre-election polls to suggest that minority voters were rather more likely to be influenced by the mainstream, non-ethnic campaigns of each of the major parties. The cultural card, therefore, may have had the effect of flattery without persuasion.

Ultimately, the Conservatives will have derived a considerable morale boost from the one in four Asians who planned to support them shown in the MORI survey. This figure is likely to be used to justify continuing efforts in this direction. In turn, it also reveals a side to the 1997 'ethnic campaign' which was evidently geared to the long term. In launching such a high-profile bid to attract such an unpromising group of voters, the Conservative aim perhaps was to lay the foundations of future encroachment on to this territory. Much was made during the 1990s of Mr Major's own belief in the viability of good race relations in Britain, and in these terms it is probable that his chief aim was to hand on to his successor reasonable odds of winning minority supporters. A notion of 'pipeline politics' was at work, which sought to convert today's Conservative sympathisers and identifiers into tomorrow's Conservative voters.[11] To be sure, fully one in five of all Asians believed that their outlook on politics in 1997 was 'more Conservative than [their] parents'', implying a genuine belief at the centre of Tory propaganda drives about the potential of younger, affluent minorities.[12] A post-election initiative to try to recruit larger numbers of minorities on to the Party's official list of approved candidates indicates that some within its ranks are moving to more serious tactics to ensure that the support of younger blacks and Asians can come on stream in future elections.[13]

Smoking guns and race cards

Thus far, we have looked at the racial dimension of the 1997 election purely in terms of the calculus of party competition for the votes of minorities. Needless to say race and electoral politics are most often associated with one another because of a historically proven track record of party exploitation of anti-immigrant and anti-minority sentiment. The contests of 1964, 1970 and 1979 are three notable cases in point.

The long run-up to the 1997 election was characterised by renewed speculation along these lines. The logic of a deeply unpopular Conservative administration turning cynically to win over voters by appealing to this sentiment could not be denied according to much informed opinion on the subject. Indeed, it was remembered that a short while after the surprise 1992 triumph, a leading Conservative strategist had accepted openly that victory had been won by negative campaigning on Labour's supposed weakness on the immigration issue.[14] The question of the Conservative race card and its deployment, therefore, became a very tangible indicator of the electoral death – or otherwise – of race in 1997.

The evidence from the 1997 campaign is consequently that much more surprising and significant. For one thing, the hints during the 1992–97 Parliament that the Conservatives would choose to play the card were both plentiful and generally reliable. After all, a bone of contention during the Parliament had been the Government's 1993 Asylum and Immigration Appeals Act followed by the drawn-out attempt to pass further legislation on asylum between 1995 and 1996. A mid-term attempt to raise the immigration issue, in terms that tried to contrast Tory efforts with alleged Labour weakness, was warmly greeted by Tory supporters in the press who had grown impatient with the leadership's re-election strategy. A move in late 1995 by the Labour leadership to kick the issue into touch – by seeking to have the Asylum Bill examined by an *ad hoc* Commons committee – reinforced the belief amongst Tory strategists that immigration would be an exceptional vote winner. Finally, it had been widely rumoured both before and during the formal campaign that Michael Howard had wanted to emphasise the immigration issue but had been overruled by John Major. The Home Secretary's standing populist instincts may have been fuelled by a more than glancing interest in the probable Conservative succession question. The conclusion drawn by many observers against this backdrop was that the electoral death of race had been greatly exaggerated.

A barkless dog

In the event the hints served to point attention in the wrong direction. The 1997 election plainly by-passed the race card on all relevant measures. Tellingly, virtually the only Conservative reference to immigration stemmed from the solitary voice of Nicholas Budgen, a right-wing hawk on the issue who went on to lose his Wolverhampton seat. Budgen made great play of the need for Conservative candidates to raise immigration as an issue in their personal addresses to their electorates. His intervention found two non-responses: first, the predicted stampede of Conservative candidates to his cause turned out to be an insignificant handful, and second, the Party leadership reacted with striking indifference. The former is more noteworthy since grassroots membership views on immigration, with which candidates might be expected to be in fairly close touch, continue to be notoriously hardline. A survey carried out in the early 1990s highlighted the issue to be anything but dead in Party members' eyes.[15]

As regards the Party leadership, several factors can be identified to explain the misfit with the Budgen intervention. The most important would appear to be the role of the Party leader in shaping – and impeding – a suitable climate for the race card scenario. John Major's reputation on race relations was a notable topic of discussion, especially in his early days as Premier. One element in this, it was believed, had been his early experience in local politics (Lambeth) in which he had bravely fought off his Party's anti-immigrant wing. Major therefore had much to live up to, and it was perhaps rather likely that he would show indecision on this issue as on so many others. In any case, a Major veto of sorts was exercised to curb, possibly kill, any planned moves to raise immigration as an election issue.

Another factor behind the barkless dog was that, all told, immigration was no longer the reliable issue it had once been for the Conservatives. That is not to say that the Party did not enjoy a clear lead over Labour on the issue, but rather that immigration mattered rather less to the electorate than it had once.[16] To be certain, no major poll was published in 1996–97 that included immigration as a 'Top Ten' issue of concern to the electorate. The passion that had been seen over the issue in the 1960s and 1970s no longer existed. Issue saliency of a much higher order than this remains a minimum condition for issue voting. To that end, the Conservatives' and Major's decision not to play immigration was based on a sound assessment of its likely impact. However, this may be to read the issue in excessively narrow terms. The Budgen line, for instance, may have not been aiming at the immigration controversies of the past but rather at today's rather more visible rows over Britain's relations with her European neighbours. After all, Budgen would not have been the first to attempt to draw such a parallel. It is worth noting that Budgen had originally been the protégé of Enoch Powell, who had held the same seat. Significantly, the latter's only intervention in the 1997 election was to issue a statement endorsing Budgen and his anti-immigration, anti-Europe stance.

A final factor is the question of whether the tactic would have been counter-productive. Immigration is supposedly one of a package of issues on which the Conservatives are said to enjoy a natural edge: crime, law and order and trade union rights being other key parts of the whole. However, the core impact of these issues is often observed in indirect terms, that is, as a secondary or subsidiary line of persuasion to deter Labour floaters.[17] The Conservatives can, under these second line terms of electoral engagement, hope to put off a large slice of their opponents' would-be supporters. The key point is that it is comparatively difficult to play the race card as a primary issue for the re-election of a Tory administration. In 1997 the futility of immigration as a primary issue was undeniable. If the chief aim was to raise a large question mark about Labour's trust and competence (on immigration), the task took on absurd proportions when prosecuted by a party that was fighting hard to defend its own trust and competence credentials on a much wider range of issues (economic management, sleaze and party unity, to name just three). Reliance on the race card as part of a primary campaign issue, in these circumstances, would have taken on an appearance of desperation and been correspondingly counter-productive (rather like, once again, the Euro-sceptic card turned out to be).

The upshot of this is that, whatever drove the Conservatives to drop immigration as an issue in 1997, they did so in a context in which several coherent arguments could be raised to justify the Party's chosen strategy. It would not take much to alter these assumptions. For one thing, the prospects for exploiting immigration ought to be rather stronger assuming (i) a different style of party leadership, (ii) the reservoir of Euro-hostility in the electorate is expanded to think of itself in openly xenophobic terms, and (iii) a closer election contest that would permit the inclusion of immigration as a Conservative secondary line of defence. None of these assumptions would be considered to be particularly reliable after the May 1997 rout.

Representation dilemmas

Following the successful election ten years ago of four ethnic minority MPs, it was widely thought that a new era in minority representation had opened. For so long, minority activists within and minority supporters of the Labour Party had argued that their votes had been taken for granted. The arrival of black and Asian parliamentarians, it was believed, would start to equalise and calm this often tense relationship. The only obstacle that potentially stood in the way was the frequent association between many minority activists and the urban left, the latter often the source of embarrassment to the Party leadership.

A decade on, it is apparent that this initial perspective seems curiously simplistic. For one thing, the role of municipal socialism in advancing the political careers of minority representatives has caused few problems, contrary to the Party's expectations during the late 1980s. Instead, the source of most of the Party's difficulties has been the question of the role of its ethnic minority membership, especially in relation to securing candidacies in promising Labour-held seats. Indeed, a succession of high-profile and damaging rows in a number of Labour constituency parties regularly punctuated the 1992–97 Parliament. The common thread running through them was the allegation that black and Asian members had hijacked local parties in order to push through minority nominations. Allegations of corruption, vote-rigging and intimidation typically followed, and many cases such as Glasgow Govan, Birmingham Sparkbrook and Small Heath and Manchester Gorton local associations found themselves under investigation from Party headquarters.

The Conservatives, by contrast, managed to keep a low profile on the thorny issue of minority representatives at this time. The divisiveness of the issue was recalled only too vividly by many within the Party who had witnessed the

John Taylor episode prior to the 1992 election. The unwritten rule from that turbulent case was that the Party's Central Office intervened in local selection affairs at great cost. That said, the Party's largely devolved selection process meant that where local opposition to a minority candidate could be successfully orchestrated, the national Party would be comparatively powerless to deflect embarrassment and damage. The racial element in the Taylor case meant that, whatever the Party leadership's desire to have minorities selected as candidates in winnable seats, it would have to take a back seat as far as the 1997 election went. Accordingly, no black or Asian hopefuls succeeded in gaining adoption in premium constituencies. Eight of the eleven Conservative candidates fielded desperately hopeless constituencies in which the huge defeat suffered by their Party nationally scarcely mattered. A further two fought contests against Labour rivals holding single-figure notional majorities and one might speculate that a good national result could have put either in reach of victory. In the event, massive swings against both (broadly in line with their respective regional averages), meant that they were discarded on to a tall heap of also rans. The single Tory incumbent – with a slim notional majority – found himself thrown out on a swing even greater than the Greater London average. Table 10.5 provides the details of contests involving incumbent MPs and successful ethnic-minority candidates.

The bleak picture for minority would-be MPs in the Conservative Party might be neutralised by a Party leadership responding to a minimal minority membership. One study has shown this membership no higher than 1 per cent, though slowly growing.[18] In the case of Labour, however, no such neutralisation option existed. Accordingly, the 1997 election featured a near doubling of the numbers of minorities in attractive seats, an increase that notably had occurred in the absence of any positive action mechanisms for selection (such as all-women shortlists involving female candidates). As Table 10.5 shows, eight black and Asian Labour candidates faced almost certain victory (including five incumbents). A ninth (Kumar) was returned in addition on the back of a swing entirely in line with his Party's regional performance. It was widely known that he had faced numerous battles in challenging assumptions amongst his Party's constituency activists equating minority candidacy with areas of high minority concentration (just 0.4 per cent of his constituents are ethnic minorities).

The telling aspect of Table 10.5 appears to be the varying fortunes of minority Labour candidates. The most startling of these was the substantial erosion in Labour's lead endured by King in the East End. The story is easy enough to decipher. The decision by both opposing parties to field ethnic Bengali candidates served to squeeze Labour from both sides on the strength of fairly powerful ethnic loyalties amongst a largely Bengali electorate. Elsewhere, Singh's candidature in Bradford experienced a similar fate with his main rival, Riaz, attracting a strong following from fellow Muslims. In Glasgow,

Table 10.5 Performance of ethnic-minority incumbent MPs and successful candidates (Conservative and Labour) 1997

Candidate and change in party's share of vote		Constituency	1992 result and majority (%)	1997 result and majority	1992–97 swing (%)
Labour (9)					
D. Abbott [a]	+ 6.4	Hackney N. & Stoke New'ton	Lab/30.9	Lab/47.6	8.3
P. Boateng [a]	+15.4	Brent S	Lab/26.5	Lab/57.1	15.3
B. Grant [a]	+13.2	Tottenham	Lab/26.7	Lab/53.6	13.4
P. Khabra [a]	+14.7	Ealing Southall	Lab/9.0	Lab/39.2	15.1
O. King [b]	−7.2	Bethnal Green & Bow	Lab/27.7	Lab/25.3	5.9 [e]
A. Kumar [b]	+11.4	Mid'boro S & Cleveland E	Con/2.4	Lab/19.8	11.1
M. Sarwar [b]	+1.1	Glasgow Govan	Lab/15.4	Lab/9.0	2.4 [d]
M. Singh [b]	−11.7	Bradford W	Lab/19.4	Lab/8.5	5.5 [e]
K. Vaz [a]	9.0	Leicester E	Lab/22.8	Lab/41.5	9.4
Conservative (1)					
N. Deva [c]	−13.7	Brentford & Isleworth	Con/2.8	Lab/25.7	14.3

Notes:
[a] Re-elected incumbent
[b] Newly elected
[c] Defeated incumbent
All swings shown are Con to Lab, unless indicated as follows:
[d] Lab to SNP
[e] Lab to Con

Sources: Author's calculations based on: 'Election results 1997', *The Times*, 3 May 1997; 'British parliamentary constituencies 1992–97' (data set compiled by P. Norris); and P. Norris, *UK Election Results: New Constituency Boundaries* (Cambridge, Mass.: Harvard University Press, 1996).

Sarwar, though elected, made little headway against an exceptionally strong campaign from the SNP, which had once held the seat.

Ethnic penalties and dividends

Generalisations about minority candidate performance – even for Labour alone – are very difficult as a consequence. Take for instance the complicating factor of the five Labour incumbents. In three cases (Boateng, Grant and Khabra) very strong local performances ensured that existing safe majorities were transformed into very substantial ones. Why this incumbency benefit was not shared in the cases of Abbott (also defending a London seat) and Vaz (who had established a tangible personal following in Leicester) seems a bit of a puzzle. It would seem that many minority candidates, even successful ones, often encounter an ethnic penalty of sorts, especially when first returned (though some – Grant and Abbott, for example – had been entangled in bitter selection contests which resulted in a demoralising impact on their local activists). This was true of many in the 1987 and 1992 intake, and 1997 was no exception. However, the encouraging news seems to be that, in many cases, established MPs can turn in performances that are not merely credible but often rather impressive. If minority candidates are an electoral liability, on the evidence from 1997 it is far from clear in what sense and to what degree this dictum applies. In many cases, from all three major parties, it simply does not apply.

The prominence of candidate selection and representation in the Labour Party means that race is far from silent as a factor.[19] The rows of recent years over 'ethnic entryism' are unlikely to fade away, especially if the arguments continue over Labour taking minority support for granted. The Conservatives for the time being have managed to dampen interest in the matter, but this shows all the signs of a temporary arrangement. To be sure, in the longer run it will be hard for the Party to extend its drive for minority supporters (and sponsors) without registering the need to see clear progress in the selection and election of minority representatives.

Conclusion

To recap, the conventional view prior to the election was that race mattered to a very limited degree, and then only in a fairly predictable range of constituencies. The immigration question, meanwhile, could be re-ignited on the back of a Conservative race card which many felt increasingly probable as the election approached. The picture therefore was one of electoral slumber, with very, very few conscious references to race by any of the leading parties either before or during the campaign.

The 1997 general election followed remarkably few elements of this pattern. To argue that race and immigration did not matter – as a purist interpretation of the 'electoral death' thesis might – would be a lopsided and imperfect account. The continuing, and arguably surprising, electoral significance of race in 1997 can be demonstrated on three grounds.

First, despite the electoral silence of the race card in the 1997 campaign, it is improbable that the political temptation of exploiting anti-immigrant feeling has been completely removed from the landscape. It is plain that the single biggest factor neutralising the race card in 1997 was the influence of an otherwise weak and demoralised leader and this alone might be enough to provide a sharply different scenario at a future election. It is true that since the early 1980s the British electorate have shown very little interest in the issue of immigration. However, this may disguise a picture in which the issue had lain dormant for half a generation. The possibility that it may be re-invoked on the crest of anti-European sentiment cannot be ruled out altogether.

Second, the 1997 election revealed that the competition for minority political loyalties has in many ways only just begun. The Conservatives' effort had many lines of internal justification. Ultimately, however, the 'ethnic campaign' was motivated by two interrelated observations: first, that Labour's monopoly must, in principle, be breakable, even in the long run; and second, that the precedent for rightward drift had already been established mid-century by the Jewish community. The Conservatives in 1997 made few attempts to disguise the ethnic basis of their campaign and in many ways the Party could be criticised for believing that ethnicity alone mattered for minority voters. Much of the empirical evidence here suggests that it does not. Future Conservative initiatives are therefore more likely to reap dividends if the Party courts its target group – middle-class Asians – without dwelling too much on the fashionable yet superficial cultural thesis. In any case, the Conservatives in 1997 ensured that the electoral disappearance of race was perhaps the last thing on their minds when appealing to black and Asian voters.

Finally, the trajectory of minority candidates standing for the major parties followed an expected and encouraging pattern. The number of minorities in the Commons today remains in single figures but the upward slope is unmistakable. The fact that this representation is now entirely on the Labour benches means that renewed pressure will be placed on the Conservatives and Liberal Democrats to make up this deficit. The race issue appeared to count for little or nothing in constituency battles beyond those forty-four seats in which a minority candidate was fielded. As such, very little broad grassroots electoral significance could be attached to the issue. Noticeably in all cases bar one the successful minority candidates were returned by constituencies containing sizeable minority electorates. The impression that race counts for ethnic minorities alone is further underlined.

The sole exception to this pattern, Kumar in Middlesbrough, is a powerful one none the less. In this case, a minority candidate effectively demonstrated his broad electoral appeal in a largely white constituency. However, this success was not bought at the price of racial invisibility and, as a consequence, it is clear that minority candidates have the potential to enter the mainstream. This is largely a question of the *political integration* of ethnic minorities. Progress on these lines is poorly linked with the electoral death of race and immigration and arguably signals the next stage in the relationship between British racial and electoral politics.

Notes

1 The term 'ethnic minority' is used more or less interchangeably with 'minority' throughout this chapter. These descriptive terms amount to shorthand for the various non-white groups identified in the 1991 General Census, the principal components of which were South Asians (Indians, Pakistanis, Bangladeshis, Sri

Lankans) and blacks (black Africans and black Caribbeans). The reader should take care to note that, whilst a lively academic and political debate exists on issues of race, ethnicity and nomenclature, no particular political or sociological inference should be attached to this chapter's use of these terms.

2 An ethnic minority booster sample, designed by Shamit Saggar (QMW) and Anthony Heath (Nuffield), was integrated into the 1997 BES cross-section. Fuller and more reliable evidence of any such differential swing will depend on the results of the 1997 BES. These data are scheduled for wider release in early 1998.

3 S. Saggar, *Race and Politics in Britain* (Hemel Hempstead: Harvester Wheatsheaf, 1992).

4 Calculated from P. Norris, *UK Election Results: New Constituency Boundaries* (Cambridge, Mass.: Harvard University Press, 1996).

5 *The Runnymede Trust Bulletin*, no. 301, March 1997.

6 A. Ali and G. Percival, *Race and Representation: Ethnic Minorities and the 1992 Elections* (London: CRE, 1993).

7 Harris Research Centre, 'Political attitudes amongst ethnic minorities', unpublished data set JN98746 (Richmond: Harris, 1987); Harris Research Centre, 'Asian poll 1991', unpublished data set JN99245 (Richmond: Harris, 1991).

8 M. Le Lohe, 'Participation in elections by Asians in Bradford', in I. Crewe (ed.), *The Political Sociology Yearbook*, Volume Two: *The Politics of Race* (London: Croom Helm, 1975).

9 *Guardian*, 8 July 1996.

10 A. Messina, 'Ethnic minorities and the British party system in the 1990s and beyond', in S. Saggar (ed.), *Race and British Electoral Politics* (London: UCL Press, 1997); A. Heath, R. Jowell and J. Curtice, *Understanding Political Change* (Oxford: Pergamon Press, 1991).

11 S. Saggar, 'Pipeline politics', *India Today*, 31 March 1997.

12 MORI, 'Asian voting: preliminary results', unpublished notes, February 1997.

13 *The Times*, 5 June 1997.

14 A. Lansley, 'Accentuate the negative to win again', *Observer*, 3 September 1995.

15 P. Whiteley, P. Seyd and J. Richardson, *True Blues: The Politics of Conservative Party Membership* (Oxford: Clarendon Press, 1994).

16 I. Crewe, 'The disturbing truth behind Labour's rout', *Guardian*, 13 June 1983.

17 S. Saggar, 'Can political parties play the "race card" in general elections? The 1992 poll revisited', *New Community*, 19 (1993): 693–9.

18 Whiteley, Seyd and Richardson, *True Blues*.

19 A. Geddes, 'Inequality, political opportunity and ethnic minority parliamentary candidacy', in Saggar, *Race and British Electoral Politics*.

Bethnal Green and Bow

Since the election of Diane Abbott, Paul Boateng, Bernie Grant and Keith Vaz as Labour MPs in 1987, the rate of increase in levels of representation of Britain's black and Asian population has been low: under-representation of Britain's ethnic minorities remains a marked feature of British politics. The 1997 general election presented an opportunity for this under-representation to be tackled. However, the issues associated with ethnic minority representation are far from straightforward, as the case of Oona King in Bethnal Green and Bow demonstrated.

Bethnal Green and Bow is an area with a history of ethnic diversity stretching back hundreds of years. When the former Labour cabinet minister Peter Shore announced his decision to retire a controversial selection contest to seek his replacement ensued. Eventually Oona King was chosen. King's father is African-American and her mother a British Jew. However, despite King's selection potentially boosting the number of women MPs from ethnic minorities (albeit from one to two), her selection provoked resentment from within the local Bengali Muslim population who thought that a member of their community should have been selected for the seat. In the Bethnal Green and Bow constituency 29.1 per cent of the population are of Bengali origin. As is often the case with inner-city constituencies, Bethnal Green and Bow also found itself at the wrong end of almost every social indicator: for example, in the top ten for unemployment and the bottom ten for car ownership.

Both the Conservatives and Liberal Democrats chose Bengalis to contest the seat. However, local Labour activists had been unable to agree on Shore's successor and King had emerged as a compromise candidate. She secured selection following a very strong performance at the final selection meeting. One anonymous Labour activist even went so far as to claim that King's selection was a 'disaster for our community' (*Guardian*, 4 April 1997). King also faced opposition from the racist British National Party. The extreme right has traditionally done relatively well in the East End of London. Bethnal Green and Bow was one of the four constituencies in which the BNP held its deposit in 1997. The most significant aspect of the Bethnal Green result was the swing to the Conservative candidate Kabir Choudhury of 5.9 per cent, which indicates the dissension within the local Bengali community. King will have to build bridges during her first term to win over disenchanted local activists, but such is the strength of support for Labour in this part of east London that her seat in the Commons looks extremely secure.

Result

Bethnal Green and Bow			
Oona King	Lab	20,697	
Kabir Choudhury	Con	9,412	
Syed Nural Islam	Lib Dem	5,361	
David King	BNP	3,350	
	Others	5,862	
Total vote		44,862	Turnout 61.20%
Lab majority		11,285	
Lab hold			
Swing Lab to Con 5.9%			

11

Women in the campaign and in the Commons

Lucy Peake

Introduction

Labour's landslide was also a breakthrough for women as the number of women MPs rose to 120. Before the 1997 election only 168 women had ever been elected. The result was even heralded as 'a women's revolution'.[1] The election also closed the 'gender gap' in voting because women and men supported the main political parties in equal proportions. Equally important, for the first time since women were enfranchised in 1918, and Nancy Astor became the first woman MP to take her seat in the House of Commons in 1919, women were recognised *both* as a critical force as voters and as a significant and visible group in Parliament. However, as we will see, women politicians were, in the main, conspicuous by their absence from the national campaigns of the main political parties.

In this chapter, the election is analysed as a long and complicated drama acted out on a political stage. Women are participants throughout – behind the scenes, on the stage, and in the audience. Gender issues are present during every scene, although their prominence varies. The political actors and script (issues) are selected and presented by the political parties, and critically evaluated by the media. The spectacular finale when women MPs became so visible largely eclipsed the election campaign, but in this chapter the stage curtains are pulled back to assess the gender issues which reached the agenda and the reasons why they gained prominence. The chapter's first section will examine the gender gap in more detail. After this, the responses of the political parties to these issues will be considered, as will participation by women in both parliamentary candidate selection processes and the election itself. Finally, the significance of the election results will be assessed for women as voters, the political parties, the new Labour Government, and the political system more generally.

The gender gap

Prior to the campaign, a number of studies combined existing academic research on women's voting patterns, opinion poll evidence, and new data from interviews and focus groups to point out that the political parties were failing to appeal to women voters and suggest that women's votes would be crucial at the 1997 general election. The 'What Women Want on Politics' survey compared the views of almost 10,000 women with the policies of the main political parties and found that women's political priorities differed markedly from those offered by political parties.[2] The study concluded that, although the parties acknowledge gender differences in their documents aimed at women, they seemed unable to incorporate these issues into their central documents and speeches. It is hardly surprising that women felt their priorities were marginalised or ignored. These findings were reinforced in February 1997 when the Equal Opportunities Commission published an NOP survey which showed that 70 per cent of women felt that political parties did not pay enough attention to issues women thought were important. These findings suggested that (i) political parties had neglected women voters, and (ii) women's votes could be crucial to the outcome of the general election. The parties clearly had a considerable incentive to court women's votes in the election campaign. The gender gap was propelled to centre-stage.

It is important to remember that women make up a larger percentage of the electorate than men: women form 52 per cent of the population. Women are also more likely to vote than men. In 1992, 82 per cent of women voted, compared with 79 per cent of men, a difference of over 1 million votes.[3] In September 1996, the Fawcett Society published a report called *Winning Women's Votes* which showed that women and men differed in terms of voting intentions and number of floating voters.[4] This pointed to a gender gap, although there had actually been a gender gap in voting in Britain since 1945. Women were more likely to vote Conservative. For instance, at the 1983 general election the Conservatives had a twenty-point lead over Labour amongst women and a twelve-point advantage amongst men (a gender gap of eight points). In 1987, the gender gap closed for the first time, only to reopen in 1992 in the Conservatives' favour. Although the press reported that it was 'Essex man' who had given the Conservatives their election victory, the votes of women made a substantial contribution to Tory success.

More detailed analysis has shown that the gender gap is actually rather complex and differs by age, occupation, social class and region. For instance, Pippa Norris examined the 'gender–generation gap' after the 1992 general election and showed that the gap was reversed by generation. Younger women favoured Labour and older women preferred the Conservatives.[5] In 1996, a MORI poll provided further evidence of this gender–generation gap: amongst women aged between eighteen and twenty-four the gender gap was three points in Labour's favour, whereas amongst thirty-five to fifty-four-year-old women, the gender gap was fourteen points in the Conservatives' direction.[6] This presented more problems to Labour than were immediately apparent: women in the eighteen to twenty-four age group comprise a far smaller proportion of the total electorate than women over the age of thirty-five. In 1992, women aged over sixty-five contributed 1.9 million votes to the total of 14 million gained by the Conservatives. In addition, younger women were less likely to vote than older women. However, the potential volatility of the women's vote was emphasised by a 1996 MORI poll which showed that 23 per cent of women compared to 16 per cent of men had yet to decide which party to support.[7] These figures provided compelling evidence that, if the parties could convince that they were committed to addressing issues of concern to women, electoral rewards could be reaped.

Interest in women's votes in the national press in the run-up to the election was unprecedented. The Fawcett Society and the Women's Communication Centre drew media attention to the gender gap by popularising already available information and updating it with opinion poll data. The results of the US presidential elections in November 1996 helped to convince some journalists that the gender gap was a story worth pursuing. President Clinton received 18 per cent more support amongst women than his Republican opponent, Bob Dole. The possibility that 'Worcester woman' – the archetypal female middle Briton – could decide the results of the British election became more tangible. The gender gap was also a sufficiently malleable notion to allow newspapers of different political persuasions to run variations on the same story. For example, the *Daily Express* ran the headline 'Inside every woman lies a natural Conservative' whilst the *Daily Mirror* proclaimed that 'Young women hold the key to a Labour victory'.[8]

An examination of the political parties' responses since the 1980s demonstrates awareness of the gender gap and a perceived need to address it. Internal research on women's voting had been undertaken and various strategies had been implemented. Even so, the efforts of the three main parties varied enormously as the following assessment of their campaigns, their candidate selection procedures, and the election results will show.

Women in the campaign: neither seen nor heard

All the main parties produced specific documents or sections of their manifestos for women: the Labour Party's 'Strategy for Women', the Liberal Democrats' 'Fair Deal for Women', the 'Opportunities for Women' section of the Conservative manifesto; but during the campaign women's issues were far less visible.

Labour policy-makers and strategists had spent years contemplating ways of increasing the Party's appeal to women after discovering that women perceived Labour to be 'masculine', and that this was a barrier to electoral success. Worryingly for Labour, more women identified with the Party on issues than actually voted for it. If Labour was to attract women's votes it needed to 'feminise' its image and consider the perspectives of women in policy-making and presentation of policy. In 1996 an attempt to gather women's political perspectives was made by Labour's 'Listening to Women' roadshow. Tessa Jowell, then Shadow Minister for Women, held meetings around Britain where women were invited to discuss issues of importance to them. The findings were published just ahead of the election campaign by Janet Anderson, who had become the Shadow Minister for Women. In her statement, she contended that political parties must try to incorporate both 'women's issues', which are issues which affect women more than men (such as stalking legislation), and 'women's perspectives' (for example, as women use public transport more frequently than men, any changes in policy would be likely to affect women and men differently).

Labour's 'War Book' – a leaked version of which was released to the media by the Conservatives in the penultimate week of the campaign – identified key target audiences: the most important group were swing voters, and the second most important were women. Labour aimed to attract women voters through policy initiatives and better presentation. During the campaign, Tony Blair made a highly publicised appeal to women voters on a key women's issue when he pledged that a Labour Government would spend £10 million to create a national network of centres for diagnosing breast cancer.

To present its more feminised image, as well as target women voters, Labour made imaginative use of women's magazines. IPC initiated this new development in political campaigning when it approached Labour's advertising agency, BMP, and the Conservatives' agency, MC Saatchi.[9] Only Labour responded: it spent £120,000 on 'advertorials' in best-selling women's magazines, including *Woman* and *Take a Break*. Tony Blair was interviewed in *Woman's Own*, and Jacqui Smith recorded her experiences as the Labour candidate for Redditch in the May edition of *Vogue*. Labour identified women as a key target audience and also recognised that women voters are not a homogeneous group. Labour's campaign could be seen as a perceptive marketing initiative as different groups of women could be targeted according to magazine readership profiles. However, Labour's strategy may also suggest that women were seen as a market niche detached from mainstream politics because, although women's issues and women politicians were given space in women's magazines, women were far less visible in the national media.

One of the key proposals in the Conservative manifesto was to allow married couples to transfer their tax allowances if one of them stayed at home. John Major hailed this initiative 'as both encouraging couples to marry and also giving a strong fiscal incentive for married women to stay at home and look after their children'.[10] The Conservative manifesto sent conflicting messages to women – the section on 'Opportunities for Women' indicated that the Party hoped to appeal to women voters who felt they had benefited from eighteen years of Conservative Government. It began by stating that 'Women have a better education, more financial independence and more opportunity than at any other time in Britain's history', and praised the successes of the 'Opportunity 2000' programme.[11] However, Major's tax proposals, coupled with Conservative rhetoric of 'Back to Basics', suggested that the Conservatives would prefer (married) women to stay at home, rather than benefit from opportunities in the workplace and education which were celebrated in their manifesto.

The Liberal Democrats, like Labour, sought to run a more 'women-friendly campaign'. Paddy Ashdown's aides claimed that he would present an alternative style to Major and Blair as he would 'listen rather than hector, suggest rather than assert and tell the truth rather than dissemble'. The *Independent* ran the headline 'Ashdown shuns machismo to catch the female vote', and claimed that 'Mr Ashdown will try for statesmanlike humility with the odd giggle thrown in. He believes that the cockfighting tactics of the other party leaders are a turn-off to voters in general, and to women in particular.'[12]

The simultaneous incorporation and marginalisation of women's issues by all the main parties were exemplified when Baroness Williams held a number of sparsely attended and poorly reported press conferences on the Liberal Democrats' 'Fair Deal for Women'. She argued that all Liberal Democrat policies were underpinned by their belief in equality of opportunity, which showed their commitment to women in all of their key policies of health, education, employment (maternity leave, and family leave for women and men), split pensions on divorce, child care, crime prevention, and a carers' charter, as well as reform of the House of Commons.

In addition to these policy-related discussions, there was also speculation about influences on women's voting. Rather ludicrously, it was suggested that women would be more likely to vote for Tony Blair if he adopted a 'less bouffant' hairstyle. On more substantive matters, experienced women politicians, including Clare Short, Dame Angela Rumbold and Baroness Williams, argued that women dislike adversarial 'yah-boo' politics, which is reinforced by media reporting.

A party seeking to present a more feminised image might ensure that women politicians were present at news conferences, on party election broadcasts, on poster advertising, and on party literature delivered directly to voters. During the election campaign the parties tried to present a more feminised image, but women politicians were scarcely visible on the national campaign stage. In order to investigate this question of the visibility of women during the campaign, the Fawcett Society monitored daily election news broadcasts on BBC1, BBC2, ITV and Channel 4 between 4 April and 10 April.[13] The number of appearances of contributors, presenters and journalists was tallied and divided by gender. The results in Table 11.1 show under-representation of women in media reporting of the campaign: women politicians made up a meagre 4.5 per cent of appearances. A Loughborough University-based study of the whole campaign emphasises this point: women made just 7 per cent of all media appearances.[14]

Table 11.1 Appearances by politicians on national news programmes 4–10 April 1997

Appearances	*Number*
Total appearances (men and women)	177
Male politicians (including party leaders)	169
Male politicians (excluding party leaders)	127
Female politicians	8

Source: Fawcett Society.

During the campaign few women politicians played prominent roles. Women who might have been expected to take a leading role were sidelined. For example, John Major encroached on Gillian Shephard's education portfolio. Other women were visible during the election campaign, but for non-political reasons. After Labour's manifesto launch, Mo Mowlam was cruelly mocked by some national newspapers about her weight gain. Following disclosure that she had been suffering from a brain tumour, the press reversed its stance and spent two days in sympathy.

Women candidates: the marginal seat effect

When assessing a woman's candidacy, the influence of local party activists who select candidates and act as 'gatekeepers' to Parliament is crucial. In the past, party recruitment procedures have not facilitated the entry of women into supposedly representative political institutions such as the House of Commons, as Table 11.2 shows.

The dearth of women MPs has been explained as the result of 'supply and demand' deficiencies in the market for parliamentary candidates.[15] On the supply side, a shortage of sufficiently well qualified women making applications would hinder women's representation. Dame Angela Rumbold, the former Conservative Vice-Chairman in charge of candidate selection pointed to supply-side problems when she said that: 'The problem is the women haven't come forward in sufficient numbers. I think that's because a lot of professional women who would make good MPs say can I give up my career for something that is much less certain – a five year contract, so to speak.'[16]

On the demand side, candidate selectors may discriminate against women, either directly or indirectly, as a result of their own perceptions of candidates' background and experience. Jacqui Smith (Labour, Redditch) describes how 'supply and demand' constraints can actually work in tandem, but also have positive effects once levels of representation begin to increase:

> It is obvious that people have tended to select MPs who are in the image of existing MPs, and until you get a critical mass, it is difficult for the world to recognise that women can be MPs. But the big change in the [Labour] Party has been that, whilst you used to hear people saying they

Table 11.2 Women MPs 1945–1997

General election	*Con*	*Lab*	*Other*	*Total*	*%*
1945	1	21	2	24	3.8
1950	6	14	1	21	3.4
1951	6	11	–	17	2.7
1955	10	14	–	24	3.8
1959	12	13	–	25	4.0
1964	11	18	–	29	4.6
1966	7	19	–	26	4.1
1970	15	10	1	26	4.1
1974, Feb.	9	13	1	23	3.6
1974, Oct.	7	18	2	27	4.3
1979	8	11	–	19	3.0
1983	13	10	–	23	3.5
1987	17	21	3	41	6.3
1992	20	37	3	60	9.2
1997	15	101	6 (inc. Speaker)	120	18.2

Source: F. W. S. Craig (ed.), *British Electoral Facts 1832–1987* (Aldershot: Dartmouth, 1989); *The Times Guides to the House of Commons 1987, 1992* (Chichester: Parliamentary Research Services); and author's calculations.

would like to select a good woman if only they could, there is no way anyone would say that today. We know that there are so many good women coming into the selection process.[17]

The political parties have adopted three main strategies to try to increase women's presence in the House of Commons.[18] First, rhetorical support is offered. For example, spokespersons will make reference to the importance of increasing the number of women in the House of Commons. The Conservatives have preferred rhetoric rather than intervention: women should be encouraged to stand, and Party members should be encouraged to select them, but the recruitment process has to be 'fair' and involve open competition. The deficiencies of rhetorical strategies are shown by the experience of a woman Conservative candidate:

> Central Office is doing a tremendous amount to encourage associations to select women. It's falling down at the stage when it goes to the general membership ... Women who have got into safe Conservative seats have not had children ... the type of people voting are generally middle-aged, middle-class, probably from the fifties and sixties age groups. If you look at that generation, they don't understand that women now have careers and children ... Until you make that cultural leap, from the people who

are selecting the candidates through to people who understand the extent to which women have a role in the workplace now, you're never going to get that change.[19]

Second, positive or affirmative action may be used. Political parties or organisations may provide special training for women applicants and candidates. For example, the '300 Group', 'Labour Women's Network', the women's organisation in Conservative Central Office, and 'Emily's List' all provide training for women. 'Emily's List' provided financial support for women Labour candidates during the 1997 election campaign, provided they were 'pro-choice'. Targets may also be set. The Liberal Democrats aimed for shortlists containing at least 33 per cent women.

The third strategy, positive discrimination, makes the representation of women (or other under-represented groups) compulsory by, for example, establishing all-women shortlists. The 1993 Labour Party Conference agreed to use such lists to ensure that women candidates were selected in half of the Party's safe and winnable seats prior to the 1997 general election. Labour aimed to reach a target of 100 women MPs after the election – and did. However, all-women shortlists were very controversial. Not surprisingly, the Conservatives and Liberal Democrats denounced the policy. For the Conservatives, David Hunt, then chair of the cabinet committee on women, claimed that 'Labour's fixation with window dressing just grows more embarrassing.' Diana Maddock, the former Liberal Democrat spokesperson on women's issues called for 'equal treatment for women, not special treatment. Our aim is equality of opportunity, not equality of outcome.'[20]

Within the Labour Party, opponents claimed that positive discrimination was undemocratic and discriminatory because male candidates were by-passed due to their sex. In January 1996, two aspiring male Labour candidates successfully challenged the policy at an industrial tribunal. This ruled that Labour had breached sex discrimination laws in preventing men from entering a profession. The thirty-five women who had been selected on all-women shortlists remained in place, but the mechanism was suspended in seats where selection had yet to be completed. The women's group of Labour's National Executive Committee reverted to a combination of rhetoric and positive action.

Being selected as a parliamentary candidate is not enough. It is also important that selection occurs in a seat where there is a realistic chance of victory. Because of all-women shortlists, more Labour women candidates than ever before were selected for safe or winnable seats at the 1997 general election. In total, Labour selected 159 women candidates: fourteen were selected in vacant Labour-held seats, ten required a swing to Labour of less than 2 per cent, eleven needed a swing of 2–4 per cent, eighteen needed a 4–8 per cent swing, and sixty-six needed a swing greater than 8 per cent. In contrast, the Conservatives selected sixty-seven women candidates, just five of whom were selected in their fifty-eight vacant seats. Moreover, women Conservative candidates were selected in less winnable seats (compounded, of course, by the dramatic anti-Conservative swing): five required a swing of less than 2 per cent to the Conservatives to win their seat, seven needed a 2–4 per cent swing, nine needed 4–8 per cent, and twenty-one needed a swing of over 8 per cent. The Liberal Democrats fared no better. They selected 140 women candidates, but few had any hope of being elected; women were not selected for the Party's six vacant seats, and only six were selected in seats requiring a 2–8 per cent swing. The SNP and Plaid Cymru also failed to select women for vacant seats. Indeed, Plaid Cymru selected seven women who all needed a swing of more than 25 per cent to win.

In Redditch, Rochdale and Slough both the principal contesting parties chose women candidates. In Hampstead and Highgate, Labour's Glenda Jackson was challenged by four other women candidates from the Conservative, Liberal Democrat, Referendum and UK Independence parties. The Speaker in the 1992–97 Parliament, Betty Boothroyd (West Bromwich West), faced no competition from the mainstream parties, who observed the rather neglected convention of not contesting the Speaker's seat.

The results: women share the limelight

Harriet Harman, the Social Security Secretary, who was also given responsibility for women's issues in the new Labour Government, told a reception of Labour's 101 women MPs that 'Women voted Labour in unprecedented numbers, and we have got to carry that momentum forward into government.'[21] Exit polls showed the gender gap had closed: women and men had voted Labour in equal proportions (45 per cent). Moreover, there was an 11 per cent swing to Labour amongst women, compared with a 9 per cent swing amongst men (BBC/NOP exit poll). Exit polls also provided evidence of a continued gender–generation gap: Labour had attracted 56 per cent of the votes of women aged between eighteen and twenty-nine; 49 per cent of those aged thirty to forty-four; and 43 per cent of forty-five to sixty-four-year-olds. In the older age group of women over sixty-five that support slipped to 34 per cent.[22]

Labour has 101 women MPs in the new Parliament compared with the Conservatives' thirteen, the Liberal Democrats' three, the Scottish National Party's two, whilst Plaid Cymru and the Northern Ireland parties have none. All thirty-seven women Labour MPs who contested the election were returned (two retired: Mildred Gordon in Bow and Poplar and Joan Lestor in Eccles). There were sixty-five newly elected women Labour MPs. These new MPs included Claire Ward (Watford), the youngest woman, at twenty-four years old; Anne Begg (Aberdeen South), the first wheelchair-bound MP; and Maria Eagle (Liverpool Garston), who joined her twin sister, Angela (Wallasey), on the Government benches. The number of women on the Conservative benches fell from twenty to thirteen. Three retired: Dame Jill Knight (Birmingham

Edgbaston), Dame Elaine Kellett-Bowman (Lancaster) and Dame Janet Fookes (Plymouth Drake). Seven women Conservative MPs lost their seats: Elizabeth Peacock (Batley and Spen), Edwina Currie (Derbyshire South), Angela Knight (Erewash), Jacqui Lait (Hastings and Rye), Dame Peggy Fenner (Medway), Dame Angela Rumbold (Mitcham and Morden) and Lady Olga Maitland (Sutton and Cheam). They were replaced by five newly elected women Conservatives: Julie Kirkbride (Bromsgrove), Eleanor Laing (Epping Forest), Theresa May (Maidenhead), Caroline Spelman (Meriden) and Anne McIntosh (Vale of York). For the Liberal Democrats, Emma Nicholson (Torridge and Devon West) retired whilst Diana Maddock (Christchurch) and Liz Lynne (Rochdale) lost their seats. Two new women Liberal Democrats were returned: Jenny Tonge (Richmond Park) and Jackie Ballard (Taunton). The SNP's two sitting women MPs were re-elected, Roseanna Cunningham (Perth) and Margaret Ewing (Moray).

Most of the women MPs in the 1992–97 Parliament had been concentrated in marginal seats, so the Conservatives' huge electoral setback in 1997 resulted in falling numbers of Conservative women MPs and greatly reduced majorities for Conservative women who had safe seats. In Norfolk South West, Gillian Shephard's majority plummeted from 17,250 in 1992 to just 2,464. Of course, incumbent Labour women MPs benefited from huge swings which turned their perilously thin majorities into safe seats. In Rossendale and Darwen, Janet Anderson increased her majority from forty-nine to 10,949. The average swing to Labour across the country was 10.3 per cent, and in marginal seats, where more women had been selected than ever before, high concentrations of switching voters swept record numbers of women to Parliament.

It is also important to distinguish between sitting incumbents and newly elected women MPs because the smooth trend of slowly rising numbers of incoming women MPs was shattered by the 1997 result. After an initial high in 1945, when fifteen new women MPs were elected, fewer than ten won seats in each election until 1987, when twenty-one women were newly elected – a rate of progress maintained in 1992. In 1997, there was a much larger cohort of seventy-two new women MPs. This could and should be a breakthrough for the representation of women in the House of Commons.

The significance of the change was underlined when new Government appointments were made. In contrast to the last Conservative cabinet, which contained only two women (Gillian Shepherd and Virginia Bottomley), five women were appointed to Blair's first cabinet: Margaret Beckett (President of the Board of Trade); Mo Mowlam (Northern Ireland Secretary); Harriet Harman (Social Security Secretary); Clare Short (Overseas Development); and Ann Taylor (Leader of the House of Commons). The quantitative increases in women's share of political posts affected the division of labour between women and men in substantive terms: Margaret Beckett, Mo Mowlam and Ann Taylor were the first women ever to hold their positions. In addition, there were nineteen women junior ministers and two women whips in the Labour Government.

The election and promotion of so many women have been celebrated in the national press. As one columnist exclaimed, 'So much joy! So much hair-spray!'[23] Indeed, much press coverage of the new women MPs was more concerned with the image of 'Blair's babes' than with their politics. Angela Smith (Labour, Basildon) said that people are not yet sure what to expect from women MPs, but things will change: 'If people ... under-estimate us, they've got a hell of a shock coming ... Once people realise women MPs can do the job just as well as men, those sorts of labels are going to disappear. I have serious constituency issues I want to address. I do not want to comment on where I get my hair done.'[24]

Conclusion

The significance of women's votes and women's political representation in the 1997 general election was unprecedented and Labour's victory facilitated the entry of a greater number of women MPs to the House of Commons than ever before. Yet, during the campaign, there was a lack of real discussion on women's political priorities and women politicians were conspicuous by their absence.

Labour claimed that more women Labour MPs would make their policies more credible and create a 'virtuous circle' by attracting the votes of more women in future elections. Janet Anderson remarked upon a striking change in the presentation of politics: 'When people turn on their televisions they will see on our side [101] women. They are less likely to feel that it is run like an exclusive gentlemen's club because it won't look like one.'[25] There were some early signs of procedural changes: the adversarial Prime Minister's Question Time was reformed and the Leader of the House of Commons, Ann Taylor, began a review of parliamentary procedures to modernise them and, amongst other things, make them more 'women-friendly'. However, the Labour Government did not honour its commitment to appoint a minister for women with full cabinet status. They claimed this was to avoid excessive bureaucracy. Harriet Harman became Minister for Women in addition to her Social Security brief, but the manner of her appointment made the job look like an after-thought rather than a central commitment by the new Government. Harman was assisted by Joan Ruddock, the junior minister for women.

Without doubt, Government policy will be closely monitored for its effects on women as well as dialogue between ministers in cabinet, other women MPs and women's organisations outside Parliament. As a result, women may have a greater impact on policy as Government priorities move closer to women's concerns, although Party allegiances will still dominate.

The election result may also usher in significant changes in the Conservative

Party. The 1997 general election showed that the Conservatives no longer enjoy a 'natural' majority amongst women voters and the number of women Conservative MPs is very low, particularly in comparison with Labour. The former Conservative MP-turned-novelist, Edwina Currie, commented, 'I hope the Conservatives will learn from Labour, otherwise we will only have old men left voting for us.'[26]

The short-term effects of the election results for women were dramatic because Labour's landslide victory thrust parliamentary women closer to centre-stage and under the media spotlight. Over the next Parliament, as the intense post-election attention fades, we will begin to see whether the election of women in 1997 is the conclusion of our political drama, or merely the end of the first act. If women politicians are to have a full and proportionate effect on British politics and policy-making, it is likely that the 1997 general election has only set the scene for future drama because, despite the breakthrough of 1997, women remain under-represented in British political life.

Notes

1 *Daily Mirror*, 2 May 1997.
2 S. Tibballs and C. Adcock, *What Women want on Politics* (London: Women's Communication Centre, 1996).
3 P. Norris, 'Mobilising the "women's vote": the gender–generation gap in voting behaviour', *Parliamentary Affairs*, 49 (1996): 333–42.
4 M. A. Stephenson, *Winning Women's Votes* (London: Fawcett Society, 1996).
5 Norris, 'Mobilising the "women's vote"'.
6 Stephenson, *Winning Women's Votes*.
7 Ibid.
8 *Daily Express*, 7 September 1996; *Daily Mirror*, 6 September 1996.
9 *The Times*, 11 April 1997.
10 *Financial Times*, 2 April 1997, p. 1.
11 Conservative Party, *You Can Only Be Sure With The Conservatives: The Conservative Party Election Manifesto 1997* (London: Conservative Central Office, 1997), p. 20.
12 *Independent*, 19 March 1997, p. 8.
13 H. Garner, *Watching Women* (London: Fawcett Society, 1997).
14 *Guardian*, 21 April 1997.
15 P. Norris and J. Lovenduski, *Political Recruitment* (Cambridge: Cambridge University Press, 1995).
16 *Guardian*, 11 April 1997.
17 Ibid.
18 J. Lovenduski and P. Norris, *Gender and Party Politics* (London: Sage, 1993).
19 Anonymous interview with Conservative parliamentary candidate as part of the British Representation Study 1997. This study of 1997 general election candidates was directed by Pippa Norris, and interviews were conducted by Lucy Peake.
20 J. Squires, 'Quotas for women: fair representation?', *Parliamentary Affairs*, 49 (1996): 71–88.
21 *Guardian*, 22 May 1997.

22 Ibid.
23 *The Times*, 8 May 1997.
24 *Daily Mirror*, 8 May 1997.
25 *Independent*, 17 April 1997.
26 *Observer*, 4 May 1997.

Rochdale

Fewer contests were likely to be harder fought than Rochdale. Defending the seat was Liz Lynne, one of the different breed of northern Liberal Democrats who had spent much of their lives fighting Labour. Lynne joined the Young Liberals at the age of eleven. Like her Liberal predecessor in the seat, Cyril Smith, she was not enthused by the Ashdown mode of leadership in the Party when it involved closer alignment with Labour. Indeed, in November 1996, Lynne had written to Paddy Ashdown seeking assurances that the Party was 'not going to be sold out for a handful of Cabinet seats'.

Antagonisms in Rochdale had been deepened by the reliance of the Liberal Democrats upon Conservative support on the local council. Now the Liberal Democrats faced their sternest challenge since the old Liberals captured the seat in a by-election in 1972. A highly capable, locally born Labour candidate, Lorna Fitzsimmons was used to tough contests, having spent her early political career fighting the far left to become president of the National Union of Students. A high-profile candidate and the youngest panellist to appear on *Question Time*, Fitzsimmons benefited locally from boundary changes which favoured Labour. A slender Liberal Democrat majority was reduced further to a notional 128. Fourth on its list of targets, Labour would win with a swing from the Liberal Democrats of only 0.1 per cent.

The decisive factor was the manner in which Labour was better able to capture defecting Conservative voters. Although the Liberal Democrat vote held up, it was insufficient to save Lynne, an MP whose acknowledged diligence had involved the tabling of 295 Parliamentary written questions since her election and elicited verbal contributions in six times as many Commons debates as the average MP.

Fitzsimmons promised to be equally belligerent on behalf of her constituents, pledging to the *Rochdale Observer* (7 May 1997) to set up an informal advisory forum of all major organisations in the town. Her constituents have elected a rising star, given her insistence to *The Times* (4 April) during the campaign: 'I am a moderniser, firmly in the Blair wing of the party and I suppose I embody new Labour.'

Result

Rochdale			
Lorna Fitzsimmons	Lab	23,758	
Liz Lynne	Lib Dem	19,213	
Mervyn Turnberg	Con	4,237	
	Others	874	
Total vote		48,082	Turnout 70.16%
Lab majority		4,545	
Lab gain from Lib Dem			
Swing Lib Dem to Lab 4.85%			

12

Northern Ireland: last chance for peace?

Jonathan Tonge

Introduction: the impact of Northern Ireland

The general election took place in Northern Ireland amidst an unpromising phase of politics in the province. Many of the hopes invested in the peace process of the 1990s appeared to have been thwarted by the IRA's return to violence in February 1996. This resumption added to a death toll already exceeding 3,000. It resulted in Sinn Fein's exclusion from inter-party talks which began at Stormont in June that year. Although the representatives of loyalist paramilitary groups had entered that dialogue, the loyalist ceasefire appeared increasingly fragile. Meanwhile the province appeared beset by the revival of sectarianism, evident in confrontations over the routes of parades and arson attacks upon Orange halls and churches.

The possible entry of Sinn Fein into all-party talks was the most important single aspect of the election in Northern Ireland. As in the other twenty-three elections held since 1973, the issue which dominated all others was the constitutional future of the province. This chapter examines the extent to which the Northern Ireland problem was salient in the wider general election campaign in Britain and interprets what the results within Northern Ireland signified for the political future of the province.

Northern Ireland made a considerable impact upon the general election in two ways. First, the support of unionists in close parliamentary votes almost certainly delayed its timing, allowing the Conservative Government to survive a full term in office. Unionist support was reciprocated by concessions from the Government. Second, the IRA used the election campaign to achieve maximum publicity. A wave of disruption began shortly after the announcement of the general election. This comprised mainly hoax bomb warnings, interspersed with occasional real devices. Motorways, airports, railways and even the Grand National all endured disruption. Activity by Irish republicans during British elections was not new. At the start of the 1979 election campaign, the Conservative Shadow Northern Ireland Secretary, Airey Neave, was killed by the Irish National Liberation Army.

Despite the prominence which the pre-election disruption gave to the IRA, Northern Ireland was, as usual, a 'dog that did not bark' during the campaign.

With the exception of a few poorly supported local Conservative candidates, none of the three main parties fielded candidates in the province. The election could not be won or lost in Northern Ireland. Nor were there differences between the main parties on the future of Northern Ireland. The insistence of Tony Blair that he would support the Conservative Government and 'not play politics with the peace process' ensured that Northern Ireland remained an arena of political bipartisanship. The result was that the constitutional future of Northern Ireland was not a matter for debate in mainland politics.

Such an exclusion was remarkable given that other, much less deadly, constitutional differences provided perhaps the main substantive distinctions between the main parties in the election. In the final week of the campaign, John Major visited Northern Ireland. The visit formed part of a trip to all four countries of the United Kingdom within a single day, as Major wished to demonstrate his unionist credentials. He spoke of the dangers of devolution as a Trojan horse for fragmentation of the United Kingdom, although his Party advocated its return in Northern Ireland.

The political background

As voters went to the polls, they could reflect upon an eventful previous five years, even by the turbulent standards of Northern Irish politics. A plethora of peace initiatives had been undertaken as part of a peace process designed to bring a permanent end to conflict. The origins of the process lay in the 1980s, with the development of dialogue amongst Irish nationalists and changes within Sinn Fein. During the 1990s the peace process was placed in the public domain, gathering momentum through declarations, ceasefires and documents, before grinding to a halt. The most significant events are listed in Table 12.1.

Table 12.1 Main events in the Irish peace process 1986–1997

Year	*Event*
1986	Sinn Fein recognises the Irish Republic
1988	Hume–Adams talks begin
1990	Britain declares no 'selfish, strategic or economic interest' in Northern Ireland
1990	Secret line of communication opens between the British Government and the IRA
1993	Downing Street Declaration
1994	Paramilitary ceasefires
1995	Framework Documents published
1995	President Clinton visits
1996	Mitchell Commission report on decommissioning of weapons
1996	IRA returns to violence
1996	Multi-party talks begin after peace forum elections
1997	IRA disrupts British general election campaign

Undoubtedly the peace process was Irish-led. Sinn Fein's abandonment of its desire to overthrow the twenty-county state in the South of Ireland allowed the Party to search for a pan-nationalist alliance which it believed might shift British thinking on Northern Ireland. In 1986 Sinn Fein, meaning 'Ourselves', abandoned its 'sole liberator' role and began to construct a nationalist alliance. This began in 1988 when John Hume, the leader of the SDLP, the moderate constitutional nationalist party in Northern Ireland, began to engage in dialogue with the president of Sinn Fein, Gerry Adams. Although the dialogue was intermittent, it symbolised that Sinn Fein might no longer be political lepers.

Anxious to foster developments, the Secretary of State for Northern Ireland, Peter Brooke, insisted that Britain had no 'selfish, strategic or economic interest' in Northern Ireland. Brooke's aim was to present an image of British neutrality and to indicate to the IRA that its 'armed struggle' was not against a colonial oppressor. Instead, the IRA had to convince pro-British Unionists, the majority in Northern Ireland, of the merits of a united Ireland. This message was reinforced in a private Brooke initiative, involving a 'Back Channel' of secret contacts between the British Government and the IRA.[1]

British neutrality was one of the avowed themes of the Downing Street Declaration (DSD) issued by the British and Irish Governments in 1993, as the peace process 'went public'. In asserting neutrality, the British Government did not distinguish in legitimacy between the nationalist aspiration to a united Ireland, or the unionist demand for retention of Northern Ireland as part of Britain.

As in all previous policy pronouncements, the DSD restated the consent principle. There was to be no change in the constitutional status of Northern Ireland without the consent of the majority. Furthermore, it was recognised that no consent to change at present existed and the British Government would not act to persuade unionists in that direction. This consent principle was always likely to be difficult for Sinn Fein to accept and the Party rejected the DSD at a special conference in 1994. For Sinn Fein, Unionist consent to a united Ireland remained a *consequence* of the establishment of such a state, not a *prerequisite*.

None the less the declaration contained enough 'green' language to interest republicans. It spoke of the need for Irish self-determination, by which the people of Ireland alone would determine their future, whilst qualifying this unsatisfactorily for Sinn Fein by insisting upon its exercise in the North and South of Ireland. On 31 August 1994, the IRA announced a 'complete cessation' of hostilities. Loyalist paramilitaries reciprocated six weeks later.

As the DSD amounted only to a broad statement of political intent, a more detailed political blueprint was required. This arrived in the Joint Framework Documents in February 1995. Part I contained the British Government's proposals for a devolved settlement in Northern Ireland.[2] It envisaged:

- an elected seventy-eight-member Northern Ireland Assembly;
- weighted majority voting;
- a panel of three members to adjudicate on controversial issues.

Part II was an intergovernmental agreement in which the British and Irish Governments attempted to bolster Anglo-Irish links in respect of Northern Ireland.[3] Specific proposals included:

- a North–South body with executive, harmonisation and consultation functions;
- compulsory membership of this body for key Northern Ireland Assembly members;
- a parliamentary forum of representatives from new political institutions in Northern Ireland and the Irish Republic;
- a permanent Anglo-Irish (East–West) intergovernmental conference.

Yet no serious attempt was ever made to sell the Framework Documents to hostile unionists.[4] Its proposals remained, but there was no immediate move towards implementation, although nationalists were more favourably disposed.

Whilst the Framework Documents represented the further political development of the peace process, the absence of all-party talks was already seen as having ominous implications. The IRA ceasefire was predicated upon the entry of Sinn Fein into all-party talks, but the absence of the word 'permanent' from the ceasefire declaration was used by the British Government as justification for a substantial 'quarantine period'. Furthermore, the Government insisted upon prior decommissioning of paramilitary weapons, whilst Sinn Fein said there would be none.

In a bid to resolve the logjam, the former US Senator, George Mitchell, was appointed to head a commission on the weapons issue. The Mitchell Commission proposed the compromise of decommissioning in parallel to all-party talks, with all participants obliged to adhere to six principles of non-violence. In response, the British Government, under unionist urging, favoured Mitchell's tentative alternative idea that there should be elections to establish mandates within all-party talks. Although there was not a consensus for such an idea, the elections proceeded in May 1996, admitting parties to talks the following month. The talks remained multi-party rather than all- embracing. Sinn Fein remained excluded by the British Government due to the IRA's return to violence in February that year, whilst the IRA blamed Sinn Fein's earlier exclusion from talks for the breakdown of its ceasefire.

British policy

British policy approaches to Northern Ireland determined the terrain upon which the general election was fought in the province. Most obviously, the

British Government insists upon non-violence and maintenance of the consent principle. Tensions exist within other aspects of the British Government's approach as it attempts to manage conflict whilst squaring a political circle between the seemingly irreconcilable demands of Ulster unionism and Irish nationalism. The main tensions appear to lie in two broad areas.

Neutrality versus integration

Much British input into the peace process was concerned with stressing neutrality over the future of Northern Ireland. There was no such thing as disloyalty within the province, as the aspiration to a united Ireland was perfectly acceptable, provided that its achievement did not violate the consent principle. Northern Ireland would be allowed to leave the United Kingdom if a majority located there so wished, an offer not tabled to Scottish or Welsh nationalists during an election campaign which promised, on the opposition side, a considerable revision of Britain's constitutional arrangements.

Against these rhetorical pledges was required a measurement of the actual policy output during the Major years. The extent to which Britain really is neutral on the future of Northern Ireland is disputed. The annual cost of maintaining the Union, the subvention, has been estimated at £4 billion.[5]

Despite the Major Government's promise of 'taking risks for peace' critics argued that policy owed more to the immediacy of parliamentary arithmetic. As its majority in the House of Commons narrowed, the Conservative Government relied upon support from the Ulster Unionist Party (UUP). Both sides denied that any deal had been enacted. In a formal sense this was almost certainly true. With the prospect of a Labour government looming, the UUP wished to maintain some distance from the Conservatives. None the less unionists were rewarded with fulfilment of two long-standing demands. The award of a select committee on Northern Ireland in 1994 was followed by a promised bolstering of the Ulster Grand Committee in 1996. Since direct rule was introduced in 1972, legislation for Northern Ireland had amounted to 'government by ministerial decree' as the Secretary of State for Northern Ireland issued orders in council.[6] The changes offered scrutiny of legislation on a par with Scotland or Wales. Throughout its history, it appeared that, in legislative terms, Northern Ireland had never been so closely integrated into the British state.

Intergovernmentalism versus consociationalism

Intergovernmentalism has dominated policy relating to Northern Ireland since the Anglo-Irish Agreement of 1985. There is an acceptance by the British Government that the problem of Northern Ireland is a joint one, requiring input from the Irish Republic. In this respect, Northern Ireland is treated as 'a place apart' from the remainder of the United Kingdom. Debate concerns the extent of influence given to the Irish Republic, not its existence.

Unionist critics wish Anglo-Irish agreements to be minimalist, centred upon security matters and minor economic co-operation in obvious areas. The Framework Documents in 1995 suggested a more substantial basis of co-operation. To such critics, Anglo-Irish intergovernmentalism imposes agreements 'over the heads' of local political parties. This was evident in the 1985 Agreement, which rendered a unionist boycott irrelevant.

Yet at the same time as seeking agreement between governments, British policy has also been to establish accommodation amongst political elites in Northern Ireland. This would involve power-sharing amongst unionists and nationalists in a local assembly. Part I of the Framework Documents suggested such consociational arrangements, encouraging a 'grand coalition' of the leaders of the main parties.[7] Using checks and balances, no one group would dominate. Part II of the Framework Document attempted to reconcile intergovernmental agreements with power-sharing. It insisted that members of this grand coalition would also have to take part in Anglo-Irish cross-border bodies. Unionists saw these proposals as coercive and based their general election campaign upon opposition.

Interpreting the election results

Northern Ireland possesses a striking association between religion and political affiliation. Slightly over 60 per cent of the population are Protestant. They overwhelmingly vote for parties in favour of the retention of the union of Northern Ireland with Great Britain. Around 40 per cent of the population are Catholic. They vote mainly for Irish nationalist parties, which support the ambition of a unitary Irish state. Within the unionist and nationalist 'families', however, there is considerable competition for votes. The 1997 election was no different, as the Democratic Unionist Party (DUP) challenged the ascendancy of the UUP as the majority representative of unionist opinion. Unionists did not challenge each other in constituencies in which one of the following scenarios applied: a unionist victory was threatened by a strong nationalist vote; one of the unionist parties had particular local strength; or, the total unionist vote in an area was minimal. As a result of this pact, the DUP did not contest half of Northern Ireland's eighteen constituencies. Only two seats, Foyle and Mid-Ulster, were uncontested by the UUP.

Amongst nationalists, no electoral agreements were forthcoming. The Social and Democratic Labour Party (SDLP) had earlier offered an electoral pact to its republican rivals, Sinn Fein, which it knew would not be accepted. Under John Hume's plan, the SDLP would not stand against Sinn Fein in certain seats, provided that the IRA ended violence and Sinn Fein ended its policy of abstentionism. The latter means that Sinn Fein MPs elected to Westminster refuse to take their seats, declining to take the oath of allegiance to the monarch. Even in an era of shifting republican tactics, this is a fundamental republican principle unlikely to alter. Change would require a two-thirds majority at Sinn Fein's *ard-fheis* (annual conference).

None the less Sinn Fein's decision announced during the campaign to open an office in London was described as a policy of 'highly diluted abstentionism'.[8] In the event, an electoral pact would have yielded only one extra nationalist seat, Tyrone West. The overall election results are shown in Table 12.2.

Table 12.2 The Northern Ireland 1997 general election result

Party	*Vote*	*Percentage*	*Seats*
UUP	258,649	32.7	10
DUP	103,798	13.1	2
SDLP	190,814	24.1	3
SF	126,921	16.1	2
UK Unionist	12,817	1.6	1
Others	90,891	12.4	–

The main feature of the results was the confirmation of the upward trajectory of Sinn Fein's vote. In winning two seats, the Party achieved its finest election result in terms of representation for forty years. Belfast West, held by Gerry Adams from 1983 until 1992, was recaptured, whilst Sinn Fein's chief negotiator, Martin McGuinness, ousted the Democratic Unionist MP, William McCrea, in Mid-Ulster. These gains were interpreted by Sinn Fein supporters as a triumph for the Party's 'peace strategy', centred upon the need for entry to all-party talks at Stormont. In the Forum elections held the previous year, Sinn Fein was successful in attracting a sympathy vote from nationalists angered at what they saw as unwarranted obstacles preventing Sinn Fein's inclusion in the peace process. Some of the support for Sinn Fein in the general election was again based upon a belief that the Party might be capable of restoring peace by delivering a new IRA ceasefire.

Some unionists and moderate nationalists attributed part of Sinn Fein's success to 'vote-rigging', arguing that duplicate voting and false registrations had bolstered the Party's tally. In Mid-Ulster, the defeated SDLP candidate, Dennis Haughey, claimed that Sinn Fein had enjoyed a '110 per cent turnout'.[9] Official turnout exceeded 86 per cent, not far short of the highest ever Westminster election figure of 92 per cent recorded in the by-election success of Bernadette Devlin in 1969. According to critics of Sinn Fein, the traditional message of 'Vote early, vote often' had been revived. It was claimed that when challenged many voters had 'turned and walked away – a sure sign they intended to use stolen votes'.[10] An alternative explanation of the high turnout, in Mid-Ulster at least, was that the contest polarised between the favoured nationalist candidate and the unionist rival. This was reminiscent of the straight nationalist–unionist contests during the republican hunger strikes of the early 1980s, when high turnouts were also evident.

Although Sinn Fein achieved one of its two gains at the expense of the SDLP, this did not prevent the steady overall increase in the nationalist vote in Northern Ireland. Fifteen years ago, the combined nationalist poll of the SDLP and Sinn Fein amounted to less than one-third of the total number of votes. Now that figure exceeded 40 per cent.[11] The nationalist vote split sixty-forty between the SDLP and Sinn Fein, the latter replacing the DUP as Northern Ireland's third largest party. Despite stiff competition from Sinn Fein, the SDLP recorded its best ever vote, discounting European elections. Again if one ignores untypical European elections, the improving electoral performance of Sinn Fein in the 1990s is striking, a feature confirmed in the local elections held only three weeks after the general election and demonstrated in Table 12.3.

Table 12.3 Electoral performance of the main parties in Northern Ireland in the 1990s (%)

Party	*1992 general*	*1993 local*	*1994 Euro*	*1996 Forum*	*1997 general*	*1997 local*
UUP	34.5	29.4	24.3	24.2	32.7	27.8
DUP	13.1	17.3	29.1	19.0	13.1	15.6
SDLP	23.5	22.0	28.9	21.0	24.1	20.7
SF	10.0	12.4	9.9	15.5	16.1	16.9
Others	19.9	18.9	7.8	20.3	14.0	19.0

On the unionist side, the results confirmed a pattern of superior UUP performance in general elections compared with other elections. This enhanced performance assists the UUP greatly in parliamentary terms, one-third of the vote yielding over half of Northern Ireland's seats at Westminster. The UUP acquired 71 per cent of the unionist vote, excluding minor parties and the Alliance, with the DUP obtaining 29 per cent. Overall, the loss of one seat and a static electoral performance compared with the 1992 election was a slight disappointment for the DUP, particularly after its strong vote in the Forum elections the previous year.

The centre ground in Northern Ireland has been described as 'mythical'.[12] The failure of the Alliance Party (APNI), a unionist party in constitutional terms but one whose support straddles the religious divide, appears to support this assertion. The APNI achieved only 7.9 per cent of the vote.

The unionist campaign

As ever, the politics of the constitution dominated the election in Northern Ireland, to the virtual exclusion of all other issues. The UUP argued the case for the Union on the grounds that it linked Northern Ireland with a 'genuinely plural, liberal democratic state capable of accommodating social, cultural and religious diversity'.[13] Which of these attributes the Irish Republic did not possess was left unsaid. Its manifesto demands included:

- replacement of the Anglo-Irish Agreement;
- establishment of an elected Northern Ireland Assembly;
- a broadcasting ban on Sinn Fein/IRA;
- the right of Orangemen to march.

The UUP claimed it had achieved 'significant progress' in ensuring greater representation at Westminster, with a record eighteen constituencies, along with the award of important legislative and scrutiny committees.[14] The Party leader, David Trimble, was irritated by the campaign tactics of the DUP, not least in their unearthing of a nine-year-old document authored by the UUP leader, entitled *What Choice for Ulster?*[15] In this, Trimble had advocated some form of independence for Ulster in the aftermath of the Anglo-Irish Agreement. This previous advocacy of dominion status led the DUP's deputy leader, Peter Robinson, to denounce Trimble as 'either a political fifth-columnist or "unsteady" on the constitution'.[16] Ironically, the DUP, whilst staunchly pro-Union, is normally seen as more pro-devolution, with the UUP seen as the party preferring Northern Ireland to integrate even more closely within the British state.

During the campaign, the DUP concentrated upon two themes. First, recent political agreements were designed to evict Northern Ireland from the United Kingdom. Fear of an Anglo-Irish conspiracy was reflected in the title of the DUP manifesto, *Democracy – Not Dublin Rule*.[17] Second, the Party insisted it alone could be trusted on the future of the Union. Its leader, Ian Paisley, declared himself 'an island of Unionist consistency in a sea of turmoil and compromise', arguing that the UUP was playing a 'loony tune' of insisting that the Union was safe, whilst accepting all-Ireland aspects of the Downing Street Declaration and Framework Documents.[18] Paisley criticised what he saw as the contradiction by which the UUP failed to condemn the Downing Street Declaration, yet derided its proposed enactment, arguing that it was 'strange to relate those who prepared the womb of the Declaration have now rejected its offspring'.[19]

The DUP's policy stances reflected the Party's hostility towards an all-inclusive peace process. They included:

- no talks with Sinn Fein prior to full decommissioning of IRA weapons;
- abandonment of the Anglo-Irish Agreement, Downing Street Declaration and Framework Documents;
- support for the Northern Ireland Forum elected in 1996 as a debating forum, rather than all-party talks.

Meanwhile the Alliance criticised the two largest unionist parties. A vote for Paisley was a vote 'for division and conflict'. A vote cast for Trimble was a vote for 'further confrontation at Drumcree and elsewhere and for endless delay and obstruction in the [peace] talks'.[20] The APNI advocated the establishment of a power-sharing executive, a Bill of Rights and implementation of the North Report's recommendation of a Parades Commission with statutory powers to determine the routes of contentious marches.

The nationalist campaign

Nationalists based their campaign upon the premise that the IRA's return to violence was a temporary diversion. There was much talk concerning the 'restoration' of the peace process. This message was underlined by a *de facto* IRA ceasefire in Northern Ireland during the election campaign, although sceptics pointed to the chaos caused by the organisation's concurrent activities in England.

Emphasis upon the need to support a 'peace strategy' dominated republican rhetoric, forming the central plank of Sinn Fein's campaign. Its manifesto, *A New Opportunity for Peace*, reaffirmed the traditional republican objective of ending British rule in Ireland.[21] Arguing that the 'six county statelet' was a 'failed political and economic unit', Sinn Fein reiterated its commitment to national self-determination and the unity and independence of Ireland.

None the less, a more conciliatory tone to Sinn Fein's language, first seen in 1992 in the document, *Towards a Lasting Peace*, was also evident.[22] That paper contained 'pluralist concepts of tone and movement'.[23] Its ideas were repeated in the 1997 election manifesto. Instead of a demand for immediate British withdrawal, there was acknowledgement that 'peace in Ireland cannot be built without the positive participation of the British Government'.[24] Insisting that Sinn Fein 'is not the IRA', the Party based the election campaign upon the need for Sinn Fein's inclusion within all-party talks. It concentrated its demands upon a series of interim measures rather than holistic solutions. These included disbandment of the RUC; better conditions for republican prisoners; the 'gaelicisation' of language; and compulsory negotiations with residents' groups before parades. The latter demand increased unionist claims that such groups were fronts for Sinn Fein. Ironically for an Irish republican party, Sinn Fein also demanded greater resources from Britain to promote Irish language and culture.

Having supported the development of a pan-nationalist alliance in furtherance of the peace process, the SDLP was confronted by the problem of how to oppose Sinn Fein. The Party campaigned on the issues of violence and Sinn Fein's relationship with the IRA. Seamus Mallon, the SDLP deputy leader, warned that support for Sinn Fein would provide a 'blank cheque to the IRA and continued violence'.[25] His message was echoed by the Irish Taoiseach, John Bruton. Flanked by SDLP MPs in Dublin, Bruton insisted:

> A vote for Sinn Fein is a vote for the IRA and the IRA's campaign of killing and murder ... I have lost patience, as everybody else who is concerned about a settlement and an agreed approach has, with the republican movement's procrastination ... Everybody knows that Sinn Fein and the IRA belong to the one movement and as long as they are committed to what they call armed struggle, a vote for them is a vote for that strategy.[26]

The SDLP supported a settlement based upon the intergovernmental and cross-border principles of the Downing Street Declaration and Framework Documents, also believing that its sister organisation, the British Labour Party, would offer nationalists a reasonable deal. Adopting a post-nationalist approach, emphasising the pooled sovereignty of a Europe of regions rather than an independent Irish nation-state, the SDLP argued for a people-based unity, rather than the territorial emphasis found in the approach of Sinn Fein.

The British party 'debate'

As in previous elections, the stances of the main parties concerning Northern Ireland did not reflect public opinion. Forty-eight per cent of the electorate favour immediate withdrawal of British troops, marginally more than those preferring troops to remain.[27] Irish reunification is the long-term constitutional option preferred by a majority of the electorate, as indicated in Table 12.4.

Table 12.4 British attitudes to the constitutional future of Northern Ireland

Option	*Supported by (%)*
Irish reunification	52
Remain part of UK	30
Other	5
Don't know	13

Source: B. Hayes and I. McAllister, 'British public opinion towards the Northern Ireland problem', *Irish Political Studies*, 11 (1996): 61–82.

Labour's election manifesto claimed 'general acceptance' that the future of Northern Ireland must be determined by the consent of the people as set out in the Downing Street Declaration.[28] Labour's official policy since 1981 had been to support Irish unity by consent. Now, despite British and Irish public opinion, the pursuit of Irish unity was no longer a Labour ambition, although *formally* it remained party policy. Pre-election it was already apparent that a Labour government would not act as a persuader to unionists that their better interest lay in Irish unity. The sacking of the pro-nationalist Shadow Northern Ireland Secretary, Kevin McNamara, in 1994 heralded this move towards a more pro-unionist position. McNamara had been interested in acting as a persuader and redefining the consent mechanism.[29] In contrast, Blair insisted:

> My agenda is not a united Ireland and I wonder just how many see it as a realistic possibility for the foreseeable future? Northern Ireland will remain part of the United Kingdom as long as a majority here wish ... I believe in the United Kingdom. I value the Union ... Northern Ireland is part of the United Kingdom because that is the wish of the majority of the people who live here. It will remain part of the UK for as long as that remains the case ... Unionists have nothing to fear from a new Labour Government. A political settlement is not a slippery slope to a united Ireland. The Government will not be persuaders for unity.[30]

Labour's spokesperson on Northern Ireland, Mo Mowlam, declared that there was a high possibility of Sinn Fein joining inter-party talks, a point also made by Tony Blair. Both made it clear that such entry required a renewed IRA ceasefire. Participation in talks would also, Blair's speech indicated, require Sinn Fein and the IRA to accept a settlement a considerable distance short of their historical objectives.

Labour's election manifesto had already made clear that there would be no change from the approach to Northern Ireland pursued by the Conservative Government. The section on Northern Ireland acknowledged that this approach had been 'bipartisan' and the 'same bipartisan approach' was expected from a Conservative opposition.[31] Labour promised a 'new political settlement' recognising that the 'option of a united Ireland does not command the consent of the Unionist tradition nor does the existing status of Northern Ireland command the consent of the Nationalist tradition'.[32]

Blair insisted upon taking office that he was committed to Northern Ireland. Acknowledgement that the current status of Northern Ireland was unacceptable to nationalists was deliberately not prefaced with the word 'constitutional'. Instead, three things were on offer to nationalists. First, there would be a continuation of the promotion of cross-border co-operation, as outlined in the Framework Documents. Optimistic nationalists hoped such co-operation would diminish the relevance of the border. Second, Labour would actively promote the idea of parity of esteem between the two communities. This would have particular resonance on the issue of parades. The Conservative Government appeared reluctant to implement the findings of the North Commission that an independent Parades Commission with statutory powers should adjudicate on the routes of individual parades. Labour promised full implementation of the North Report, welcoming its emphasis upon local mediation.[33] Finally, Labour offered a package of reforms relating to security matters, including increased accountability within the Royal Ulster Constabulary; incorporation of the European Convention of Human Rights into United Kingdom law; and changes to the Prevention of Terrorism Act (PTA).

Controversy over the PTA provided an isolated intrusion of party politics on Northern Ireland into the election campaign. Labour's previous opposition to the annual renewal of the PTA was cited by the Home Secretary, Michael Howard, as evidence that Labour was 'soft' on terrorism. Such an allegation enraged Labour, Tony Blair arguing that it broke the bipartisan approach to the Northern Ireland problem. In defence, the Conservatives cited remarks by Labour's John Prescott blaming the breakdown of the peace process upon the reliance of the Major Government upon unionist favours, duly reciprocated.

The Conservative manifesto insisted that the Party continued to 'cherish' the Union and Northern Ireland.[34] The document faced the potential difficulty of explaining why devolution was good for Northern Ireland, but disastrous for the remainder of the United Kingdom, by referring to 'special circumstances which require further action to be taken'.[35] Perhaps the only surprise in the brief restatement of existing policy was the use of the term 'broad consent' when discussing the requirement for constitutional change.[36] This was slightly vaguer than the previous insistence upon majority consent. It could be interpreted as an indication that any settlement would proceed even in the face of a substantial renewal of republican hostilities. Alternatively, it might be construed as a phrase indicating that hardline unionists would not be able to prevent any settlement with a substantial all-Ireland dimension.

In their manifesto column devoted to Northern Ireland, the Liberal Democrats reiterated their commitment to an internal consociational, power-sharing settlement long advocated by its APNI sister, reform of the judicial system and implementation of the North Report.[37]

Conclusion

If the importance given to constitutional issues was an unusual feature of the election elsewhere in Britain, in Northern Ireland it was business as usual. This election was different in an important respect, however, in that it was as concerned with the prospects for all-party talks about the constitution as it was with actual party stances on the constitution. All-party dialogue will form the basis of Labour's approach to conflict management, although it remains doubtful whether sufficient agreement will be received to translate the process into one of conflict resolution.

Certainly the most important feature which emerged from the election was the continued rise of support for Sinn Fein. An optimistic assessment of this was that support for Sinn Fein's new, more moderate strategy of seeking inclusive dialogue was a tacit acceptance that the 'armed struggle had run its course' and a new IRA ceasefire would result.[38] Sinn Fein might now be encouraged towards a new, non-armed, constitutionalism. A more pessimistic reading pointed to the fact that Northern Ireland's constitutional problem was unresolved. Sinn Fein had a clear mandate which might, IRA ceasefire permitting, grant a place at all-party talks on Northern Ireland's future. Yet this begged the crucial question. Would the republican movement accept peacefully an unsatisfactory outcome to those talks?

Notes

1 E. Mallie and D. McKittrick, *The Fight for Peace: The Secret Story behind the Irish Peace Process* (London: Heinemann, 1996).
2 HM Government, *Frameworks for the Future* (Belfast: HMSO, 1995).
3 Ibid.
4 P. Bew and G. Gillespie, *The Northern Ireland Peace Process 1993–1996: A Chronology* (London: Serif, 1996).
5 M. Tomlinson, 'Can Britain leave Ireland? The political economy of war and peace', *Race and Class*, 37:1 (1995): 1–22.
6 W. A. Hazleton, 'A breed apart? Northern Ireland's MPs at Westminster', *Journal of Legislative Studies*, 1:4 (1995): 30–53.
7 A. Lijphart, 'The Framework Document in Northern Ireland' *Government and Opposition*, 31:3 (1996): 267–74.
8 P. Bew, 'After the mayhem', *Guardian*, 22 April 1997.
9 *Irish World*, 9 May 1997.
10 *News Letter*, 2 May 1997.
11 *Independent*, 18 May 1997.
12 P. Arthur and K. Jeffery, *Northern Ireland since 1968* (Oxford: Blackwell, 1996), p. 51.
13 Ulster Unionist Party, *General Election Manifesto 1997* (Belfast: UUP, 1997), p. 1.
14 D. Trimble, 'UUP believes in positive approach to repair Union', *News Letter*, 30 April 1997.
15 D. Trimble, 'What choice for Ulster?' (Belfast: Ulster Clubs Movement discussion paper, 1988).
16 *News Letter*, 30 April 1997.
17 Democratic Unionist Party, *Democracy – not Dublin Rule: Election Manifesto 1997* (Belfast: DUP, 1997).
18 I. Paisley, letter to the *News Letter*, 30 April 1997.
19 I. Paisley, 'Measured and consistent action', *The House Magazine*, 22:755, 17 March 1997.
20 Alliance Party of Northern Ireland, *Agenda for Change: Election Manifesto 1997* (Belfast: APNI, 1997), p. 2.
21 Sinn Fein, *A New Opportunity for Peace: Election Manifesto 1997* (Belfast: Sinn Fein, 1997).
22 Sinn Fein, *Towards a Lasting Peace* (Belfast: Sinn Fein, 1992).
23 K. Bean, 'The new departure? Recent developments in republican strategy and ideology', *Irish Studies Review*, 10 (1995): 1–10, at p. 3.
24 Sinn Fein, *A New Opportunity for Peace*, p. 4.
25 *Observer*, 4 May 1997.
26 *Irish News*, 10 April 1997.
27 B. Hayes, and I. McAllister, 'British public opinion towards the Northern Ireland problem', *Irish Political Studies*, 11 (1996): 61–82.
28 Labour Party, *New Labour: Because Britain Deserves Better. Election Manifesto 1997* (London, 1997).
29 P. Bew and P. Dixon, 'Labour Party policy and Northern Ireland', in B. Barton and P. J. Roche, *The Northern Ireland Question: Perspectives and Policies* (Aldershot: Avebury, 1994).

30 *Daily Telegraph*, 17 May 1997.
31 Labour Party, *New Labour*, p. 35.
32 Ibid., p. 35.
33 *Irish Post*, 5 April 1997.
34 Conservative Party, *You Can Only Be Sure with the Conservatives: Election Manifesto 1997* (London: Conservative Central Office, 1997), p. 57.
35 Ibid., p. 51.
36 Ibid., p. 51.
37 Liberal Democrat Party, *Make the Difference: Election Manifesto 1997* (London: 1997).
38 *Independent*, 8 May 1997.

Belfast West

It was widely expected that Gerry Adams, Sinn Fein MP for West Belfast from 1983 to 1992, would recapture his seat. The size of his victory was none the less significant. It confirmed that there was majority support for a party which continued to give tacit support to the IRA's 'armed struggle'. Across Belfast as a whole, Sinn Fein narrowly outpolled the SDLP, an unprecedented feat.

During the campaign Adams, President of Sinn Fein since 1983, emphasised the organisational separation of the Party from the IRA. Furthermore, Sinn Fein's support in a trio of elections, the 1996 Forum and the 1997 general and local elections was boosted by the desire of the nationalist electorate for its inclusion in peace talks.

Joe Hendron, the SDLP candidate, doubted that a vote for Sinn Fein might be construed as support for the conversion of republicans to Adams's vision of a non-armed political movement. Despite enduring a loyalist car bomb attack in 1994, Hendron spent the final evening of the campaign attempting to canvass loyalist votes in the Shankill district, hoping for a repeat of the tactical anti-Adams vote thought to assist the SDLP in 1992. During that contest, the number of such tactical voters could only be guessed. Now there were in any case fewer such potential voters. Boundary changes, accounting for about 20 per cent of the former constituency, had instead absorbed two republican estates.

SDLP candidates in Belfast tend to take a jaundiced view of Sinn Fein activities. This is due to the close nature of electoral contests and is also a consequence of intimidation. Hendron's previous office was burned down by republicans. Whilst such activities had waned, the defeated candidate did not care to distinguish between Sinn Fein and the IRA, insisting also that multiple registering boosted Sinn Fein's poll.

Notwithstanding the assertion of Gerry Adams that 'Joe is a lovely bloke' the bitterness of the contest highlighted the limits of pan-nationalism when set against IRA violence, including local 'punishment attacks'. Its main message, however, was to confirm the steady rise of Sinn Fein as an electoral force.

Result

Belfast West			
Gerry Adams	Sinn Fein	25,662	
Joe Hendron	SDLP	17,753	
Frederick Parkinson	UUP	1,556	
	Others	914	
Total vote		45,885	Turnout 74.27%
Sinn Fein majority		7,909	
Sinn Fein gain from SDLP			
Swing SDLP to Sinn Fein 9.74%			

Conclusion

Andrew Geddes and Jonathan Tonge

The 1997 general election produced one of the most sensational results in British political history. By 2 May, the recall vote appeared to be producing an even bigger landslide. Wishing to be associated with victory, almost *everyone* appeared to be claiming that they had voted Labour. The result heralded the end of perhaps the most influential period of Conservative Government this century, eighteen years in which many of the post-war political orthodoxies had been challenged. Four questions need to be addressed. First, why did the Conservatives lose? Second, how did Labour manage to revive its electoral fortunes in such spectacular fashion? Third, why did certain issues achieve particular salience in the 1997 election? Fourth, what does the huge reversal of electoral fortunes in 1997 indicate in wider terms concerning the nature of the electorate?

Only by answering all four questions can the wider implications of the 1997 election be fully addressed. Labour's last landslide in 1945 offered significant prospects of change. Is the same true of 1997? Labour was elected pledging caution and realism. There was talk of an 'absence of politics' in a contest which appeared to take place in an ideological vacuum. Has the 'people's party' recognised that the people's priorities have changed; has Labour accepted key aspects of the Conservative revolution; have both these developments occurred?

Conservative collapse

Surely the most striking aspect of the contest was the collapse of the Conservative vote. Solid at 42 per cent in the four previous elections, the vote share of the Party fell by a staggering 11 per cent, to its lowest proportion since 1832. Disunity has been commonly cited as a major factor, but this is too general an explanation. As Philip Cowley has indicated, Conservative parliamentary dissent, measured in aggregate terms, was not exceptionally high. What mattered was the qualitative nature of dissent. Unity on milder issues paled into significance compared with the fracture on Britain's relationship with the EU. Division on this issue was laid bare by leaks, public rows in the media and, bizarrely, the issue of personal manifestos by over one-third of Conservative candidates expressing dissent with the 'wait and see' policy endorsed by the Party leadership on the question of Britain's entry into a single

European currency. The Conservative Party's internal wrangling and the leadership's unwillingness to address difficult questions contributed to its forfeiture of the right to take such decisions.

The task of this book has been to analyse the 1997 general election, not to predict future developments. None the less, it must be regarded as inconceivable that the new Conservative leader, William Hague, will permit such autonomy amongst candidates. Local constituency associations may also find their autonomy curtailed as a result of their pre-election activities. The 'trade-off' is likely to be the extension to constituency parties of a limited stake in the election of a Conservative leader, a move supported by Hague during his leadership bid.

An overhaul of the Conservative Party appears overdue. Its election success in 1992 merely papered over cracks all too evident five years later. These problems included a declining and ageing membership; numerous local election reverses which damaged the fabric of the Party and left it with fewer local councillors than the Liberal Democrats; a less secure financial base than was once evident when the Party could comfortably field hundreds of full-time election agents; and a lack of professionalism set against the slickness of new Labour's greatly increased membership and vigorous campaigning approach.

Sleaze proved the other Achilles heel of the Conservative Party, a problem less predictable than that of Europe and one perhaps peculiar to the 1997 election. Increased regulation of the outside interests of MPs following the recommendations of the Nolan Report may reduce instances of political sleaze. The issue of sleaze remains sensitive, a fact reflected in the speed of investigation undertaken by the Labour Party in respect of allegations made against two of its election victors, Mohammed Sarwar and Bob Wareing. Furthermore, Nolan has rather less control over the sexual peccadilloes of Conservative MPs. A prurient media may ensure that sleaze and politics remain in touch, in an era where press attention is very firmly focused on the grey area between the public and private lives of public figures.

Overall, therefore, the Conservatives threw away any remaining prospects of an unprecedented fifth term of office through matters of image and substance. A party unable to unite on the important question of European integration was further unbalanced by the willingness of certain of its MPs to exploit the rewards of their position. Highly publicised internal animosities were exemplified by John Major's talk of 'bastards' within his Cabinet provoking a leadership contest with less than two years remaining before the general election. This friction, allied to dubious personal and political practices of some Conservative 'honourable members', ensured that the objective criterion by which the election might have been decided – the relative strength of the economy – was not decisive. A party victorious in the midst of recession in 1992 was trounced during the boom of 1997. Statecraft, centred upon the art of winning elections and presenting an image of governing competence, had been abandoned in favour of ideological internal antipathy.

Why did Labour win?

Such was the extent to which the Conservatives imploded that it is legitimate to ask whether Labour won merely by default. Indeed, it is possible to construct an argument based upon the myth of landslide. There are two main aspects to this. The first is that Labour's polling strength was markedly exaggerated by the vagaries of Britain's first-past-the-post electoral system. Under a strictly proportional system, Labour would have been denied an overall majority, possessed 128 fewer MPs and been confronted by thirty-nine extra Conservative and sixty-six Liberal Democrat MPs. Forty-four per cent of the vote yielded 63 per cent of parliamentary seats. Second, Labour did not receive the votes of a majority of Conservative defectors. Of the 4.5 million such Conservative losses (one-third of the Conservatives' 1992 total vote), Labour gained up to 1.5 million. Most of the remainder are accounted for by non-voters (up to 2 million, which accounted for a significant – 5 per cent – fall in turnout, despite fine weather) and defectors to the Referendum Party, accounting for many of that party's 800,000 total.

Despite the above caveats, Labour none the less polled 13.6 million votes, a figure which appeared a remote prospect in the wilderness years of the 1980s. Furthermore, as David Denver has indicated in Chapter 1, the Party is likely to have attracted a significant number of vote switchers. Turnout fell less in Conservative areas, indicating that at least part of the explanation for Labour's success lies in a shift in allegiances. Why did voters return to the Party in such numbers?

Labour appeared to have lost the previous election partly as a legacy of its unpopular offerings in 1992. The Party also lost because it had a less convincing leader. Neil Kinnock made Labour electable by ditching the ideological baggage and gesture politics of the 1980s. However, he had begun his political career on the left of the Party and could not distance himself sufficiently from such roots. In contrast, Blair, not prominent until the Labour Party began its reforms, carried no such ideological baggage. This factor allowed him to negotiate without damage a useful question he was asked by David Dimbleby in a bruising interview on BBC television, in which the interviewer attempted to develop a 'Tony Turncoat' theme: were people right to vote Labour in the 1980s, the era when Blair decided to become a Labour MP on an agenda entirely alien to 'New Labour'?

By 1997, under Blair, the Labour Party could scarcely have distanced itself further from its politics of the 1980s, which had begun to fade from memory. As Steven Fielding has noted, the process of transformation within the Labour Party was based upon a project of appeal to aspirants rather than allure to the excluded. In attempting to gain the support of 'Sierra man' much traditional baggage was ditched. Clause Four, overwhelming reliance upon trade unions and even the word 'socialism' were all jettisoned. This switch to 'New Labour' made the Party an extraordinary difficult target for the Conservatives to attack. First, the target was continually moving, to the extent that Labour even indicated in the campaign that they might 'outprivatise' the Conservatives. Second, it was impossible to maintain a credible argument that Tony Blair was really a closet socialist with a hidden agenda behind his seeming moderation. Equally, it was impossible to pretend that the Labour Party as an entirety had not changed. With some legitimacy, the Conservatives might claim that many of their clothes had been stolen. However, their own internal divisions were a greater distraction than this argument, which in any case was of limited value.

Labour's managerial approach to policy issues signified a decisive break with its ideologically driven approach of former years. This partly reflects a Blairite belief that radicalism is not associated with old left dogma. It also reflects wider feeling concerning the redundancy of the old left–right dichotomy, as these terms have become increasingly meaningless. Nowhere was Labour's new managerialism and moderation more apparent than in its proposals for the management of the economy. During the 1970s and 1980s, Labour had promised a fundamental shift in the balance of wealth in Britain. Now, the Labour Party refused to raise the top rate of tax beyond 40 per cent. Tax-and-spend had been replaced by prudence and caution.

Such moderation and the careful nature of Labour's campaign were juxtaposed against Blair's belief in the viability of a *radical* centre. The essential caution of Labour's five main campaign pledges reflected its belief in moderate populism – modest but significant improvements in health, education, youth employment and law and order which would offend no one. Emphasis was placed upon policy delivery, producing in effect a Blairite 'Contract with Britain'. In contrast to the ill-fated Newt Gringrich version in the United States, Blair's contract was based upon pragmatism and realism.

The dominant issues and the nature of the campaign

The 1997 campaign was fought on much more suitable terrain for Labour than had occurred in previous campaigns. The Party's claims that the Conservatives had imposed twenty-two tax rises since 1992, a mantra similar to the Conservatives' claims of Labour's threatened tax 'double whammy' in 1992, pre-empted a Conservative strike on this issue. Defence policy, the issue on which the Conservatives had enjoyed the biggest lead during the 1980s, in Labour's years of support for unilateral nuclear disarmament, was no longer a salient concern in a post-Cold War era.

In determining what were the dominant issues in the 1997 campaign, some caution should be exercised. Europe was a crucial issue in the sense that it exposed Conservative Party divisions, but less so in terms of inter-party policy difference. Other policy areas such as welfare and pensions provided 'mock show' which barely concealed an underlying consensus and acceptance of the need for change, as Ian Holliday demonstrates in Chapter 8.

Plans for constitutional reform provided the most striking distinctions between the parties. Under John Major, the Conservatives adopted a Burkeian defence of the constitution as the embodiment of the collective wisdom of our ancestors. The wipe-out of Conservatives in Wales and Scotland suggested that the so-called peripheries of Britain were less than impressed with this approach. Labour's comparative radicalism in this arena helped the Party in two ways. First, it provided an image of a modern party possessing reforming zeal. Second, support for devolution allowed the Party to acknowledge nationalist sentiment to a sufficient extent to prevent a great upsurge in support for the SNP or Plaid Cymru. Yet even on plans for devolution, Labour was cautious, insisting upon referendums for its enactment and the transfer of tax-raising powers. Blair's comparision of the prospective Scottish Parliament with a parish council, whilst an obvious gaffe, none the less gave some indication of Labour's preference for modest change.

Labour was able to put its message across effectively. Its victory was not merely a triumph of slick marketing. In 1987, the Party had run an impressive campaign but the weight of its policy burdens was such that the Conservatives won an overall majority of over 100. There were three crucial aspects to Labour's marketing operation, facilitated by concomitant policy changes. First, the Party enjoyed unprecedented newspaper support, most crucially from the *Sun*, whose change of allegiance provided an immediate boost at the outset of the campaign. Even amongst the tabloids opposed to Labour, pro-Conservative coverage was lukewarm. Vilification of Labour was rare. Only the *Daily Mail*, with its apocalyptic eve-of-election warning of the 'end of one thousand years of history' injected some anti-Labour vigour into press coverage. Second, Labour's Millbank operation was widely regarded as successful in promoting Party unity and cohesiveness and preventing the Party from being forced on to unfavourable political territory. Third, Millbank's operation would not have been possible without an effective 'on the ground' Labour campaign. Talk of 'television elections' or elections determined by political advertising has been overdone. Bolstered by a rising, youthful membership (average age below forty) Labour mounted a huge canvassing operation, useful not only in 'getting the vote out' but also in relaying doorstep concerns to Millbank. It was these canvass teams who, for example, informed Millbank that Europe appeared far less an immediate concern than pensions. This led to Labour's concentration upon the latter in the closing stages of the campaign, provoking the Conservatives into defensive 'scare story' allegations examined in Chapter 8 by Ian Holliday.

The implications of the 1997 election

Elections in Canada and France in recent years have indicated the seeming volatility of modern electorates, capable of huge swings and able to cause the 'meltdown' of governing parties. Increased electoral volatility means that, despite the size of its majority, Labour does not enjoy an impregnable position. This is especially true in Britain where increases or decreases in vote shares are exaggerated in representative terms. Also, the 1997 election represented the most sophisticated display yet of tactical voting, a factor which benefited the Liberal Democrats and one which is likely to greatly assist second-placed candidates in constituencies in future years.

Labour won by capturing all its key seats. The Party won so *handsomely* because it regained the confidence of voters in London and the South East, the area of biggest Conservative to Labour swing. Ironically, most of the seats captured there were not on Labour's target list, highlighting the abandonment of the Conservatives. Labour benefited from its ability to recognise what is entailed in the modern commodification of politics, in which voters elect the most attractive package of policy and image. Labour, cautious, reformist and modern, was preferred to a Conservative Party, many of whose policies had been endorsed, but which failed on the image part of the package. The Party appeared tired, disunited and at times disreputable. Only a substantial period in opposition may allow a renewal of the Conservative Party. In common with all parties, however, its fate may be determined by the attitude of the public to proportional representation in a referendum. Will we see the Conservatives, or any other party, govern alone after future elections?

Appendix

The new House of Commons

Party	*MPs*	*Male*	*Female*	*< 40*	*40+*	*Oxbridge*	*Other Univ*
Lab	419	318	101	64	355	68	171
Con	165	152	13	20	145	84	45
Lib Dem	46	43	3	16	30	13	19
UUP	10	10	0	1	9	0	3
SNP	6	4	2	1	5	0	6
PC	4	4	0	0	4	0	4
SDLP	3	3	0	0	3	0	1
DUP	2	2	0	0	2	0	0
SF	2	2	0	0	2	0	0
UKUP	1	1	0	0	1	0	1
Speaker	1	0	1	0	1	0	0
Total	659	539	120	102	557	165	250

Source: *The Times*, 3 May 1997; *Observer*, 4 May 1997. Authors' calculations.

The new cabinet (twenty-two posts)

Prime Minister	Tony Blair
Deputy Prime Minister and Secretary of State for the Environment, Transport and the Regions	John Prescott
Chancellor of the Exchequer	Gordon Brown
Foreign Secretary	Robin Cook
Lord Chancellor	Lord Irvine
Home Secretary	Jack Straw
Education and Employment Secretary	David Blunkett
President of the Board of Trade	Margaret Beckett
Minister of Agriculture, Fisheries, and Food	Jack Cunningham
Secretary of State for Scotland	Donald Dewar
Secretary of State for Defence	George Robertson
Secretary of State for Health	Frank Dobson
President of the Council and Leader of the House of Commons	Ann Taylor
Secretary of State for National Heritage	Chris Smith

Secretary of State for Social Security	Harriet Harman
Secretary of State for Northern Ireland	Marjorie Mowlam
Secretary of State for Wales	Ron Davies
Secretary of State for International Development	Clare Short
Lord Privy Seal and Leader of the House of Lords	Lord Richard
Chancellor of the Duchy of Lancaster	David Clark
Minister of Transport	Gavin Strang
Chief Secretary to the Treasury	Alistair Darling

Index